IMAGES
of America

The Floyd Collins Tragedy at Sand Cave

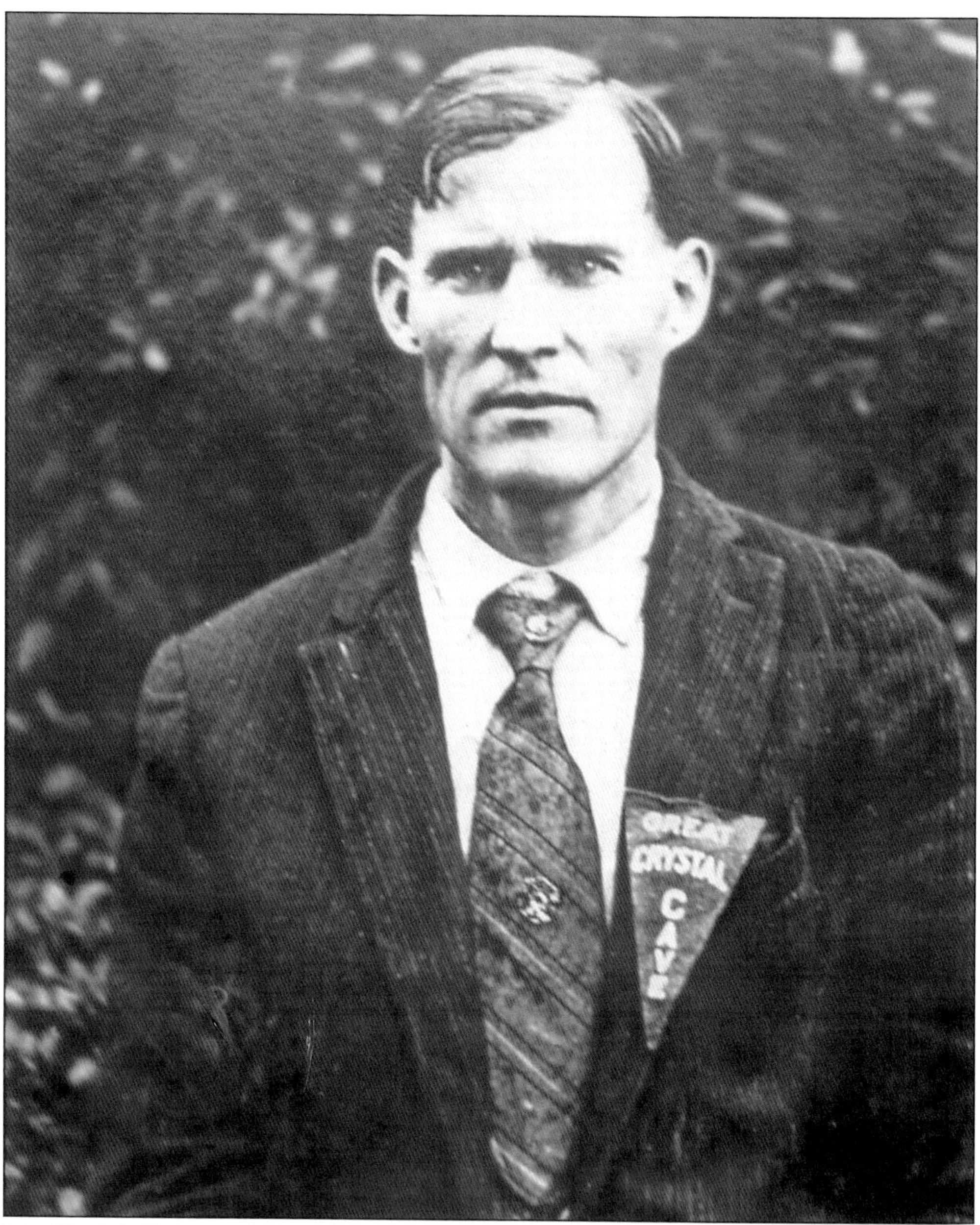

The Floyd Collins tragedy at Sand Cave was one of the country's most bizarre and tragic events. The story of a Kentucky cave explorer becoming trapped, then buried alive, and ultimately dying alone in a cave held a powerful grip on the nation for 17 days in 1925. The Collins story is still alive today for those who seek out the history of one man's passion for exploring caves. (Neville Collection, Cave Research Foundation.)

ON THE COVER: The casket of Floyd Collins, just after being removed from the hearse, is on the way to his resting place on the Collins homestead above Great Crystal Cave on April 26, 1925. Floyd Collins was trapped in Sand Cave on January 30, 1925, but because of the instability of the cave, his body was not recovered until April 23, 1925. (Courtesy of National Cave Museum.)

IMAGES
of America

THE FLOYD COLLINS TRAGEDY AT SAND CAVE

John Benton, Bill Napper,
and Bob Thompson

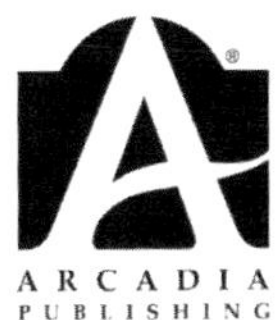

ISBN 978-1-4671-2442-3

Published by Arcadia Publishing
Charleston, South Carolina

Printed in the United States of America

Library of Congress Control Number: 2016945806

For all general information, please contact Arcadia Publishing:
Telephone 843-853-2070
Fax 843-853-0044
E-mail sales@arcadiapublishing.com

Visit us on the Internet at www.arcadiapublishing.com

CONTENTS

Acknowledgments

We want to thank the many individuals and institutions that helped this project come together, including Sharon McKinney and Udolph Highbaugh, Wade Highbaugh Collection; Stan Sides, Russell T. Neville Collection, Cave Research Foundation; Gordon Smith, National Cave Museum; Jonathan Jeffery, Nancy Richey, and William R. Reynolds Jr., Library Special Collections, Western Kentucky University; Terry Langford, Mammoth Cave National Park, National Park Service; Library of Congress; Minnesota Historical Society; United States Geological Survey; Roger Brucker; Tom Chaney; Scott Cundiff; Tim Donley; William Halliday; Cyndi Hanes; Alex and Jenny Hicks; Richard Hobart; David Jones; William Gross Magee; Dean Snyder; Judi Thompson; Norman Warnell; and Pamela Jeter Wilson.

Introduction

William Floyd Collins (1887–1925) was one of the most prominent cave explorers of the Mammoth Cave region. His explorations laid the foundation for others to later discover that Mammoth Cave was the longest cave in the world. At a very young age, Collins wandered around the sinkholes of his father's farm looking for a cave to rival the nearby famous Mammoth Cave. His interest in caves was an obsession, and he spent much of his free time caving, either alone or with his brothers and friends.

The area surrounding Mammoth Cave in south-central Kentucky was a key vacation destination in the early part of the 20th century after the discovery of new caves. By 1925, and at the time of Floyd Collins's entrapment in Sand Cave, at least seven caves were open to the public in the counties of Barren, Edmonson, and Hart. They include Mammoth Cave, New Entrance to Mammoth Cave, Great Onyx Cave, Great Crystal Cave, Diamond Caverns, Mammoth Onyx Cave, and Hidden River Cave. Except for Diamond Caverns, Mammoth Onyx Cave, and Hidden River Cave, all are located today within the boundaries of Mammoth Cave National Park.

Mammoth Cave was one of America's first tourist attractions. The long tradition of guiding underground tours there has been going on since 1816 and is still occurring today, 200 years later. As with all of the caves in the area in the early 1920s, Mammoth Cave was under private ownership before it became a national park in 1941. The private caves within the cave area, especially Great Onyx Cave, Floyd Collins' Crystal Cave, and New Entrance to Mammoth Cave, competed with Mammoth Cave for the area's tourist business.

Cave tourism, when successful, did far more than bring in money. The worldwide awareness of Mammoth Cave demonstrated quite conclusively to the local people of the Mammoth Cave area, including Floyd Collins's family, that it could bring something just as sought after as fortune—fame. Mammoth Cave had achieved worldwide recognition as a tourist attraction more than 50 years before Floyd Collins was born. As the years went by, word of Mammoth Cave spread and resulted in a steady growth of tourism even into the present day.

Floyd Collins's life, and certainly his front-page death, had dramatic impact throughout the Kentucky Mammoth Cave region. Seldom in history has there been such a main character where so many aspects of the complete story are best told through the life of one central figure. Not since Jesse James robbed the Mammoth Cave stagecoach in 1880 had there been so much excitement in the area.

Floyd Collins discovered Great Crystal Cave in 1917 on his family's Flint Ridge farm. Even though it was a magnificent cave, it was also the last cave on the main road and past Mammoth Cave. Floyd Collins's entrapment in Sand Cave in 1925 came as a result of Collins wanting to find a new cave closer to the main road leading to Mammoth Cave. Climbing into a tight passageway in a cave on land owned by a friend, Collins's foot became trapped by a dislodged rock, and it took a little more than two weeks before anyone could reach him closely enough to get him out. It took another two months after that before anyone actually pulled Collins's body out of the cave.

The tragedy itself became a media event for the whole nation as each day's news at the cave became front-page headlines. The area around Sand Cave had a carnival-like atmosphere that became a social gathering for sightseers. Remarkably, 90-plus years later, the tragic event is still noteworthy thanks to books, film documentaries, and theater productions. The Floyd Collins tragedy was so memorable that in 1975, Kentucky residents voted it the top statewide news story of the century.

The exceptional images used in this book come primarily from four photographers who were either there at the time of the Collins entrapment or shortly thereafter. Photographer Wade Highbaugh was a good friend of Floyd Collins who lived two miles from the Collins homestead and one mile from Sand Cave. Highbaugh took pictures of Great Crystal Cave in the early 1920s, the Collins Sand Cave entrapment in February 1925, the removal of Collins from Sand Cave on April 23, and the Collins funeral on April 26. Photographer Russell T. Neville from Kewanee, Illinois, also developed a friendship with Collins, as the Neville family visited the Mammoth Cave area regularly. Neville took pictures of Great Crystal Cave for three days in July 1924 (with Floyd Collins) and in July 1926 (with Marshall and Homer Collins) and the Sand Cave aftermath in July 1925 and July 1926. Photographer William R. Reynolds Jr. from Cave City took pictures on April 26, 1925, as Collins's body was taken from the funeral home in Cave City to the Collins homestead for burial. Photographer and geologist Willis T. Lee took pictures of Great Crystal Cave in May 1925 as part of a commission to help establish the cave area as a national park.

The historical images featured in this book not only present a complete picture of the man himself, but also reveal the bigger picture of how the best and worst of the entire Kentucky Mammoth Cave region—its hopes and dreams, exploration and discovery, business and economics, rags to riches, successes and failures, and in the end, tragedy and death—fell upon the shoulders of one man, the "Greatest Cave Explorer Ever Known," Floyd Collins.

One

The Mammoth Cave Region

Where Natural Wonders Offer Fame and Fortune

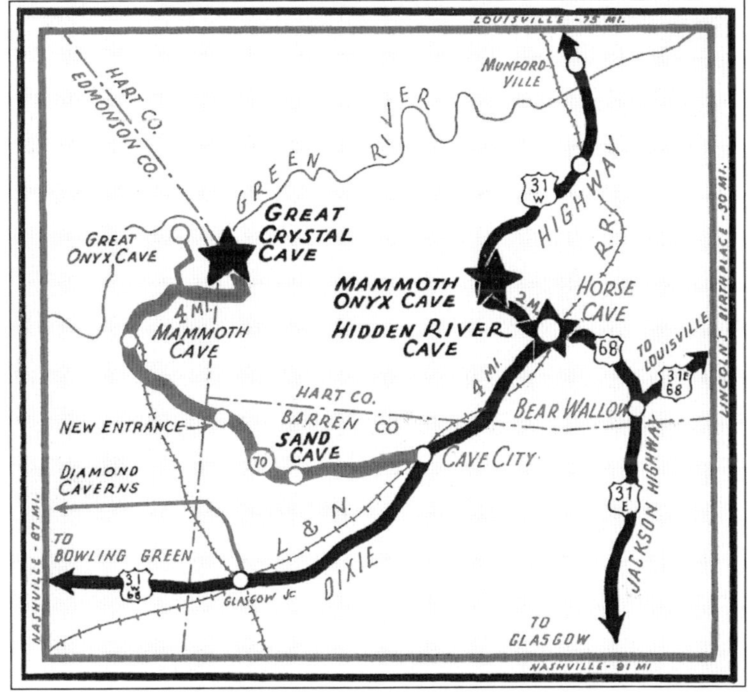

Floyd Collins' Crystal Cave was just one of seven caves in the Mammoth Cave region of south-central Kentucky that were open in 1925 during the time of his entrapment in Sand Cave. Mammoth Cave, New Entrance to Mammoth Cave, Great Onyx Cave, Great Crystal Cave, Diamond Caverns, Mammoth Onyx Cave, and Hidden River Cave all competed with each other for the tourist dollar. (Bill Napper Collection.)

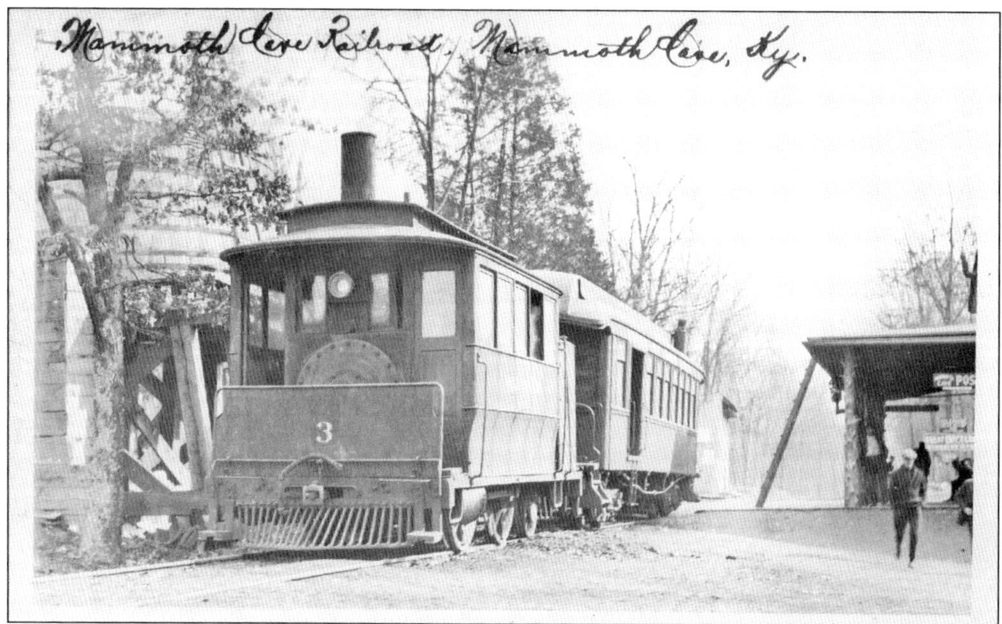

By the 1920s, improvements in transportation made it easier for visitors to reach the cave area. Trains were an option by 1859 and automobiles by 1904. The Mammoth Cave Railroad played an important part in getting tourists to Mammoth Cave, as well as other caves in the region. The train operated from 1886 to 1931 on an 8.7-mile extension from Glasgow Junction (Park City) to Mammoth Cave. (National Cave Museum.)

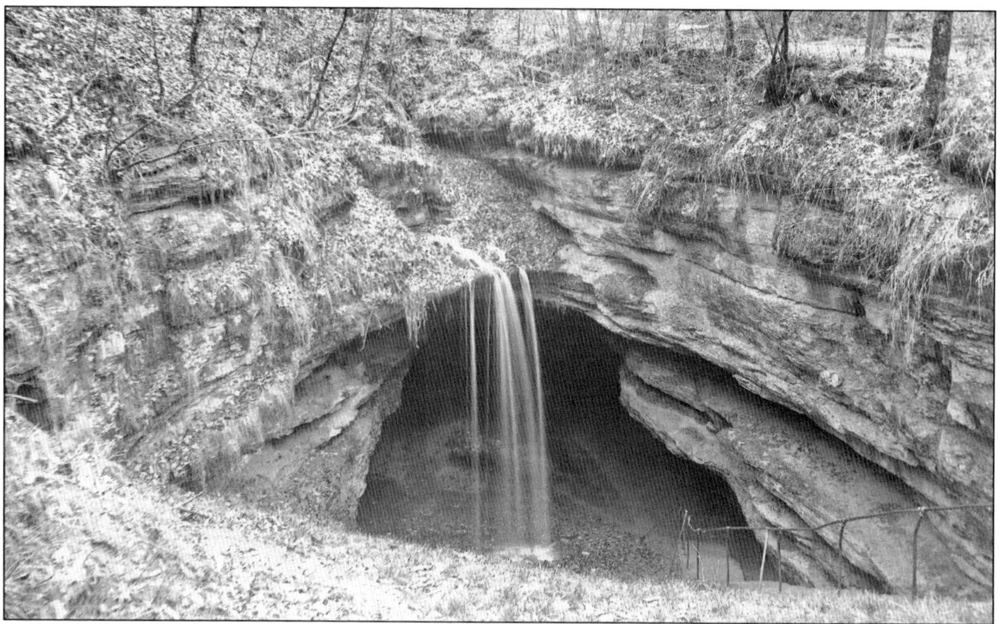

Mammoth Cave is one of America's oldest tourist attractions. The cave was an attraction long before it became a national park in 1941. Since its discovery around 1797, a total of 405 miles have been explored and mapped, making it the longest cave system in the world. Floyd Collins' Crystal Cave was connected to Mammoth Cave in 1972, along with other caves in the area. (Wade Highbaugh Collection.)

For the past 200 years, guided tours have been given in Mammoth Cave by knowledgeable guides. Floyd Collins and other cave explorers followed in the footsteps of Stephen Bishop, a famous cave explorer and early African American slave and guide of Mammoth Cave. Many of the early cave guides of Mammoth Cave were also cave explorers. (Mammoth Cave National Park, Kentucky, Park Museum Collections.)

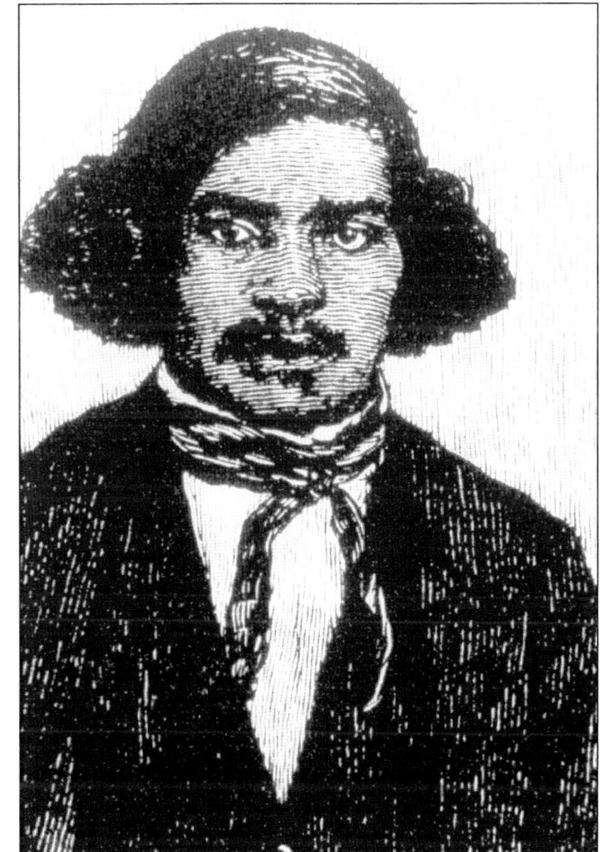

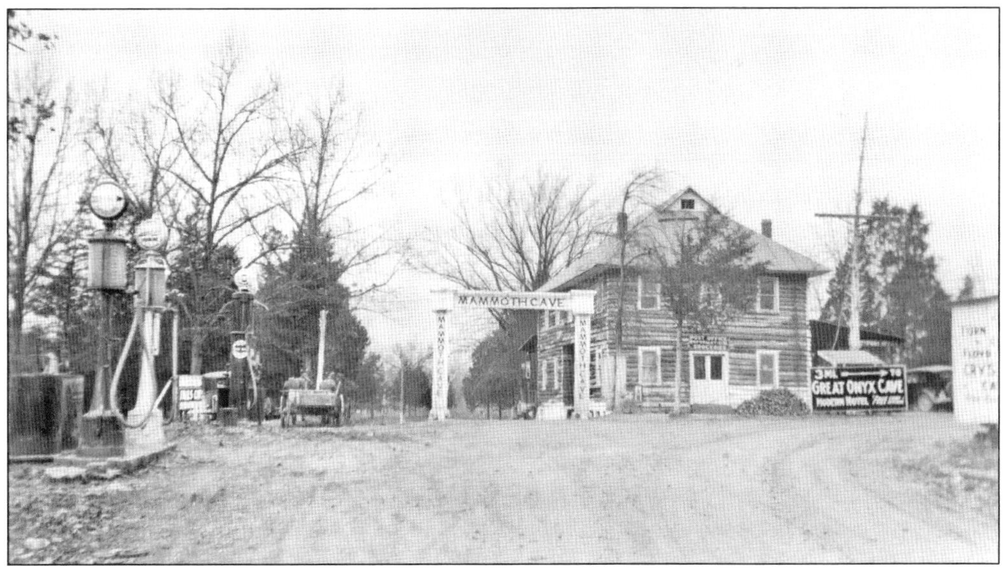

Floyd Collins's family lived on a farm four miles from the main entrance of Mammoth Cave. The large building on the right served as a general store, post office, and train depot for visitors coming to and from Mammoth Cave. Note the directional signs for Great Onyx Cave and Floyd Collins' Crystal Cave to the right of the 1920s arch entrance to Mammoth Cave. (Norman Warnell Collection.)

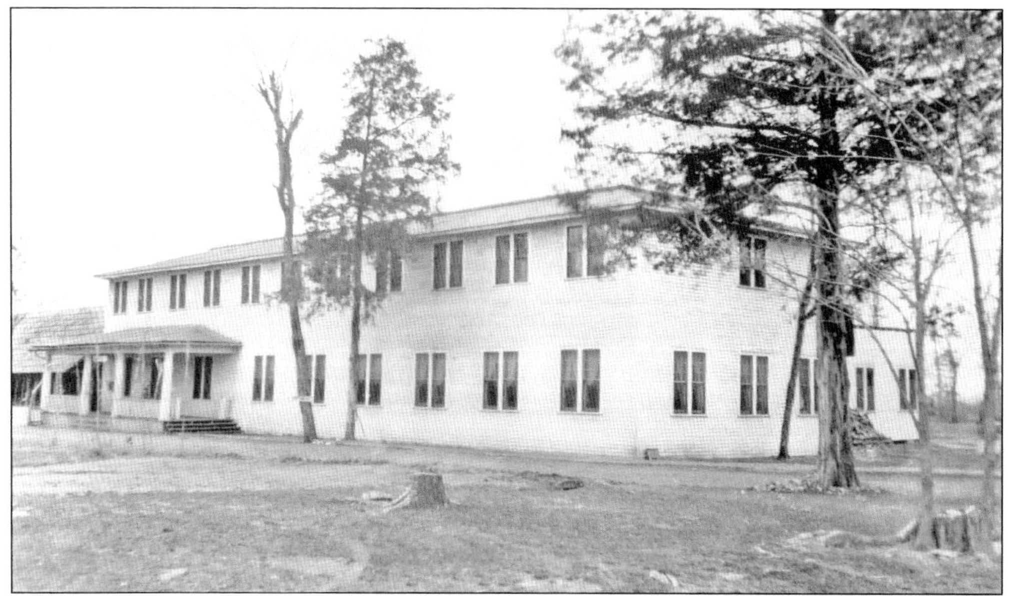

Mammoth Cave was one of three caves in the area that had a hotel in the 1920s. The first Mammoth Cave Hotel was built in 1841 and burned to the ground in 1916. The second hotel, shown here, was built in 1925. The Collins family, as well as other families in the region, occasionally made additional income as a result of Mammoth Cave tourism. (Norman Warnell Collection.)

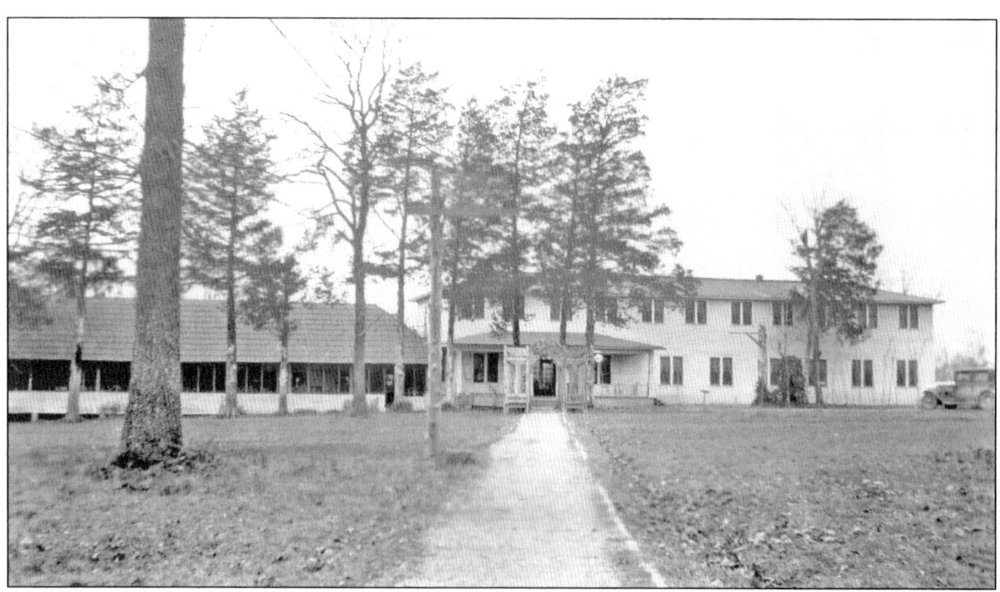

The Collins family sold eggs, among other things, to the Mammoth Cave Hotel to help support their needs. Floyd Collins would often go with his father to make deliveries to the hotel. Floyd Collins' Crystal Cave was the only cave in the area not to have a hotel, but it did have a two-story, 12-room boardinghouse from 1922 to 1924. (Norman Warnell Collection.)

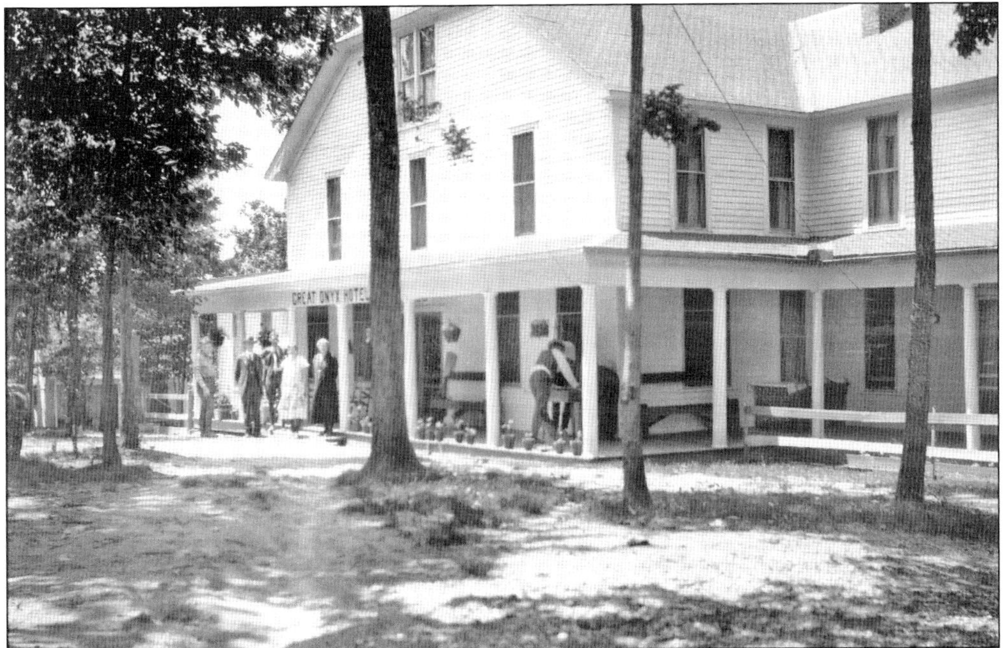

Great Onyx Cave was one of three caves in the area that had a hotel in the 1920s. The hotel was built in 1920 and was used until the National Park Service purchased the privately owned cave in 1961. The cave was located three miles from the main entrance to Mammoth Cave and one mile from Floyd Collins' Crystal Cave. (United States Geological Survey.)

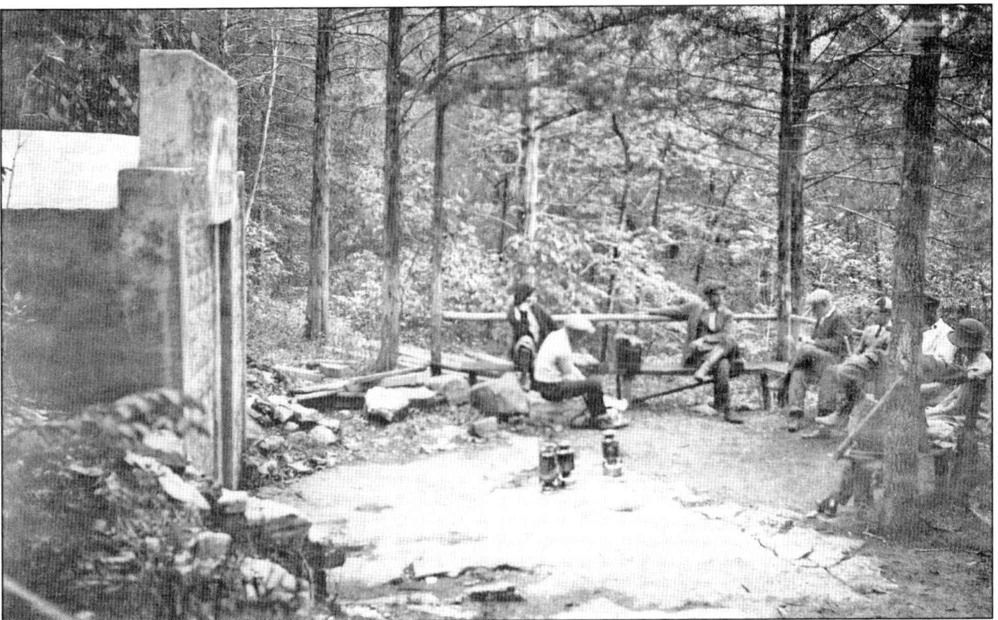

Great Onyx Cave (entrance to the left) was one of the caves Floyd Collins' Crystal Cave competed against. Cave explorer Edmund Turner discovered the cave in 1915. Recent evidence suggests that Floyd Collins may have discovered Great Onyx Cave in 1914 with Turner. Great Onyx Cave is still in operation today and is usually shown seasonally at Mammoth Cave National Park. (United States Geological Survey.)

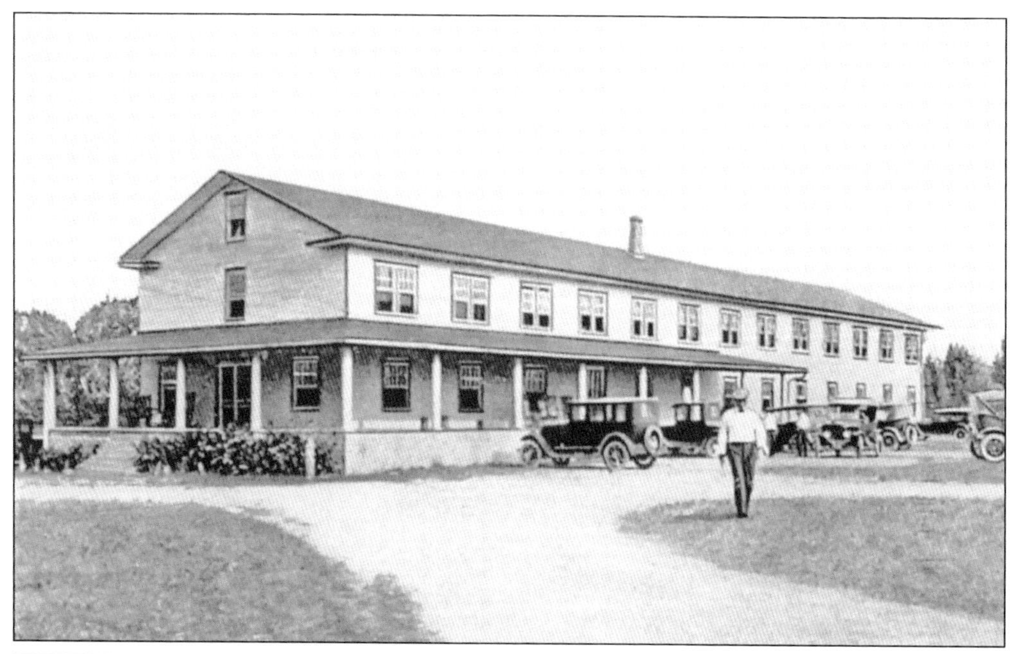

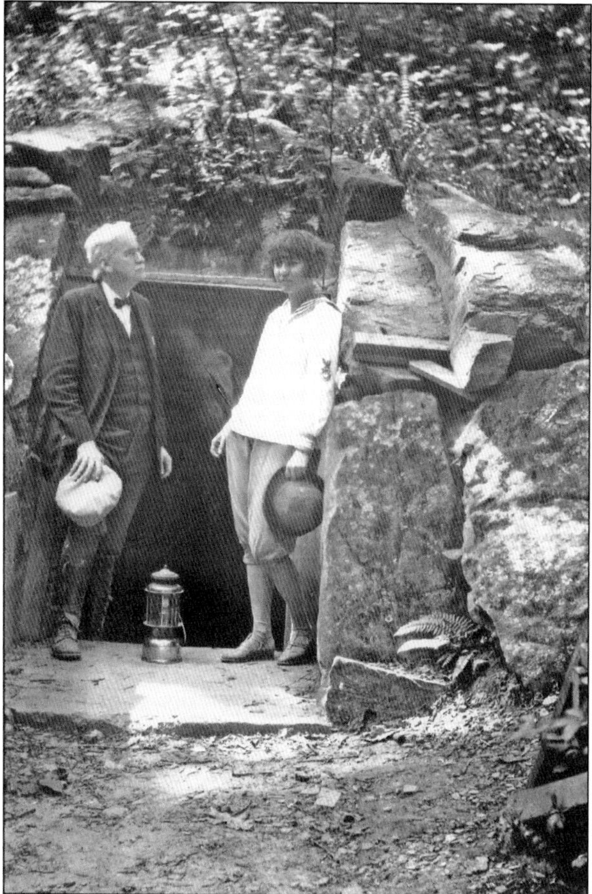

New Entrance to Mammoth Cave, the first cave on the main road to Mammoth Cave, was one of three caves in the area that had a hotel in the 1920s. The hotel was built in 1923. After the Kentucky National Park Commission purchased the privately owned cave in 1931, Mammoth Cave had two hotels for guests until 1941, when this one was demolished. (Bob Thompson Collection.)

New Entrance to Mammoth Cave was discovered after it was blasted open by its owner, George Morrison. It was one of the caves that Floyd Collins' Crystal Cave was in competition with. New Entrance to Mammoth Cave is actually part of Mammoth Cave but was not discovered until 1921 and was owned and operated privately until the state National Park Commission bought the cave in 1931. (United States Geological Survey.)

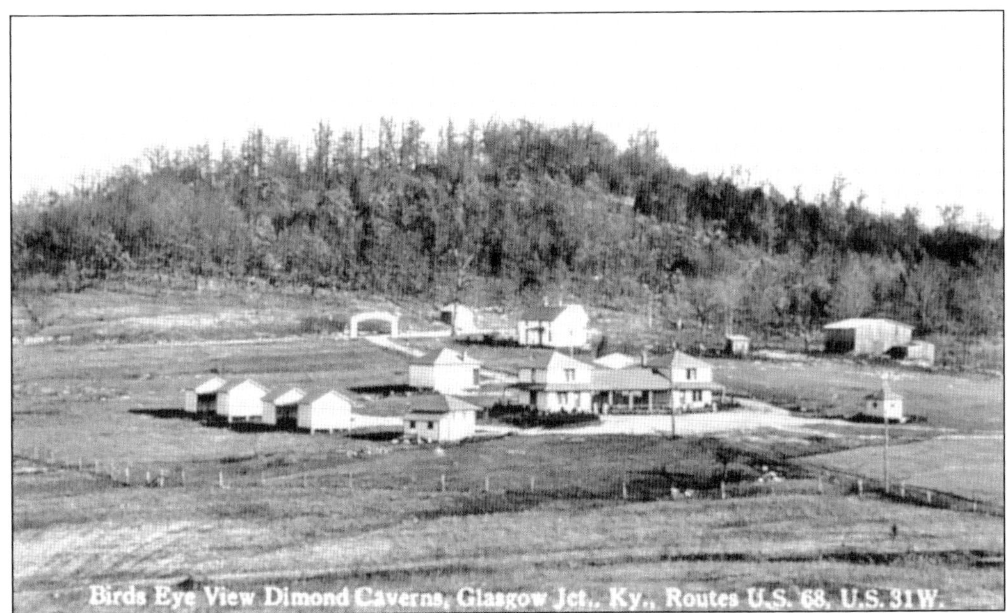

Diamond Caverns, opened in 1859, was another cave that competed with Mammoth Cave, New Entrance to Mammoth Cave, Floyd Collins' Crystal Cave, and Great Onyx Cave, even though the cave was not on the same road as the others. Diamond Caverns was one of the stops for the Mammoth Cave Railroad on the way to Mammoth Cave. (National Cave Museum.)

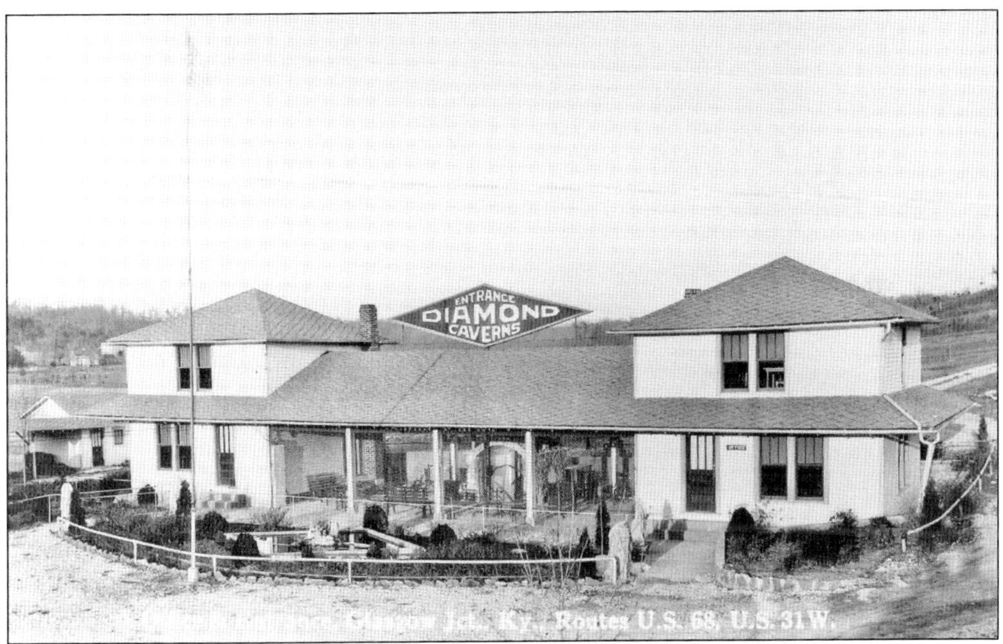

Diamond Caverns was first called Richardson Cave after one of the cave's original explorers. The stone arch entrance to the caverns can be seen just under the building overhang at center. Diamond Caverns is still in operation today as a tourist attraction and is the home of the National Cave Museum. (National Cave Museum.)

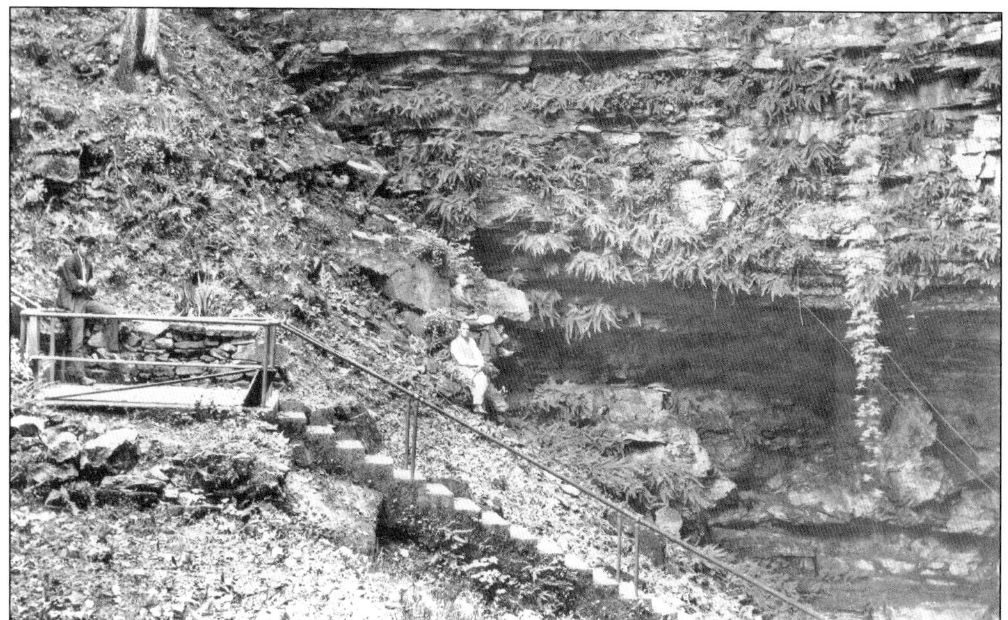

Hidden River Cave, opened in 1916, was the first cave owned and operated by dentist Dr. Harry Thomas of Horse Cave. Thomas was the man who bought Floyd Collins' Crystal Cave in 1927 from the Collins family. Formerly called Horse Cave, from which the town took its name, Hidden River Cave is still in operation today and is part of the attraction known as the American Cave Museum. (United States Geological Survey.)

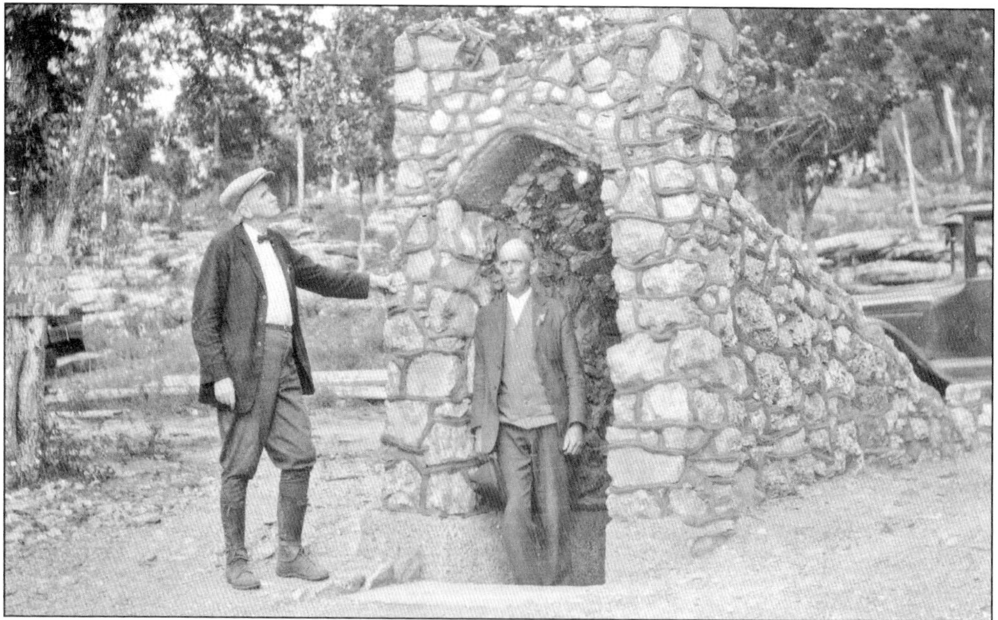

Mammoth Onyx Cave was the second cave owned and operated by Dr. Harry Thomas. The cave was opened in 1921 and competed with Mammoth Cave, New Entrance to Mammoth Cave, and Great Onyx Cave, as well as Great Crystal Cave when it was owned by the Collins family. Mammoth Onyx Cave is still in operation today and is part of the Kentucky Down Under attraction. (United States Geological Survey.)

Two

The Cave Explorer

Visions of Rags to Riches

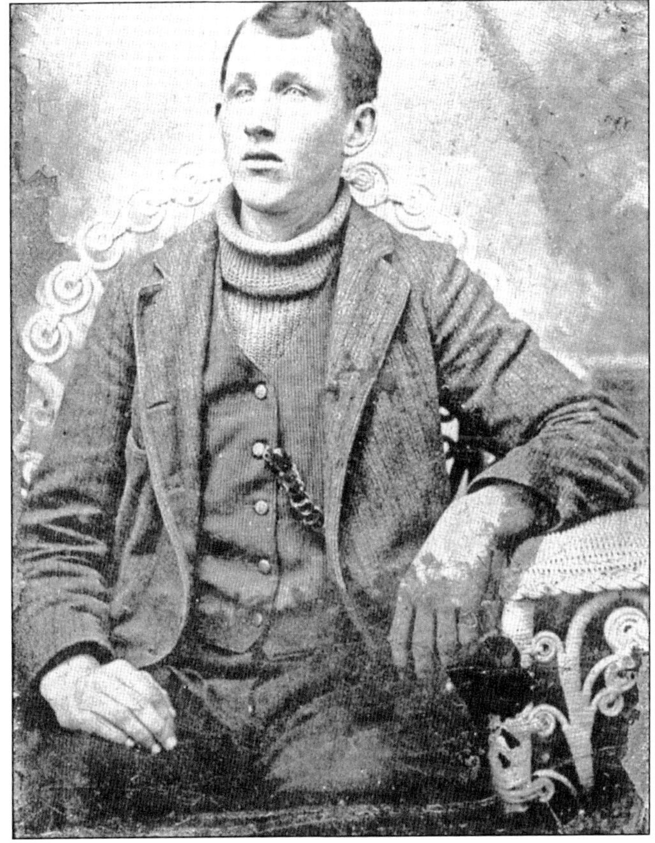

Floyd Collins, born in 1887, was the child of a typical cave country family. The majority of their time was spent farming, hunting, trapping, logging, cutting timber, and other hard work associated with daily survival. Formal education beyond grade school was a dream rarely achieved by the locals, but through hard work and perseverance, families survived. This photograph shows Floyd Collins as a young man. (Library Special Collections, WKU.)

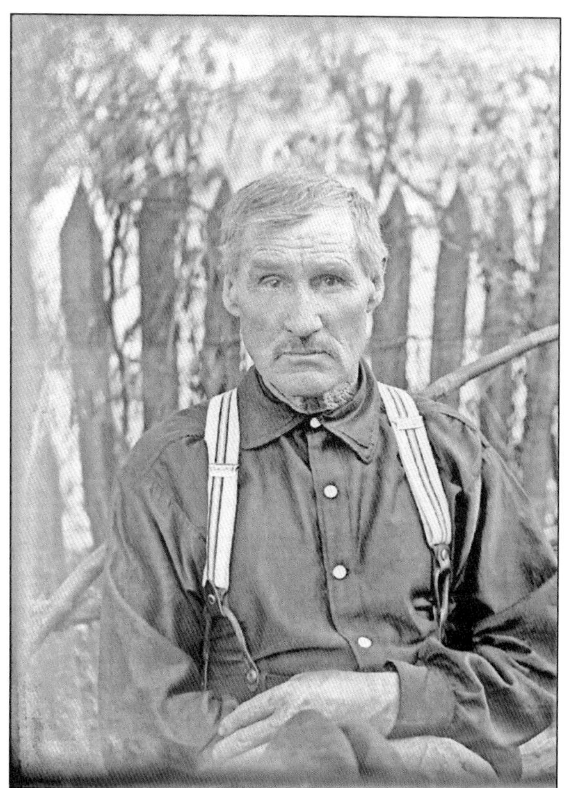

Floyd Collins was the third of eight children of Lee (shown at left) and Martha Collins. They were, in order of birth, Elizabeth, James M., William Floyd, Annie B., Andy Lee, Marshall E., Nellie, and Homer Collins. Lee Collins owned the farmland around what would be Floyd Collins's first big cave discovery. (Wade Highbaugh Collection.)

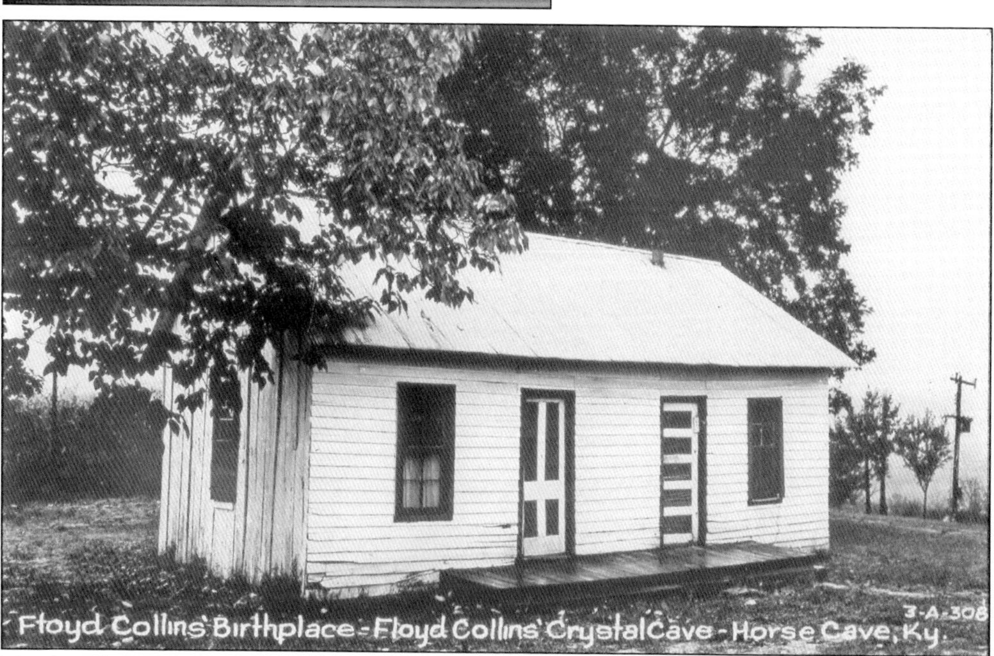

Floyd Collins grew up in this house, on land just above the entrance to Great Crystal Cave, which he would soon discover. The house was a one-story frame structure with a rear addition. The main structure had two rooms. This house was also used as the first ticket office for Great Crystal Cave. (John Benton Collection.)

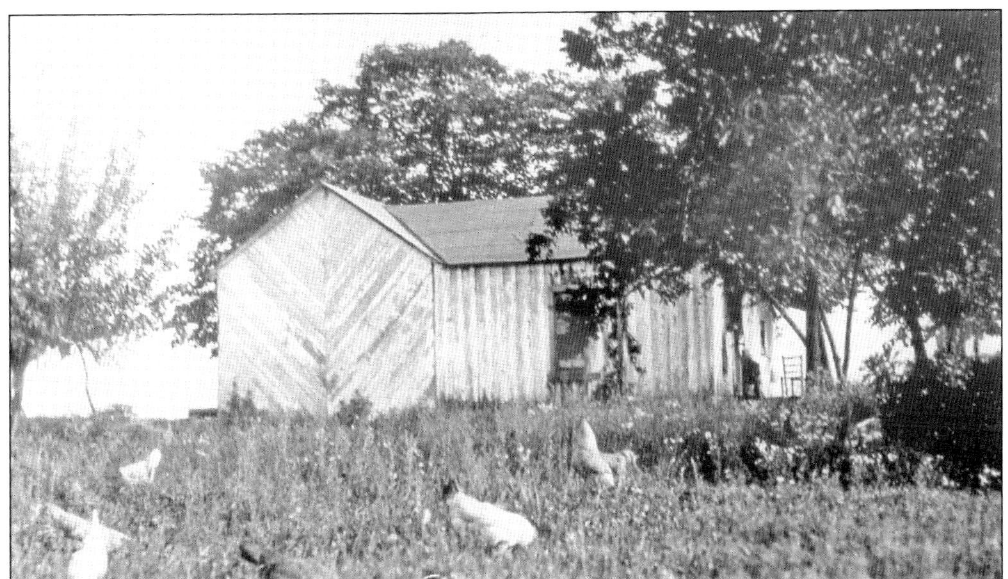

The Collins house sat on a fieldstone foundation, had a corrugated metal gabled roof, two front doors, and two front double-hung sash windows. The family raised chickens and had a garden and orchard on the farm to help support their needs. (Neville Collection, Cave Research Foundation.)

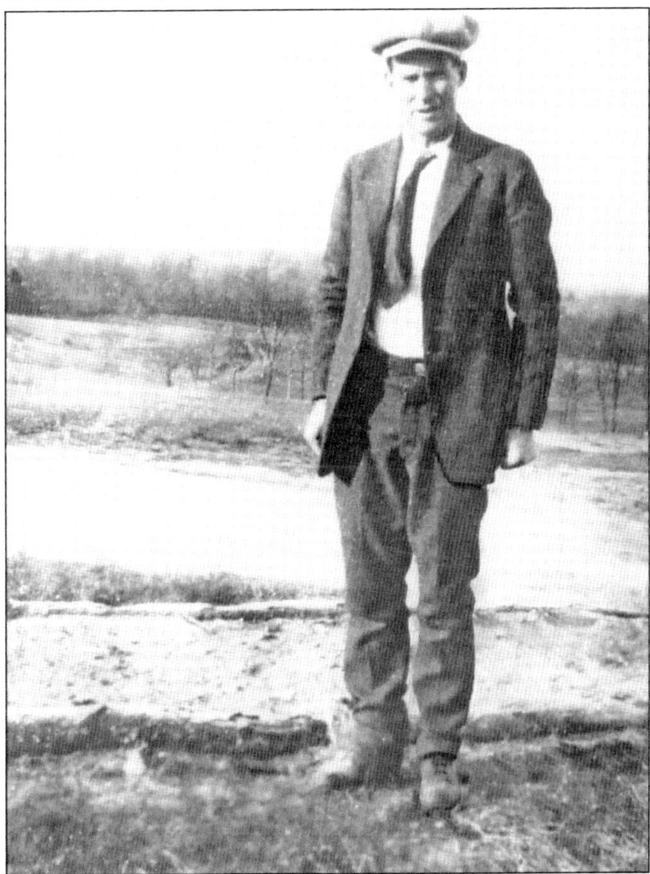

Floyd Collins had been going into caves since the age of six. His brothers Homer, Marshall, and Andy would often go caving with him around the Flint Ridge area where they lived. Floyd Collins's first discovery was a small cave on the Collins property known as Donkey's Cave or Floyd's Cave. Plowing with a mule in 1910, Collins fell into the sinkhole entrance. A cabin was built over the cave entrance. (Richard Hobart Collection.)

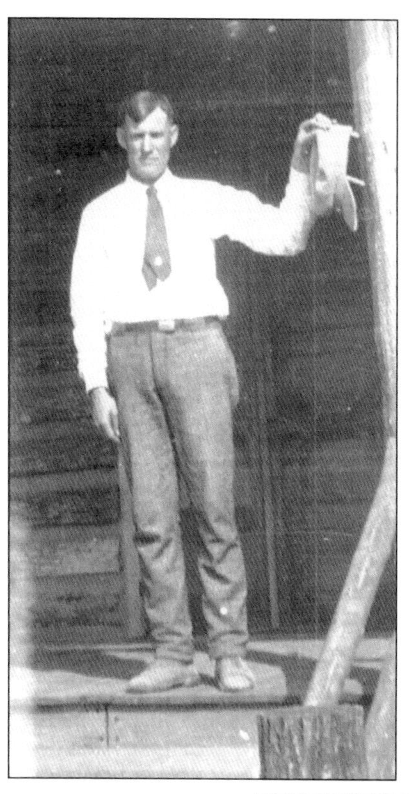

Cave explorers like Floyd Collins were important in the discovery of new caves in the Mammoth Cave area. Motivated to make a few extra dollars from tourists, Collins explored nearby Salts Cave and discovered a treasure trove of artifacts. Floyd Collins is shown here in front of the Crystal Cave ticket office. (National Cave Museum.)

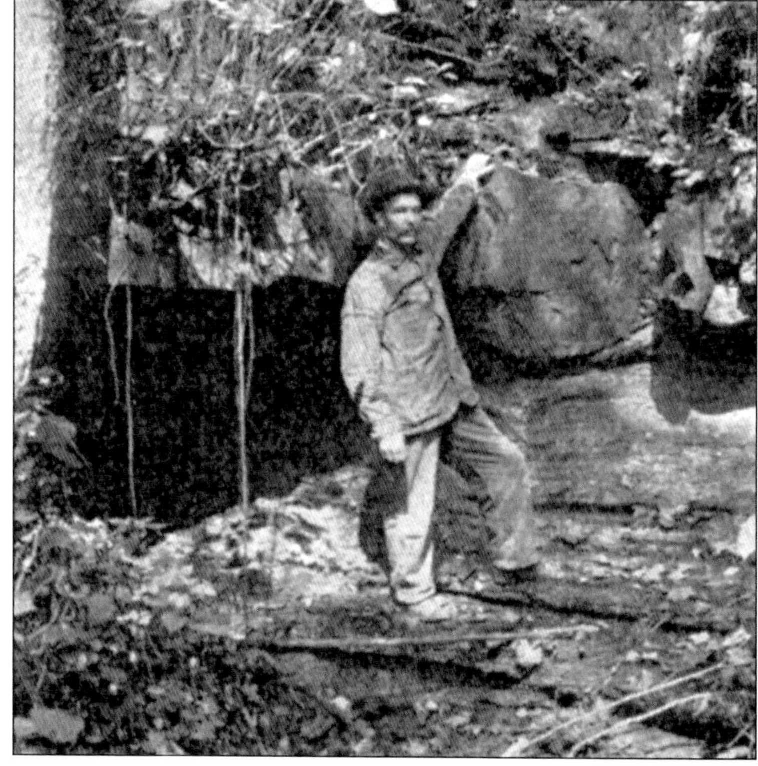

Edmund Turner, a young geologist from New York, came to the Mammoth Cave area in 1912, looking for caves to explore. Turner hired Floyd Collins to show him some caves and stayed at the Collins house. Edmund Turner and Floyd Collins assisted in the discovery of Dossey's Dome Cave in 1912 and Great Onyx Cave in 1915. Turner is shown here above the Salts Cave entrance. (Bill Napper Collection.)

Three

GREAT CRYSTAL CAVE

THE DISCOVERY OF A LIFETIME

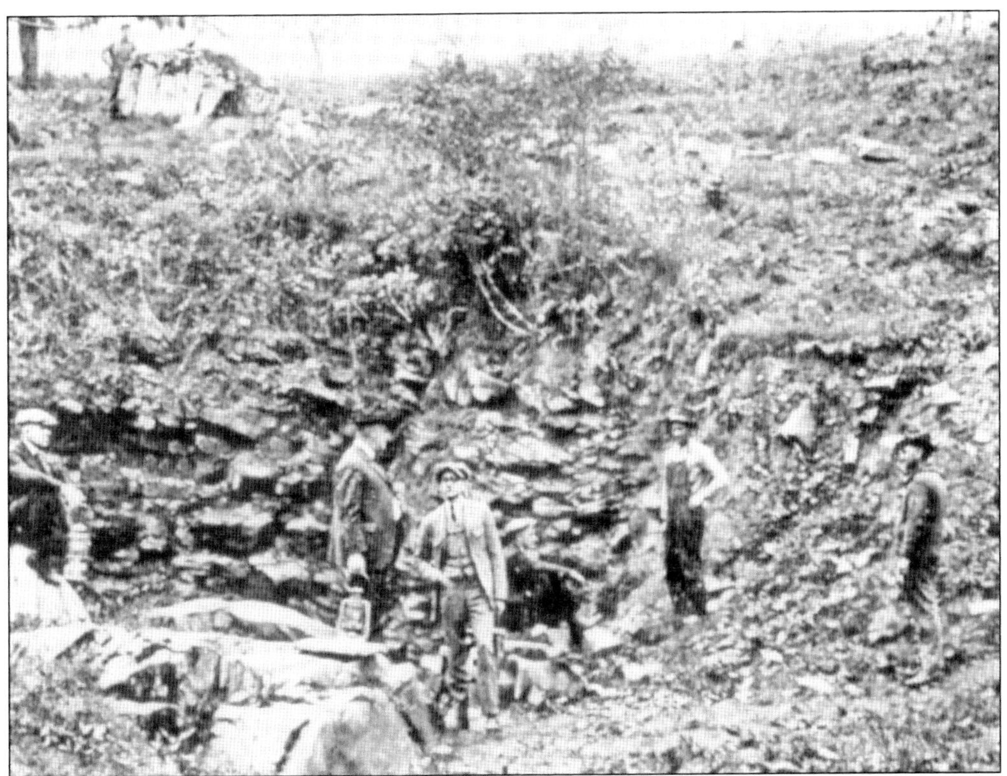

In September 1917, Floyd Collins noticed cool air coming from between the sandstone boulders in the bluff below the Collins home. He immediately began removing debris and encountered a pit filled with rocks. He worked intermittently for a few months removing rocks and opened a passage that was used as a root cellar to store foods. This photograph shows the entrance to Great Crystal Cave. (National Cave Museum.)

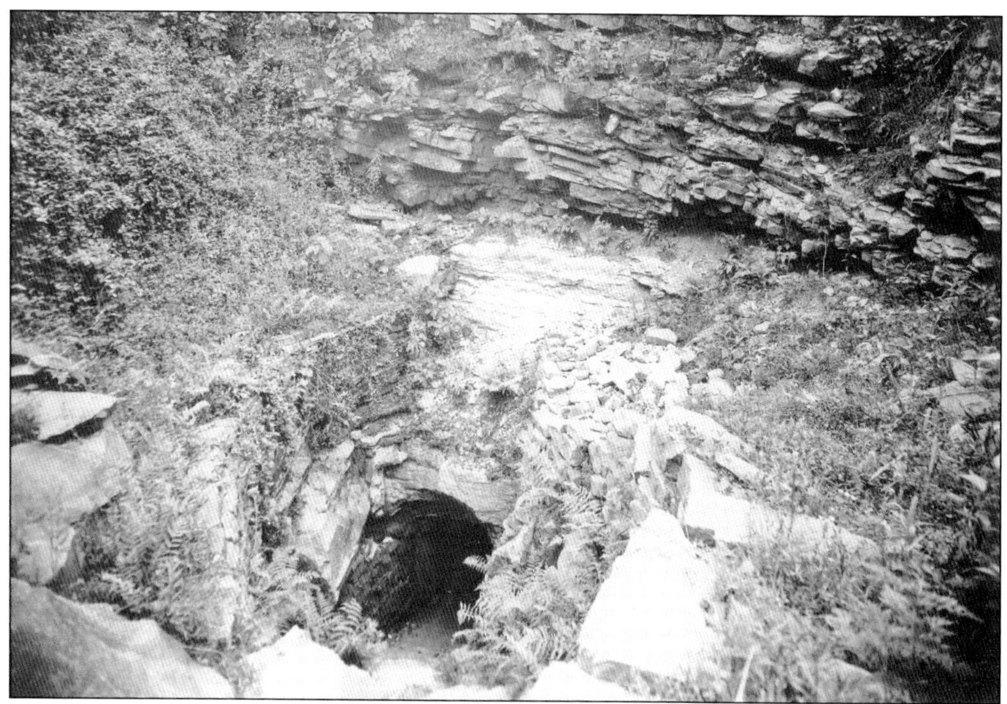

Eventually, Floyd Collins renewed his efforts to dig more after finding packrats had carried apple scraps through the rocks. On December 17, 1917, as more rocks were removed, Floyd Collins discovered the sinkhole entrance to Great Crystal Cave. Collins first named his new discovery Wonder Cave and Great Gypsum Cave, but after some advice from a friend, he renamed it Great Crystal Cave. (National Cave Museum.)

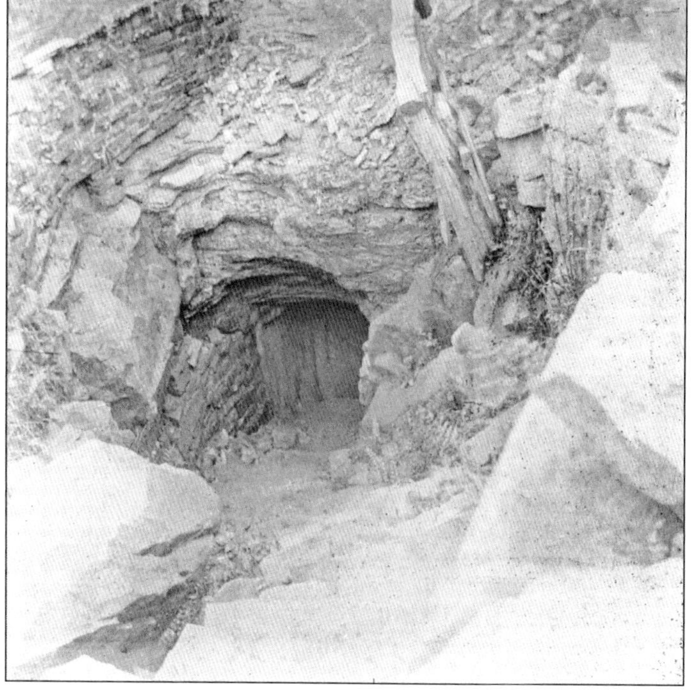

Floyd Collins immediately realized the significance of the discovery and worked out a plan with his father to open the cave to tourists. Making the cave suitable was difficult and expensive. With very little money, the Collins family had to do most of the work themselves. The Collins brothers enlarged and improved the sinkhole entrance with retaining walls, a stone stairway, and a door. (National Cave Museum.)

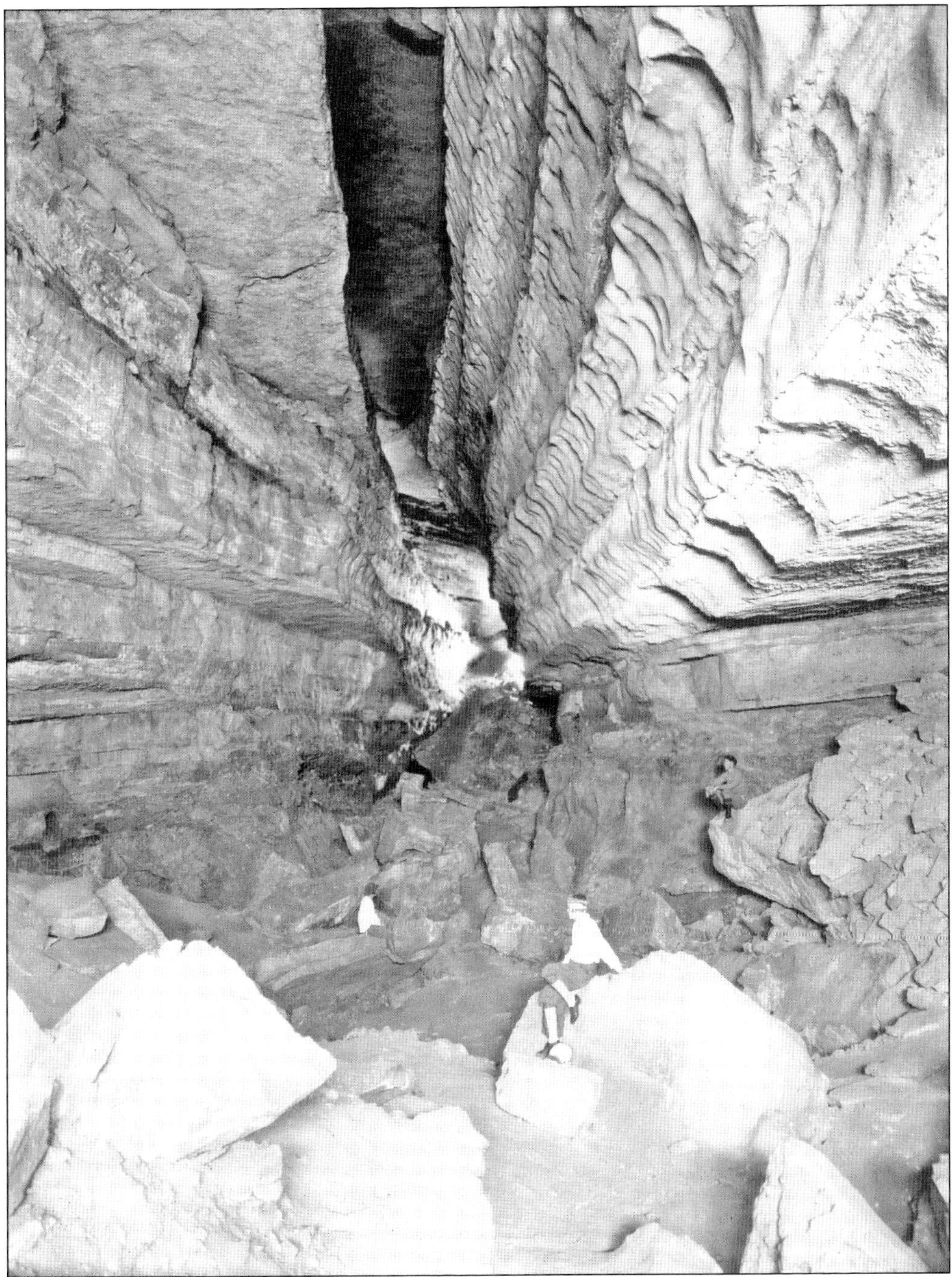

In April 1918, after rigorous effort by the entire Collins family to prepare the cave for tourists, Great Crystal Cave was opened for tours. In the first couple years of operation, the cave was leased out in the summer to others, but none could make it a success. Here is the large passageway known as the Grand Canyon looking toward the entrance. Great Crystal Cave was equal to Mammoth Cave in size and beauty. (United States Geological Survey.)

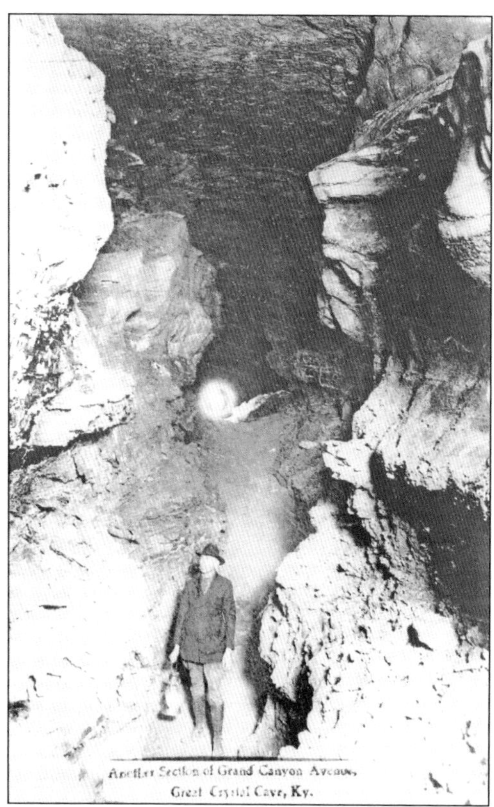

A large gypsum passage is shown in Great Crystal Cave. The view is looking out toward the entrance. This was the first large cave passageway that Floyd Collins explored in the cave with his brothers Marshall and Homer. (Dean Snyder Collection.)

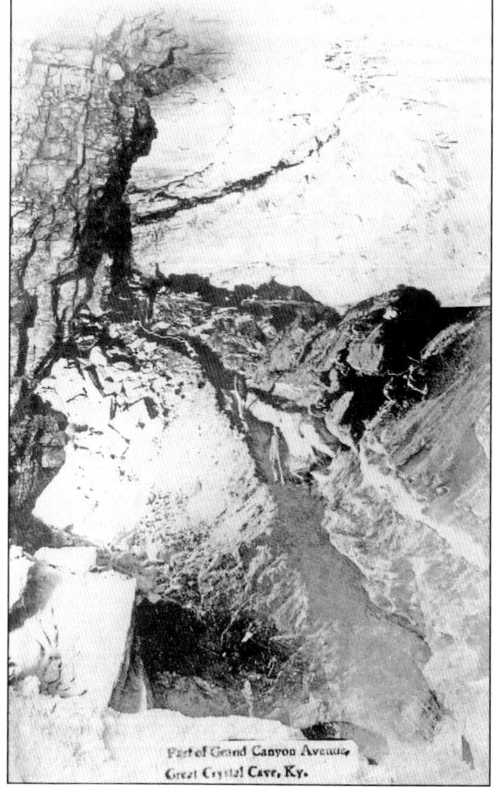

Floyd Collins is shown walking in the Grand Canyon passageway of Great Crystal Cave. The huge trunk passage, 20 feet high and 30 feet wide, was formed by an underground stream. Lanterns were used for lighting the cave, as an adequate system of electric lights was not installed until 1954. (Dean Snyder Collection.)

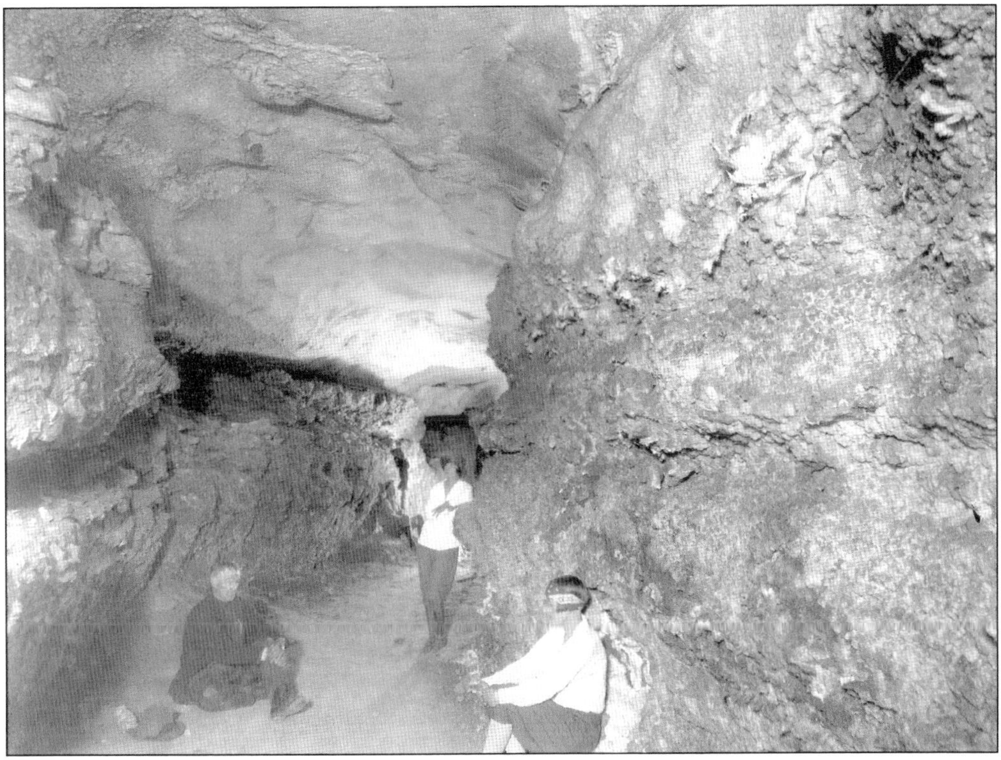

As Floyd Collins crawled his way further into his newly discovered cave, he discovered big passageways and beautiful white gypsum. It did not take long for Collins to realize that tourists would pay for cave tours, as well as souvenirs. He made money selling rocks, arrowheads, and other items of local interest. These photographs show some of the gypsum- and onyx-crusted walls in the interior of Great Crystal Cave. Floyd Collins's father, Lee, sits at left above. (Both, United States Geological Survey.)

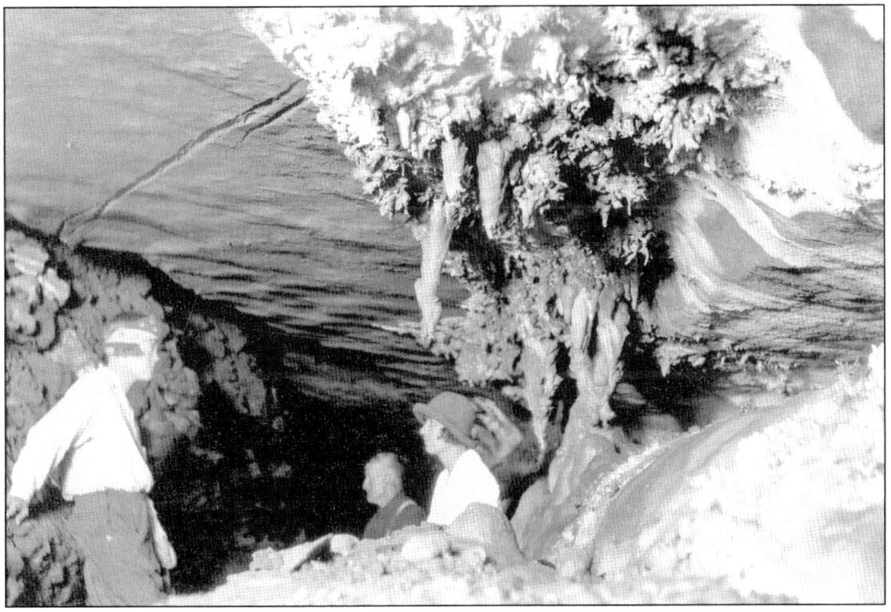

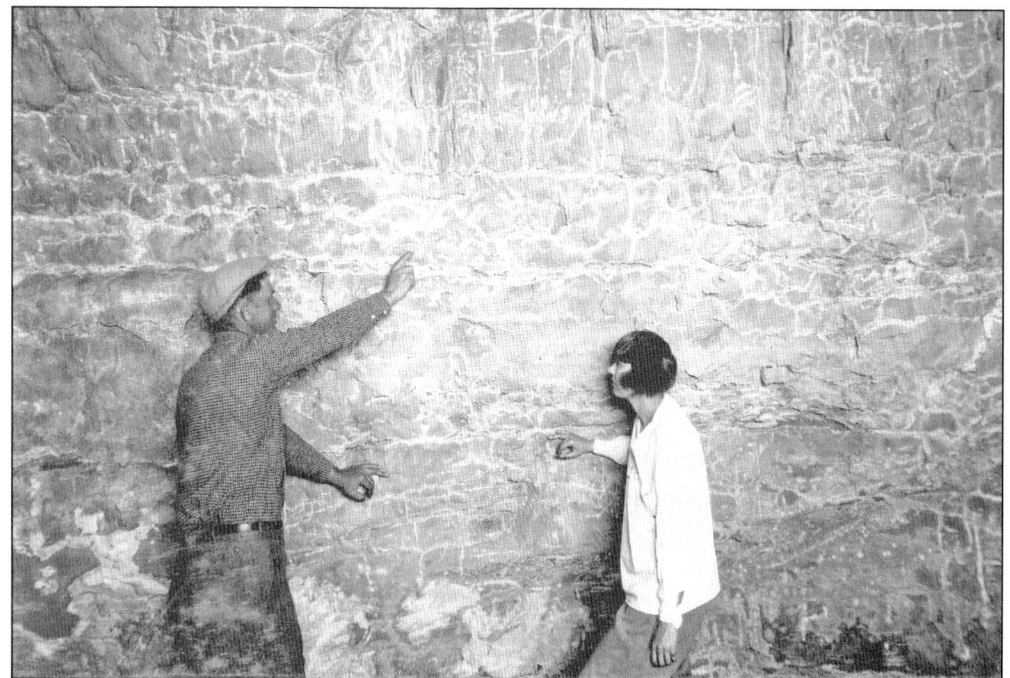

Calcite crystals enclosed in the cracks of the caves' limestone walls are shown in Great Crystal Cave. Some of these incrustations have been interpreted by those unfamiliar with them as being picture writing of prehistoric people. (United States Geological Survey.)

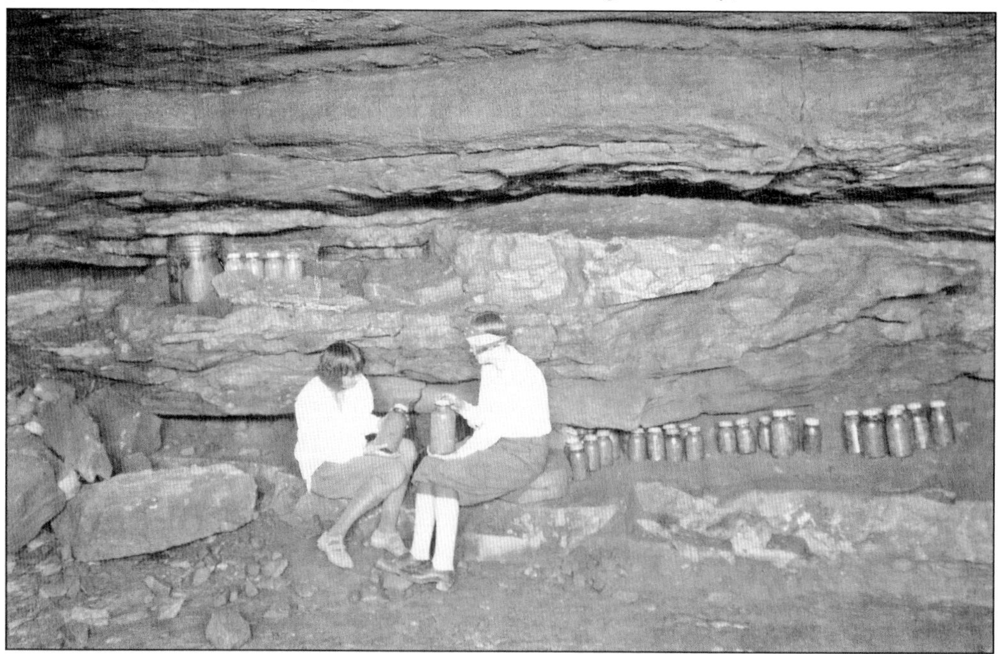

Even with the opening of Great Crystal Cave, the Collins family still had to do farm work just to survive until the newly opened cave started generating some money. Great Crystal Cave was utilized as a refrigerator by the family for storing and selling canned goods. The all-year temperature of 54 degrees Fahrenheit kept supplies of canned fruits and vegetables cold. (United States Geological Survey.)

Floyd Collins is shown in the area of the cave known as Crystal Springs. He is seen at top left holding a coal oil lantern and taking a water break in Great Crystal Cave. Tour guides would often dip up a drink for tourists who wanted to taste the pure cold water. (National Cave Museum.)

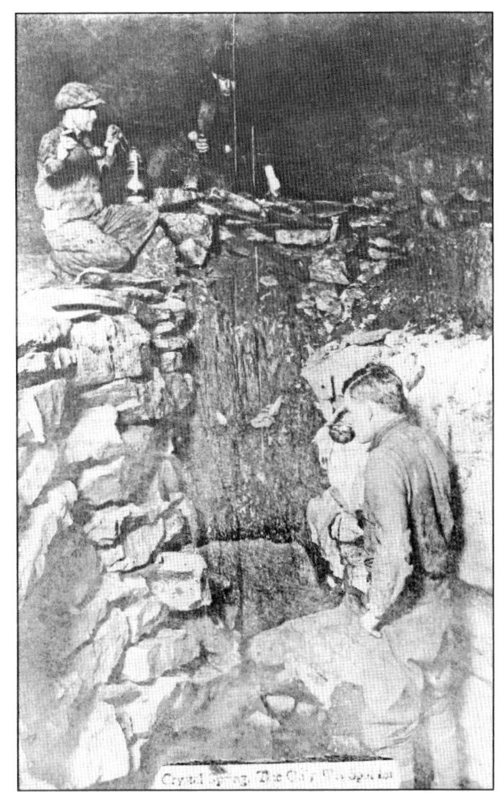

In the many months it took to develop the cave for tourists, Floyd Collins relentlessly explored the cave, often alone. To Collins, caving was a calculated risk, and he was willing to take that risk. If he was not guiding tourists, Collins would spend his days underground exploring. This photograph shows Collins behind some beautiful gypsum formations in Great Crystal Cave. (National Cave Museum.)

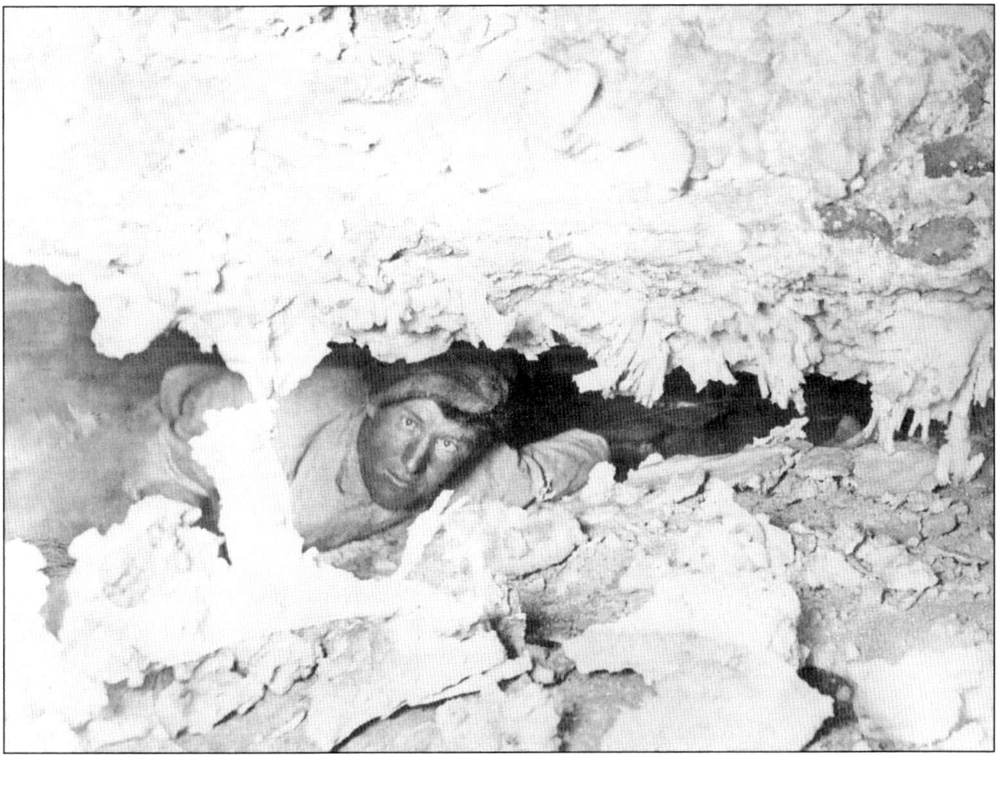

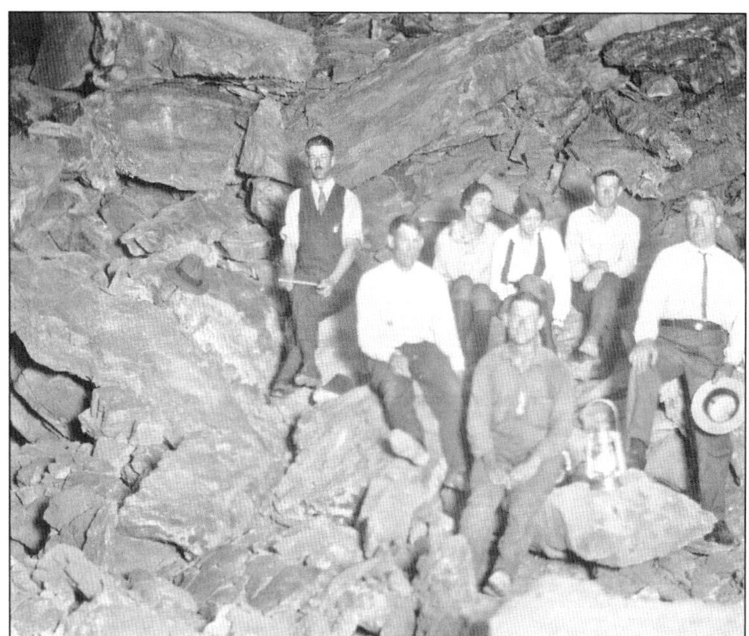

This 1924 photograph shows Floyd Collins and the Russell T. Neville party in Great Crystal Cave. From left to right are unidentified, Floyd Collins, Hazel Neville, Julia Neville, Homer Collins, Russell T. Neville, and unidentified (front). (Neville Collection, Cave Research Foundation.)

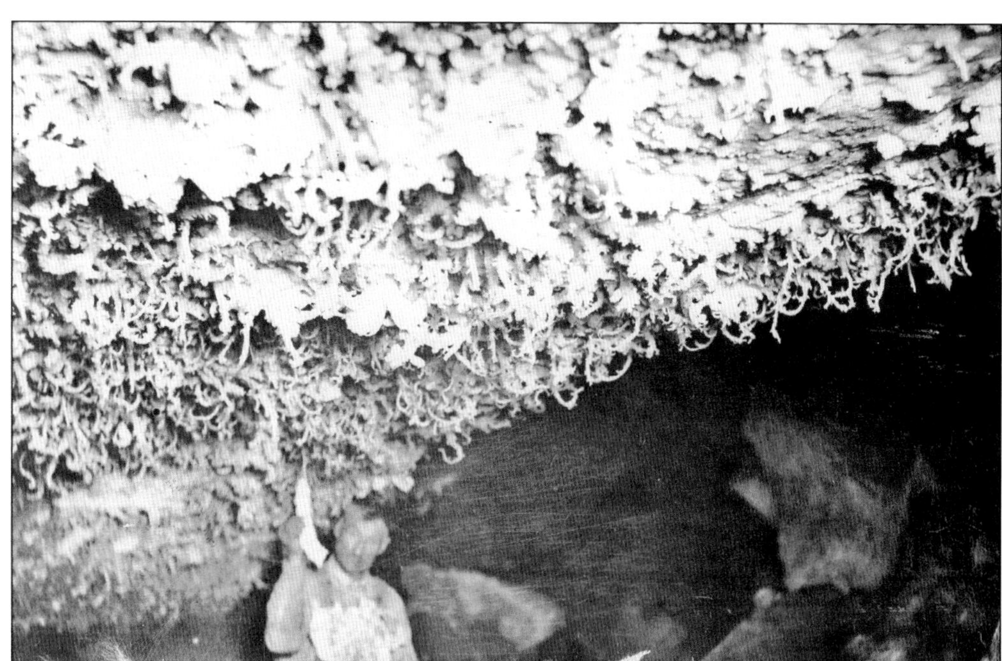

Floyd Collins's father, Lee Collins, is in a section of the Great Crystal Cave known as Nanny Ramsey's Flower Garden. This section of the cave was named after it reminded one visitor of her grandmother's flower garden at home. The "flower garden" displays beautiful white gypsum flowers growing from every inch of the wall and ceiling. (National Cave Museum.)

- See The -
New Onyx
Discovery
In

The Great Crystal Cave

The Most Beautiful Onyx Formations Yet Discovered In Any Cavern. ൳ New Avenue of This Beautiful Formation Shown This Year For The First Time

To help advertise the cave, a promotional brochure of Great Crystal Cave was put out by the Collins family between 1918 and 1925. According to the brochure, one could "wear your silk dresses if you like or your evening suit as no change of clothing is necessary." Representatives for the Great Crystal Cave solicited information to tourists at Mammoth Cave and Cave City. After Floyd Collins's death in 1925, the name of the cave was changed by Collins's father, Lee, to Floyd Collins' Crystal Cave. (National Cave Museum.)

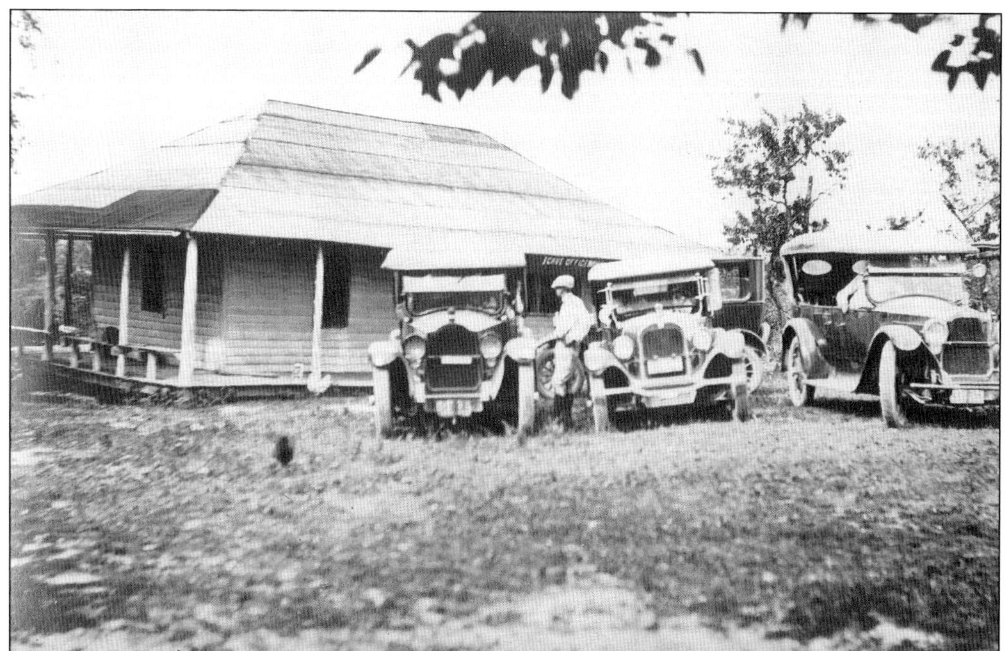

The Collins family constructed a second ticket office in 1921 near the Collins home and the path to Great Crystal Cave. The Great Crystal Cave ticket house, with hip roof, dog trot, wraparound porch, and clapboard siding, was used for selling cave tickets and souvenirs to tourists visiting Great Crystal Cave. (National Cave Museum.)

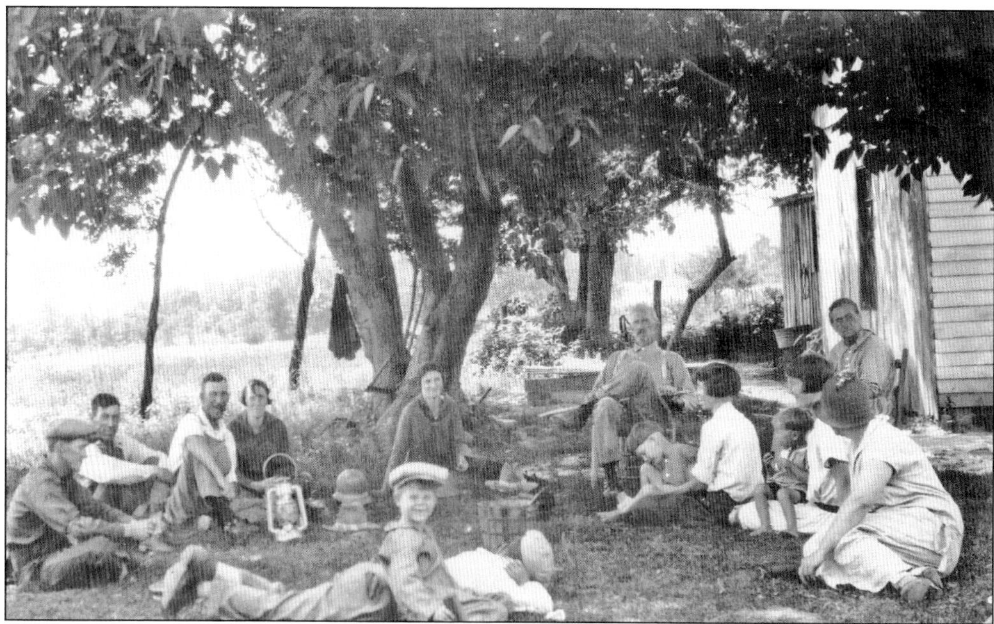

This 1920s photograph shows the Collins family on the west side of their home on Flint Ridge. From left to right are Marshall Collins, Andy Collins, Floyd Collins, Nellie Collins, and Homer Collins (face down on the ground). Lee and Jane Collins (Lee's second wife) are sitting in chairs. This is the only known photograph of the Collins family together as a group. (Pamela Jeter Wilson Collection.)

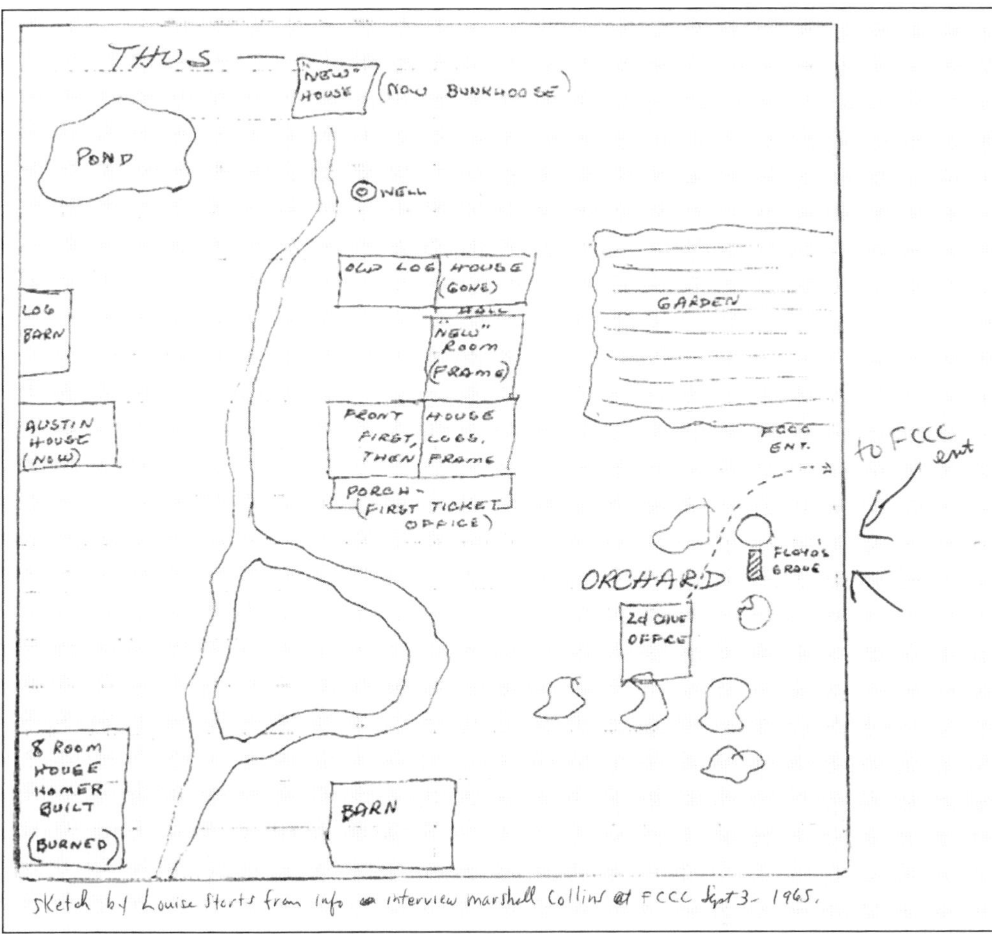

This is a 1965 sketch of the Collins homestead area according to Floyd Collins's brother Marshall. The sketch includes the location of the Collins family home, the first and second ticket offices, Floyd Collins's grave, and Great Crystal Cave. Also included is the boardinghouse that was built by Homer Collins in 1922. The boardinghouse caught fire, along with the barn, in 1924. (Sketch by Louise "Micki" Storts, Cave Research Foundation.)

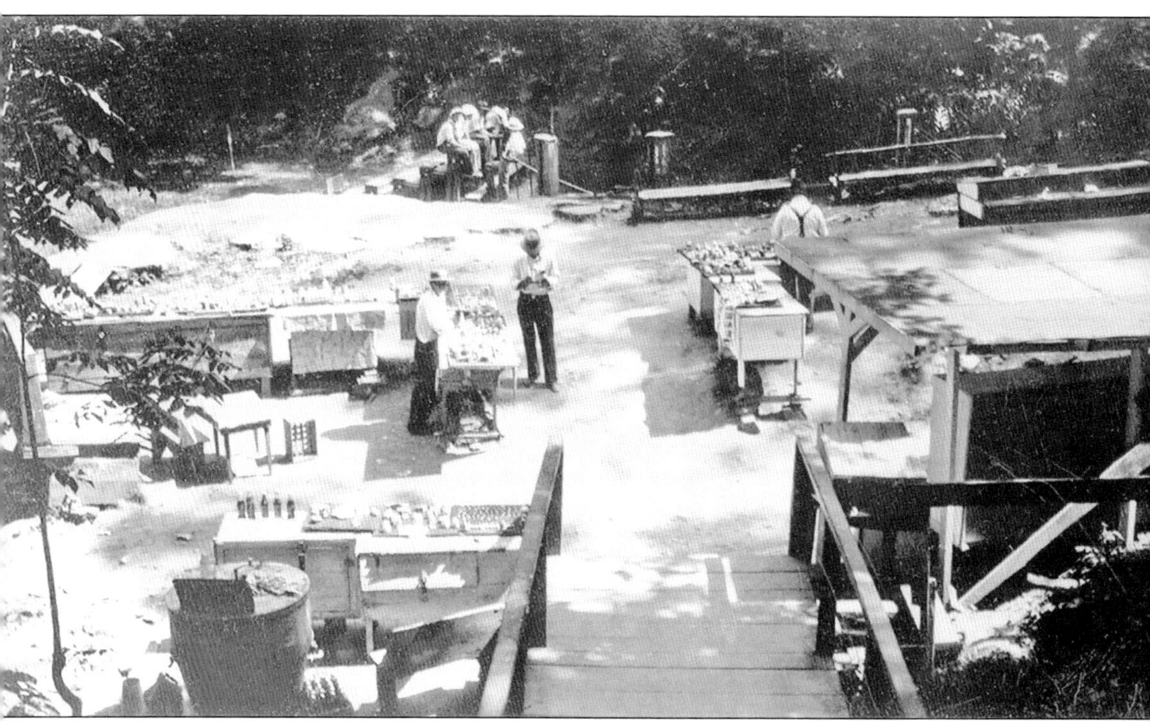

Souvenir stands like these were common on the public road leading to Mammoth Cave, which, at the time, extended all the way to the entrance of the cave. Floyd Collins, as well as other locals, sold rocks and formations from these stands to tourists to help bring in more income for their families. The selling of cave formations is forbidden by law today. (John Benton Collection.)

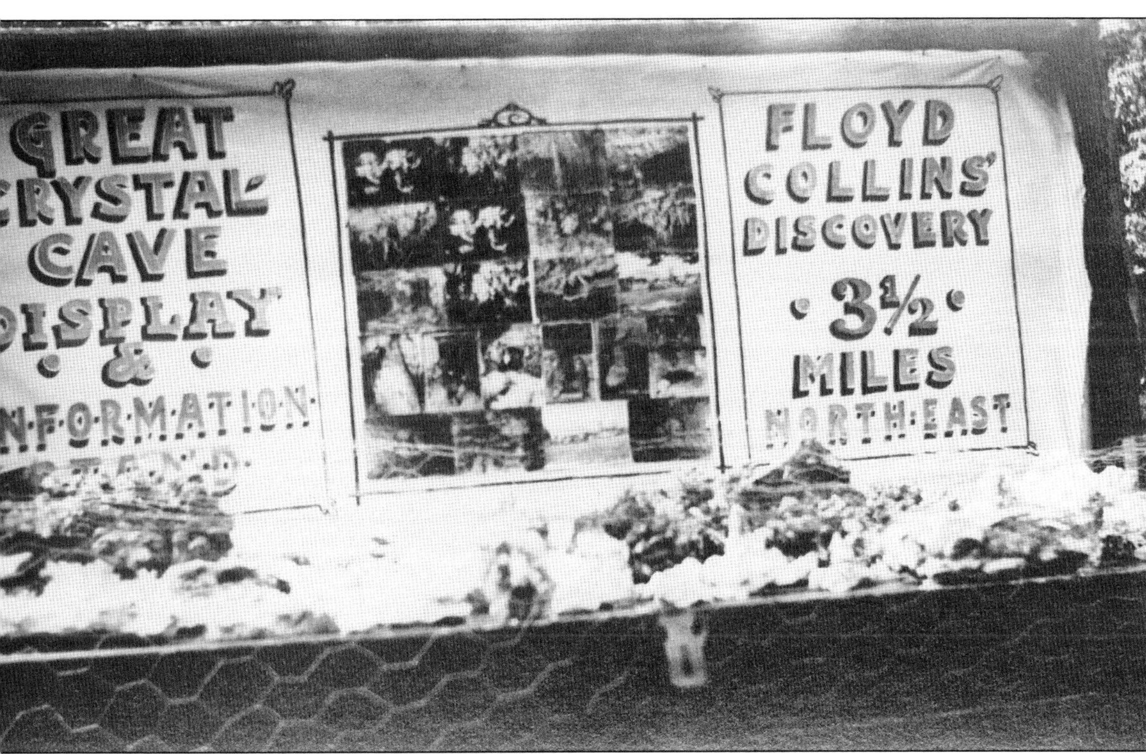

Great Crystal Cave used this display to show photographs and specimens from their cave. Great Crystal Cave had a display at Mammoth Cave along the public road and a second display located in Cave City. Floyd Collins would occasionally break off a piece of gypsum (also forbidden by law today) in Great Crystal Cave to give to a tourist as a souvenir. (National Cave Museum.)

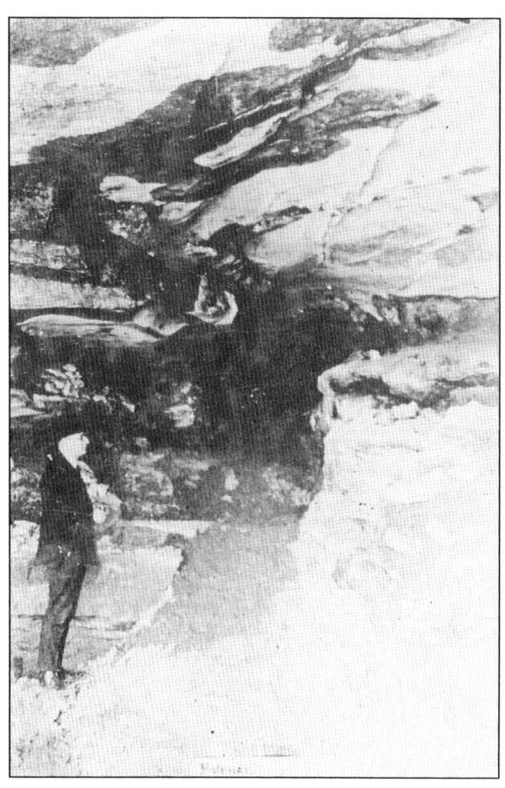

Buzzard Cave was another small cave on the Collins property that the Collins brothers explored. The cave was later renamed Cathedral Cave after it was sold to Dr. Harry Thomas, the same man who bought Floyd Collins' Crystal Cave in 1927. A single strand of electric lights was run to this short cave; it was advertised as being electrically lit. The Buzzard Cave entrance, looking in, is shown at left and the entrance, looking out, is shown below. (Left, Bill Napper Collection; below, National Cave Museum.)

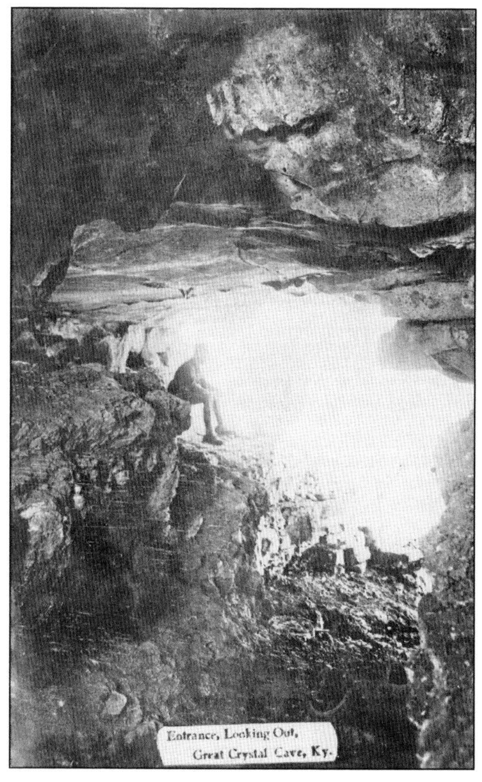

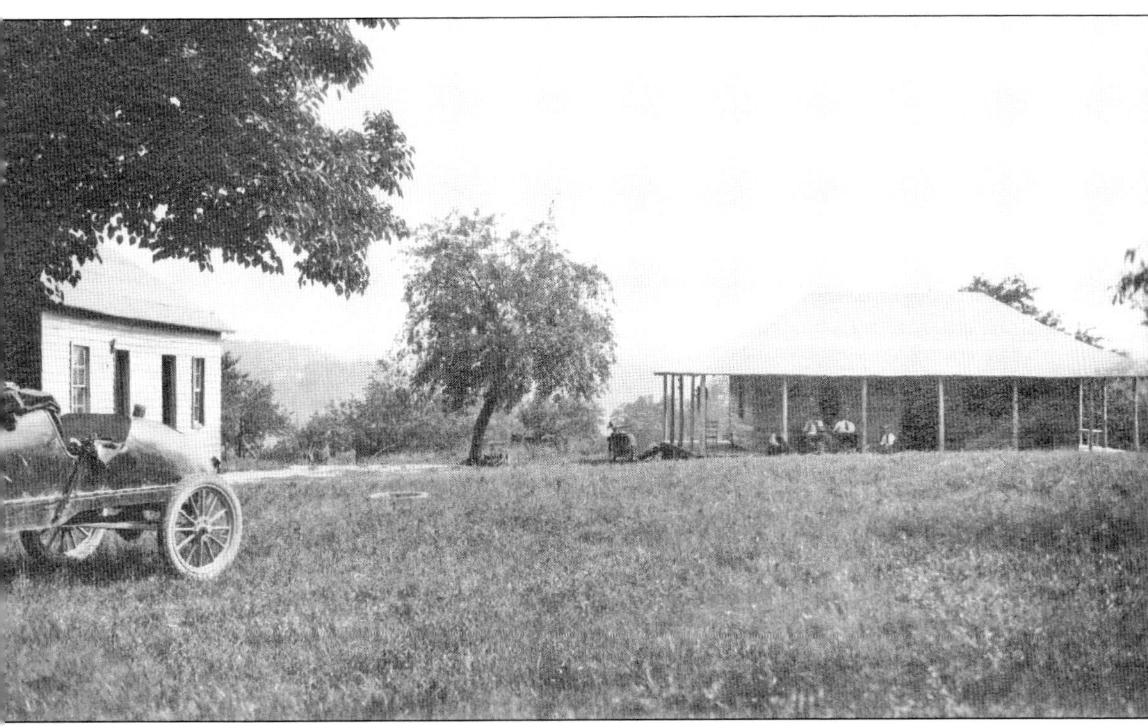

Charles A. Lindbergh, the American aviator, paid a visit to the cave region of Kentucky in 1921 while he was attending officer training school at Camp (later Fort) Knox. Lindbergh, with a couple of friends, visited Mammoth Cave and Great Crystal Cave. They were guided through Great Crystal Cave by Homer Collins, Floyd's brother. Lindbergh was an unknown at the time of his visit; his transatlantic flight from New York to Paris was not made until 1927. Lindbergh took this 1921 photograph of the Collins home (left) and ticket office (right), along with Lindbergh's 1919 Excelsior Big X motorcycle (next to ticket office) and his companion's Ford Speedster. Even though it has been written that Lindbergh was present at the 1925 Collins entrapment, there are no photographs or documentation to support this claim. Lindbergh was stationed in Texas as an Army Air Service Reserve pilot at the time of the Collins tragedy. (Minnesota Historical Society, catalog number 001676963.)

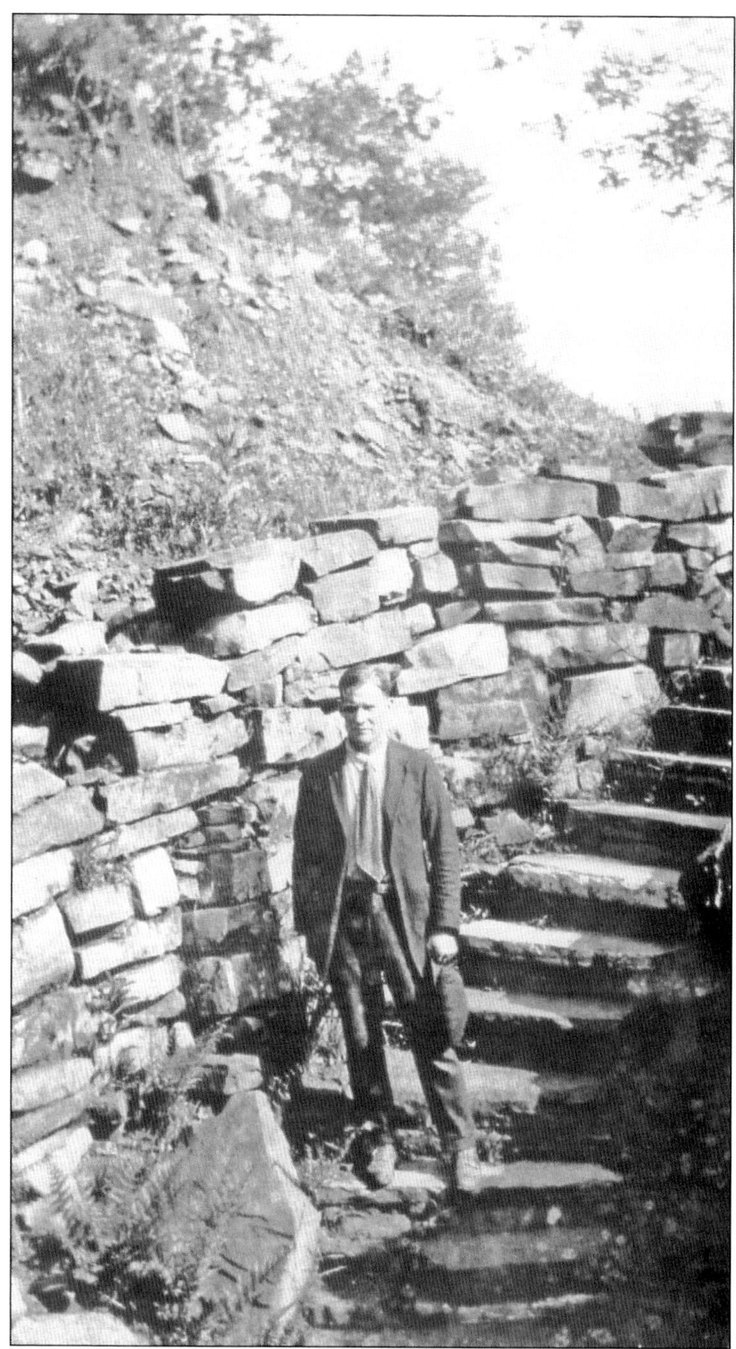

It became obvious to Floyd Collins that although Great Crystal Cave was the most spectacular cave in the area, it was too far from the main road to be a booming success. Tourists had to pass New Entrance to Mammoth Cave, Mammoth Cave, and Great Onyx Cave before they came to Great Crystal Cave. Also, the road to the cave was narrow and hilly, with mud holes, rocks, and ruts. Great Crystal Cave had been owned and operated by the Collins family since 1918 but had never made a profit. Floyd Collins is shown here going down the steps to Great Crystal Cave. (Neville Collection, Cave Research Foundation.)

Four

Trapped in Sand Cave

A Nation Becomes Gripped in One Man's Struggle

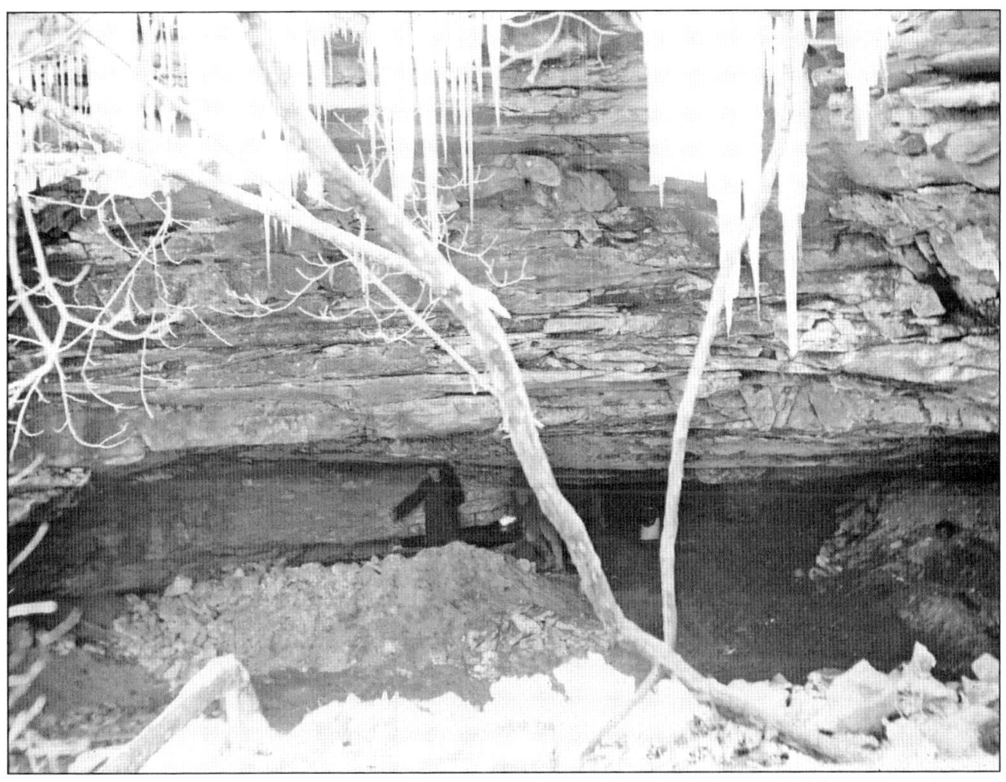

Floyd Collins continued his explorations in an attempt to find a more profitable cave to show to tourists. He eventually found a promising small cave (pictured) close to the main road to Mammoth Cave on the land of Bee Doyel, Ed Estes, and J.L. Cox. Collins struck a deal with the men to give them half interest if he found a cave on their land. (Wade Highbaugh Collection.)

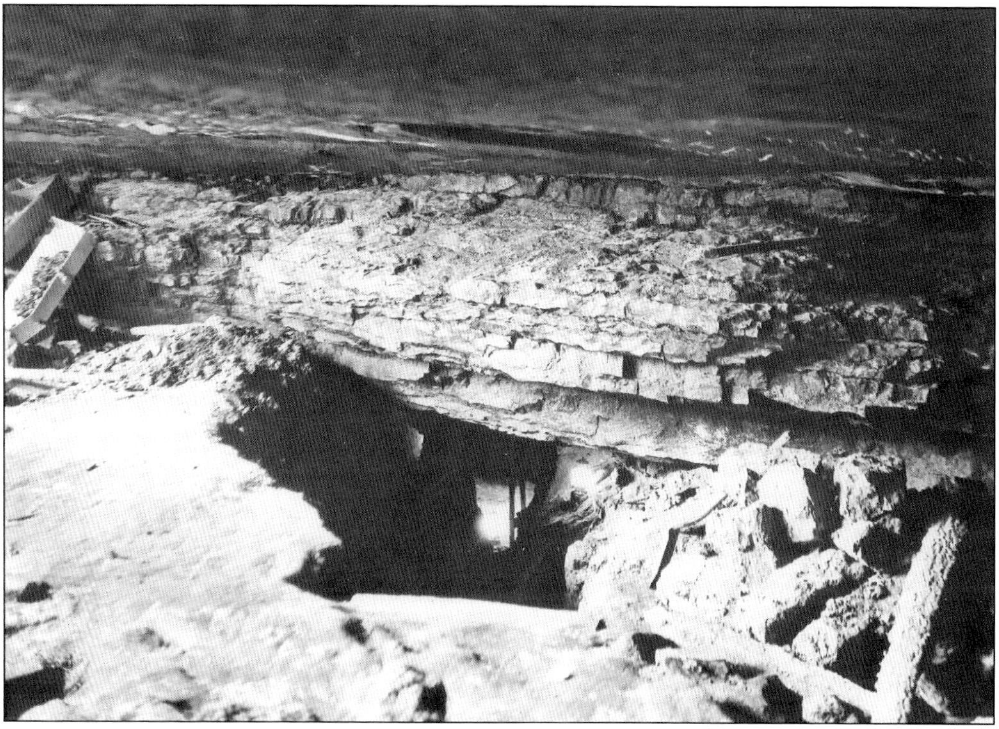

On Friday, January 30, 1925, Floyd Collins began exploring Sand Cave. He had given the cave this name after he found white sand in the layers of rock, and the name stuck. Collins was trying to find his way through a jumble of rocks in a small passageway where he had to crawl, hoping to find a large open cave passage or room. (Neville Collection, Cave Research Foundation.)

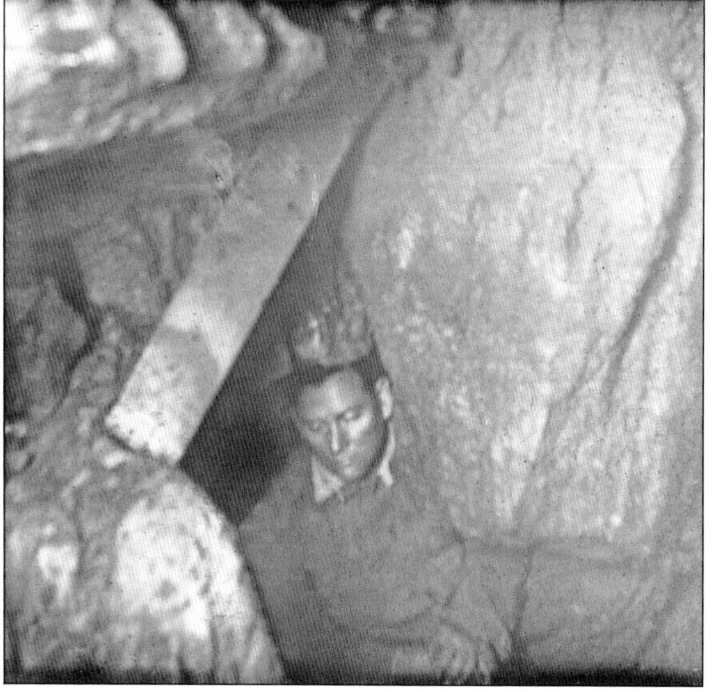

As Collins began to exit from Sand Cave, a 27-pound rock fell from a pocket in the cave ceiling and caught his foot from behind. Collins was in a prone position of about 45 degrees and there was not enough room for him to reach over his body to dislodge the rock. He tried his best to maintain his composure and avoid panic. The individual pictured is unidentified. (Wade Highbaugh Collection.)

Floyd Collins had been stuck in caves before, but he had always been able to free himself quickly. As the last drop of fuel in his coal oil lantern ran out, Collins was now in total darkness. He continued to struggle and try to free himself. All he could do was pray and wait for help to come in the constant 54-degree temperature of the cave. (National Cave Museum.)

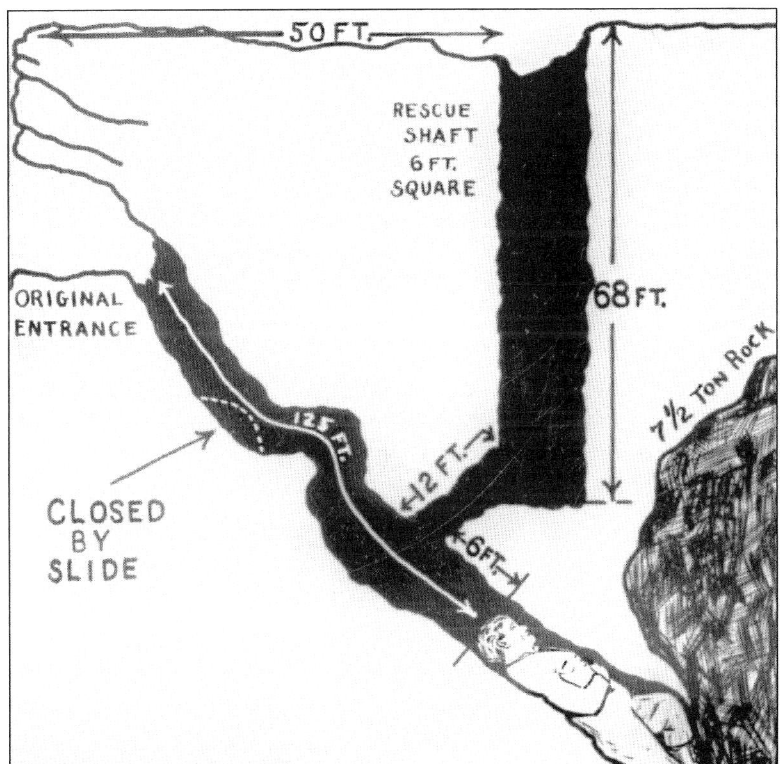

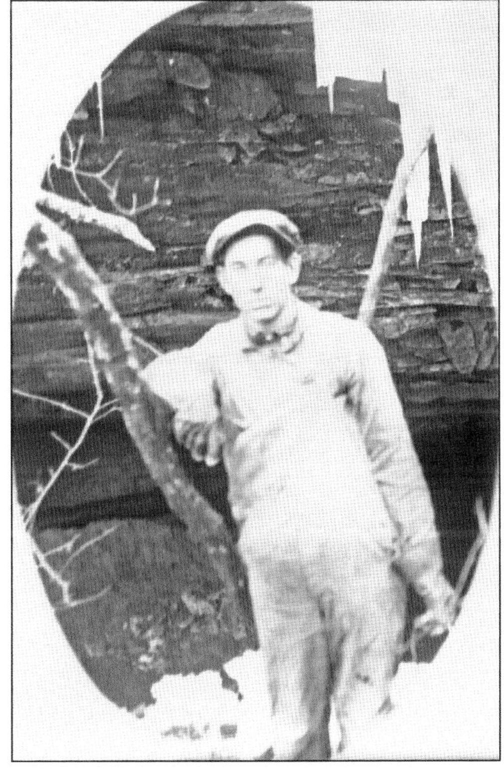

On Saturday, January 31, 1925, Bee Doyel checked Floyd Collins's sleeping quarters to find that Collins was missing. Jewell Estes (pictured), the 17-year-old son of Ed, went to the cave to check on Collins with Doyel and found Collins's coat and cap still hanging on a ledge just outside the entrance to Sand Cave. Jewell, being the most slender person of the group, started into the crawlway to find Collins. (Wade Highbaugh Collection.)

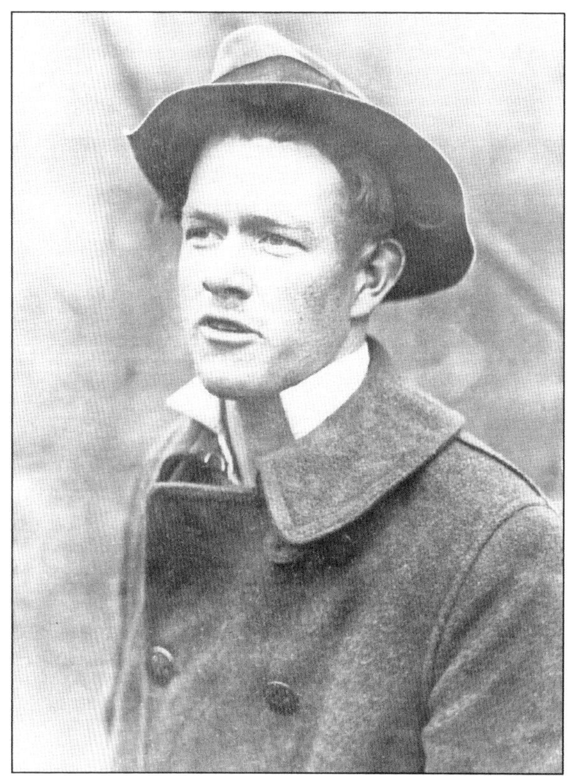

Jewell Estes entered Sand Cave and got within 20 feet of Floyd Collins, finding him trapped. Collins's brother Marshall arrived and crawled down with a crowbar but could not free him, being unable to reach over Floyd to dislodge the rock holding his foot. One of Floyd's other brothers, Homer (pictured), was contacted in Louisville; upon his arrival, he immediately headed to the cave entrance. (David Jones Collection.)

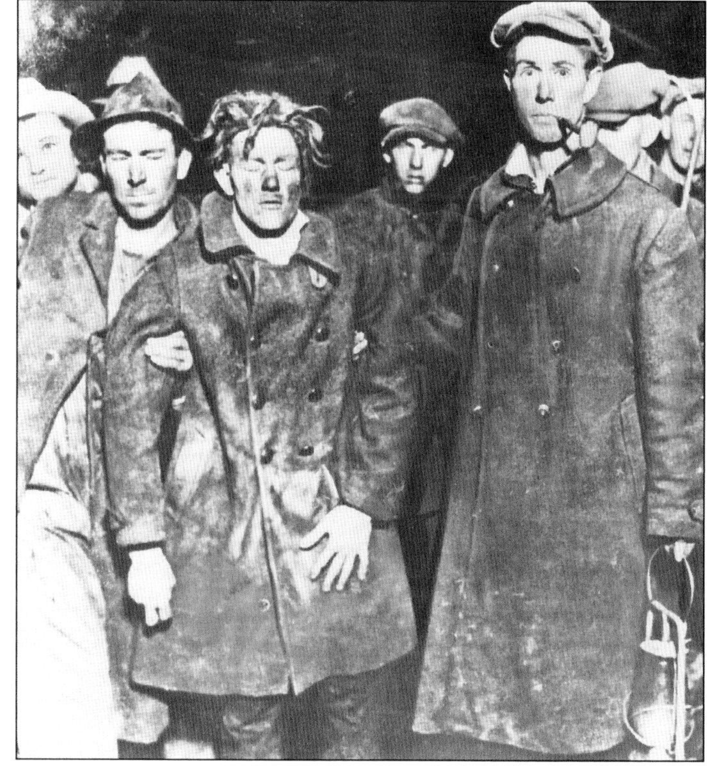

Homer Collins (pictured being helped out) was the first man to go inside the cave with food and drink for his brother. Homer worked eight terrible hours, removing about two bushels of loose rock, clay, and gravel around the upper portion of Floyd's body. Exhausted, Homer had to be persuaded to leave the cave around dawn the next morning. (David Jones Collection.)

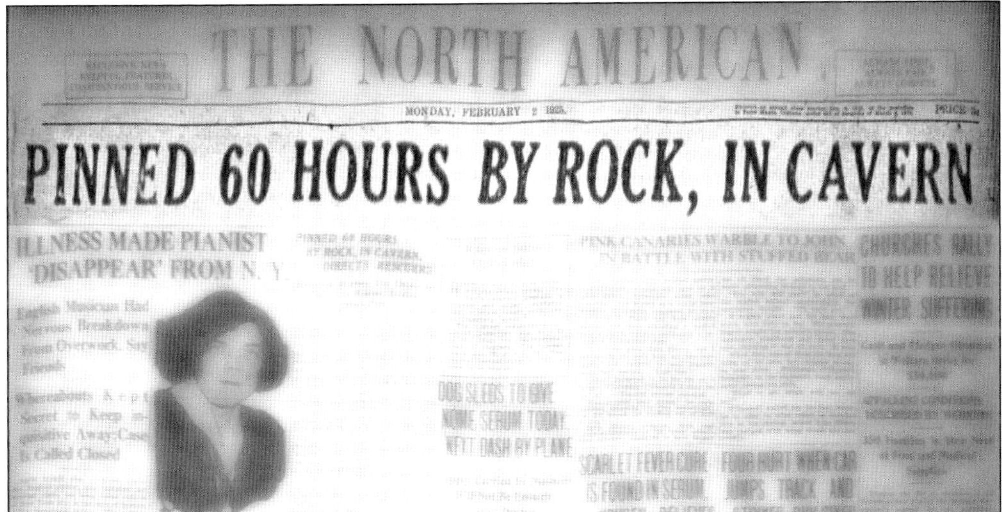

THE NORTH AMERICAN

MONDAY, FEBRUARY 2 1925.

PINNED 60 HOURS BY ROCK, IN CAVERN

ILLNESS MADE PIANIST 'DISAPPEAR' FROM N. Y.

DOG SLEDS TO GIVE NOME SERUM TODAY

CHURCHES RALLY TO HELP RELIEVE WINTER SUFFERING

SCARLET FEVER CURE IS FOUND IN SERUM

On Sunday, February 1, 1925, Homer Collins and Johnny Gerald, Floyd's good friend, went into Sand Cave but were unable to free Collins. Newspapers from all over the country started printing daily accounts of the Collins entrapment story on their front pages. No one knew who Floyd Collins was, but the stories about him captured everyone's attention. Newspapers included full layouts and photographs. (National Cave Museum.)

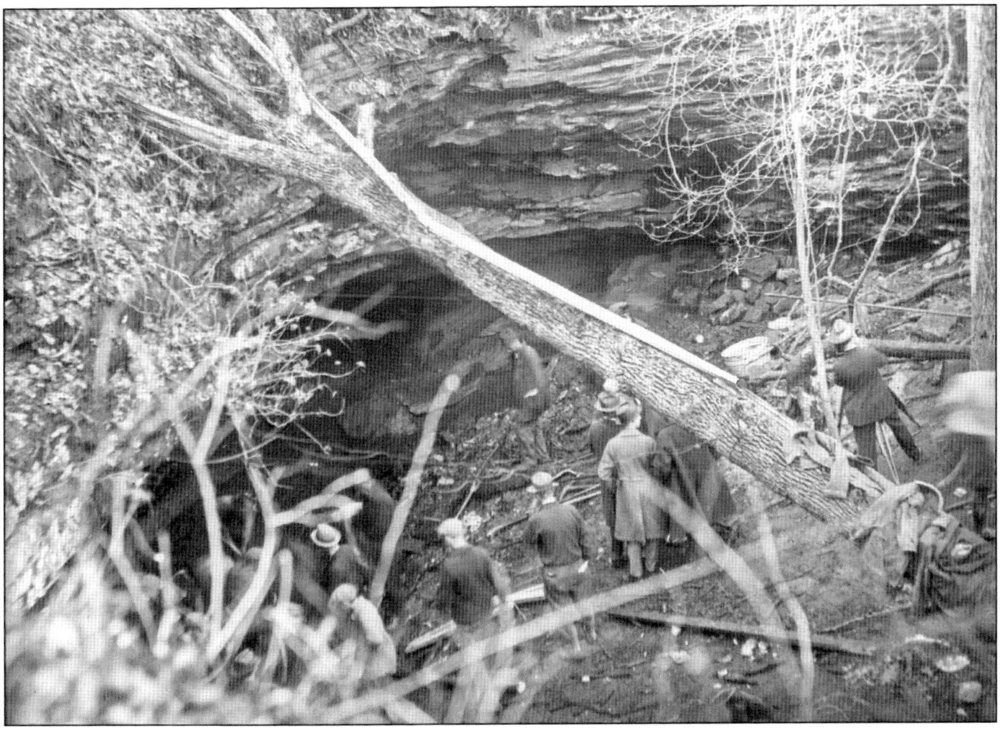

Interest from all over the country came in the form of volunteers, encouraging letters, and money. Onlookers continued to grow in number around Sand Cave, and so did the presence of moonshine. Cave City magistrate Clay Turner and William Hanson, town marshal, worried about the crowds and events getting out of control and sent a telegram to Kentucky governor William J. Fields for assistance. (Wade Highbaugh Collection.)

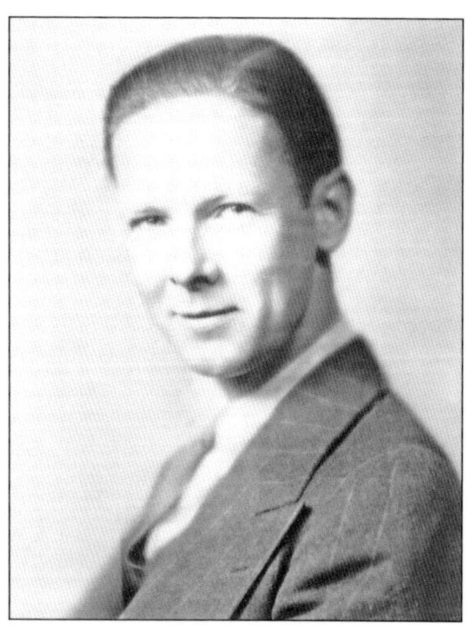

On Monday, February 2, 1925, *Louisville Courier-Journal* reporter William Burke "Skeets" Miller arrived at Sand Cave. Miller made seven trips into the cave throughout the ordeal to interview and feed Collins. Miller described Collins's entrapment as being like a cork in a bottle, with precious little room to work around his body to free his trapped foot. Miller, who was only five feet, five inches and 120 pounds, became a story unto himself and received a Pullitzer Prize for his coverage of the rescue attempt. (Bob Thompson Collection.)

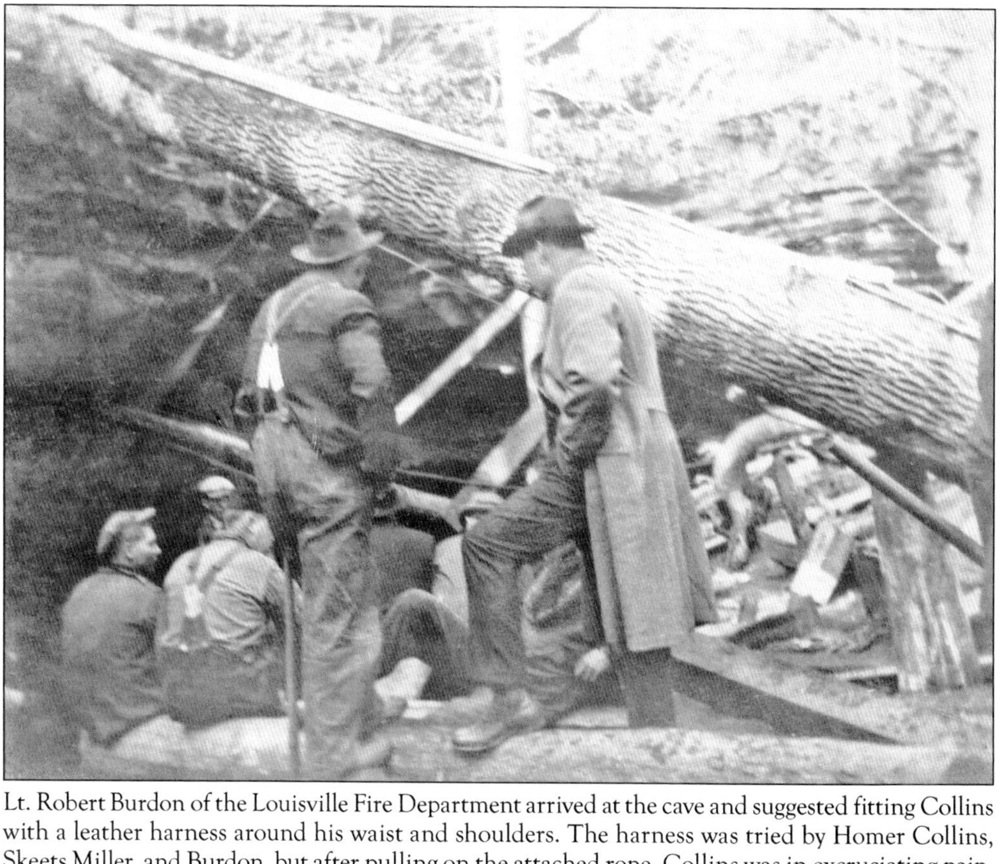

Lt. Robert Burdon of the Louisville Fire Department arrived at the cave and suggested fitting Collins with a leather harness around his waist and shoulders. The harness was tried by Homer Collins, Skeets Miller, and Burdon, but after pulling on the attached rope, Collins was in excruciating pain, so the plan was stopped. An award was offered by Homer Collins to anyone who could bring his brother out alive. (National Cave Museum.)

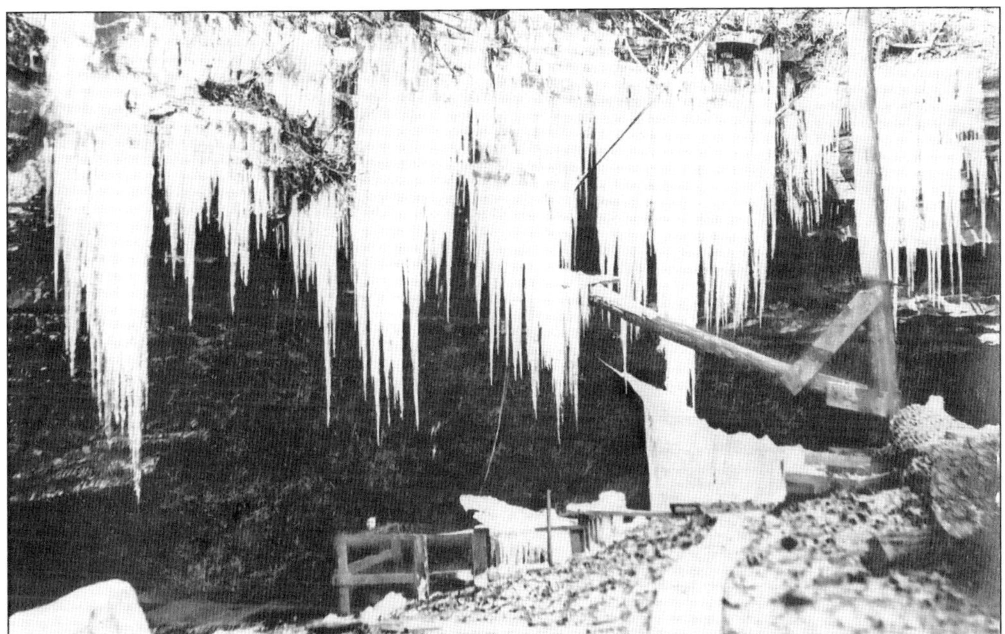

Many haphazard rescue parties entered Sand Cave. Later it was learned some never even made it to Collins, as stashes of milk, food, and coffee were found along the route or pushed into crevices or rock ledges. H.C. Lane, who had a Delco lighting outfit, ran a set of wires with a light bulb inside the cave. It was placed on Collins's chest. (Dean Snyder Collection.)

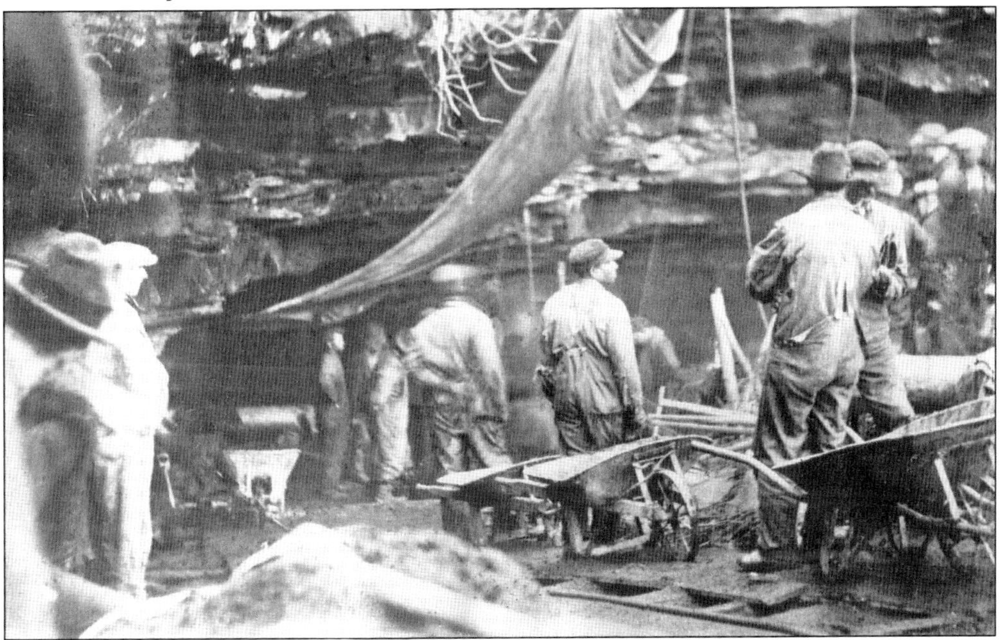

On Tuesday, February 3, 1925, in contrast to much drinking and rowdiness on the surface, Johnny Gerald, along with West Point graduate Lt. Ben Wells and Charles E. Whittle, the 25-year-old president of Ogden College in Bowling Green, entered Sand Cave just after midnight and for over five hours removed much rock and gravel from around Collins's body. It was tough, physically demanding work. (National Cave Museum.)

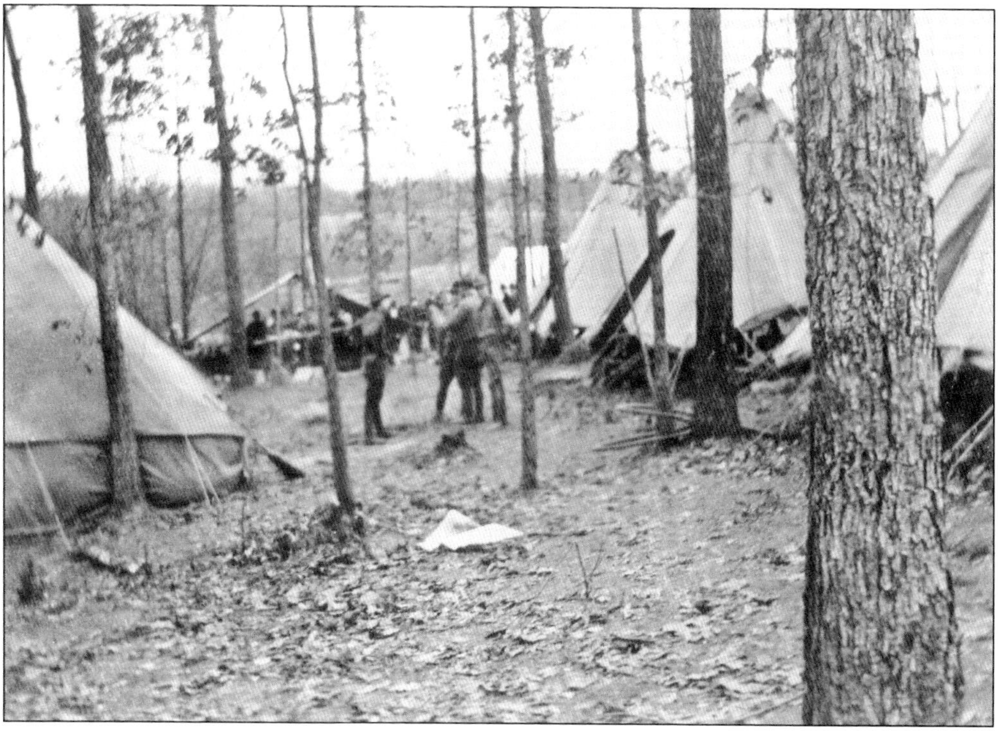

Workers started bringing in emergency supplies, including food and tents. A hospital tent was set up with Dr. William Hazlett from Chicago in charge. Injured persons were given treatment, and the unit would be ready to move Collins, if he stayed alive, to the hospital in Glasgow. Below, Hazlett (at center) is shown talking to Homer Collins and the reporters about Floyd Collins's situation. (Both, National Cave Museum.)

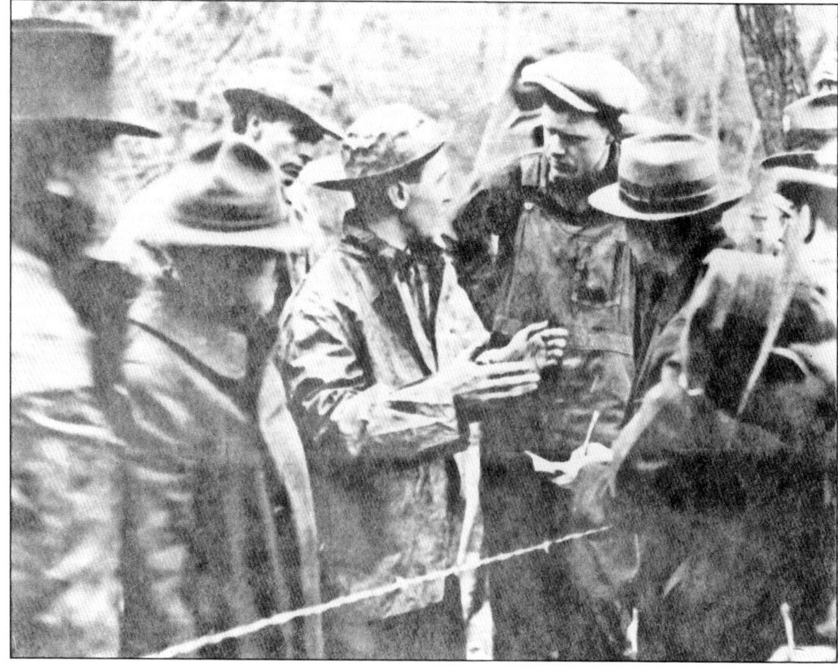

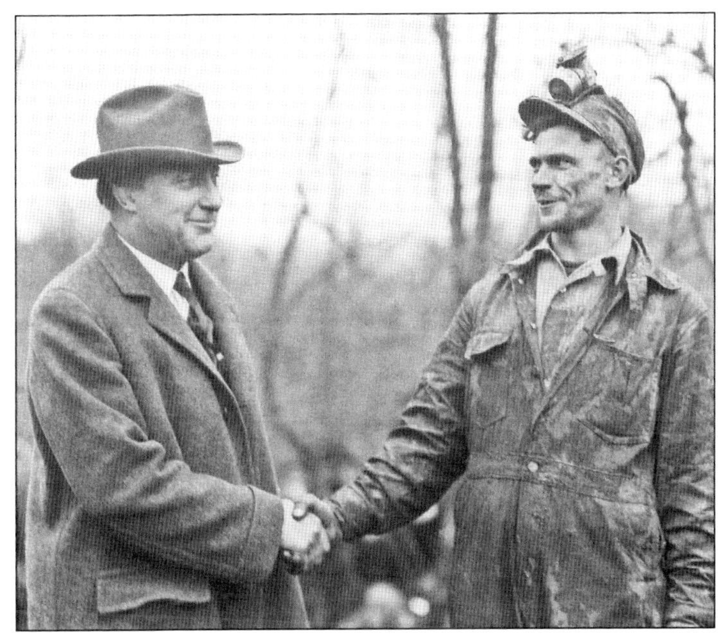

Kentucky governor William J. Fields assigned the lieutenant governor, Brig. Gen. Henry H. Denhardt (left), to take control of the rescue operations. Denhardt was not well liked, seeming arrogant and controlling to the locals. An unhealthy competitive environment between the locals and outsiders began. Denhardt would not allow Homer Collins or Johnny Gerald into Sand Cave, although both did reenter later in the rescue attempt. (David Jones Collection.)

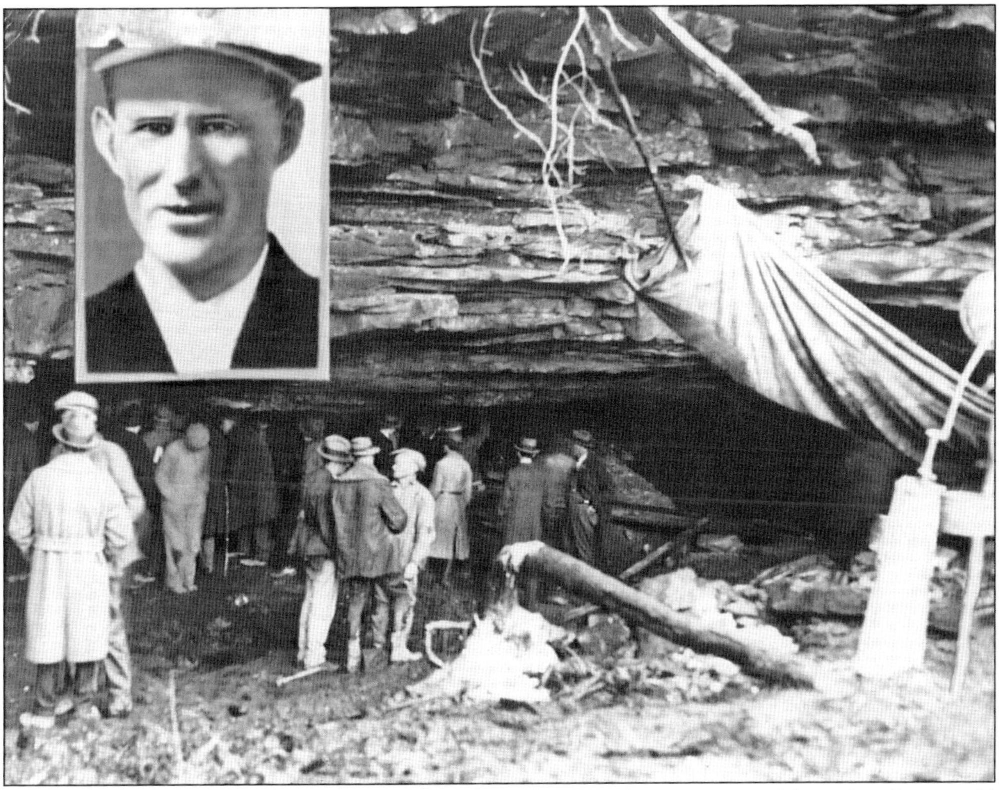

Skeets Miller went into Sand Cave three times in one day and came out confident that they would get Collins (inset) out. On the first trip of the day, Miller and 13 other men crawled in and used a chip hammer to enlarge the cave. As each piece of rock was broken off, it was passed to another and relayed out to the entrance. (Dean Snyder Collection.)

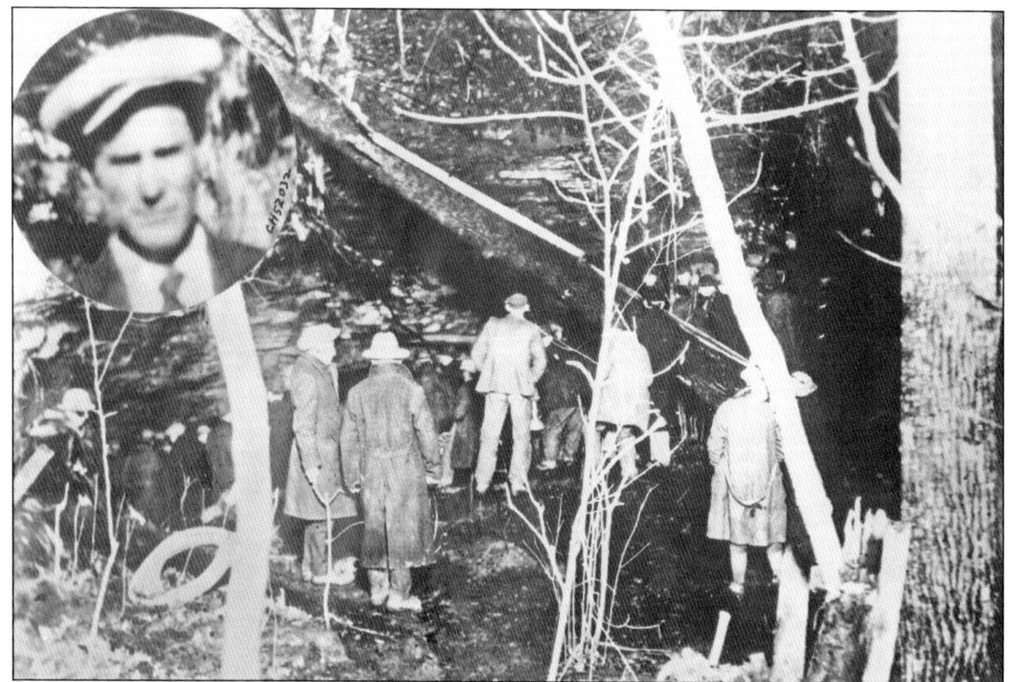

On his second trip into the cave, Skeets Miller brought Collins (inset) milk and whiskey. It seemed the liquids helped, as Collins began to talk as though he would make it out alive. The third time in, the workmen passed an automobile jack to Miller, hoping to be able to raise the rock, but the jack slipped each time. (Dean Snyder Collection.)

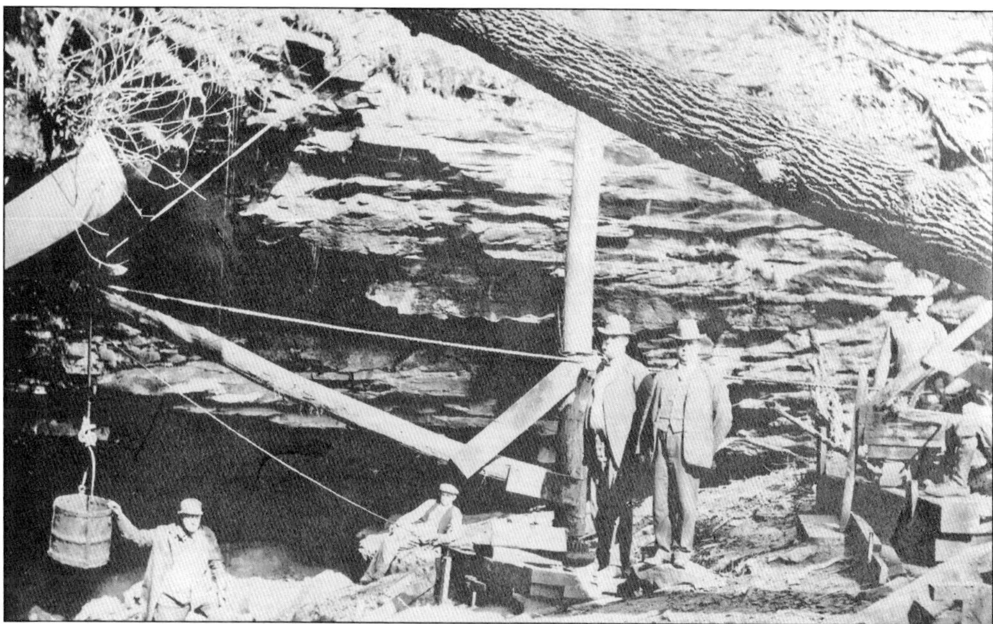

On Wednesday, February 4, 1925, Everett Maddox and Ben Fishback, part of the jack rescue attempt, stayed behind and talked to Collins. Maddox and Fishback reported a rock fall that blocked the cave passage where Collins was trapped. Rescuers could talk to Collins through the narrow passage, but could no longer get to him as they had before. (Wade Highbaugh Collection.)

Johnny Gerald, with a small crew, tried to shore up the cave passage where the collapse had occurred. As others were starting to give up hope on rescuing Collins, Skeets Miller was still planning a way to get Collins out. Everett Maddox, a miner, helped Miller lead trips into the cave. (National Cave Museum.)

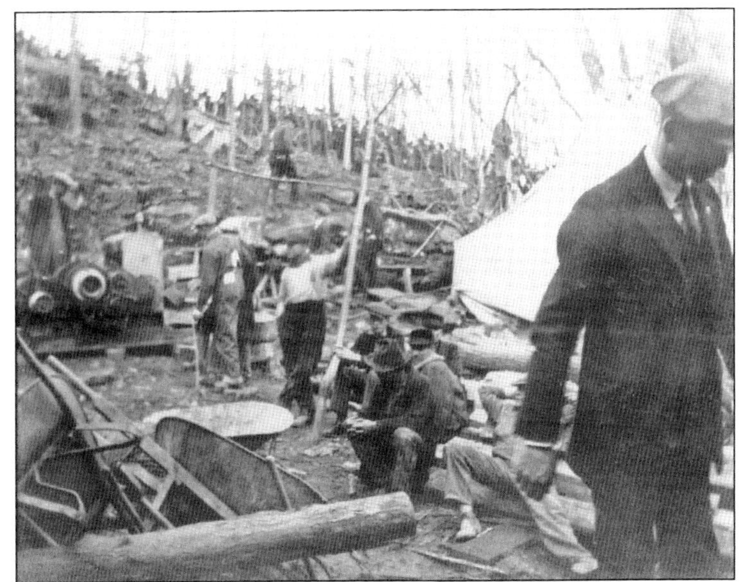

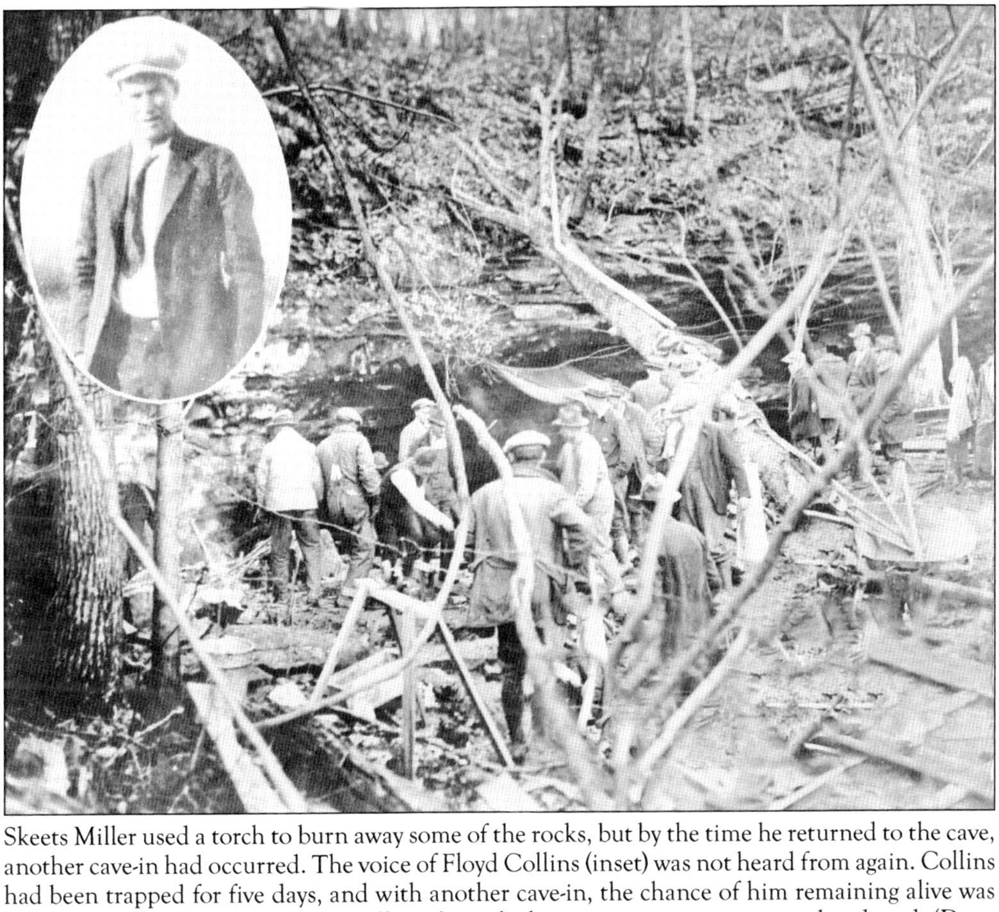

Skeets Miller used a torch to burn away some of the rocks, but by the time he returned to the cave, another cave-in had occurred. The voice of Floyd Collins (inset) was not heard from again. Collins had been trapped for five days, and with another cave-in, the chance of him remaining alive was now slim. The attempt to rescue Collins through the narrow passageway was abandoned. (Dean Snyder Collection.)

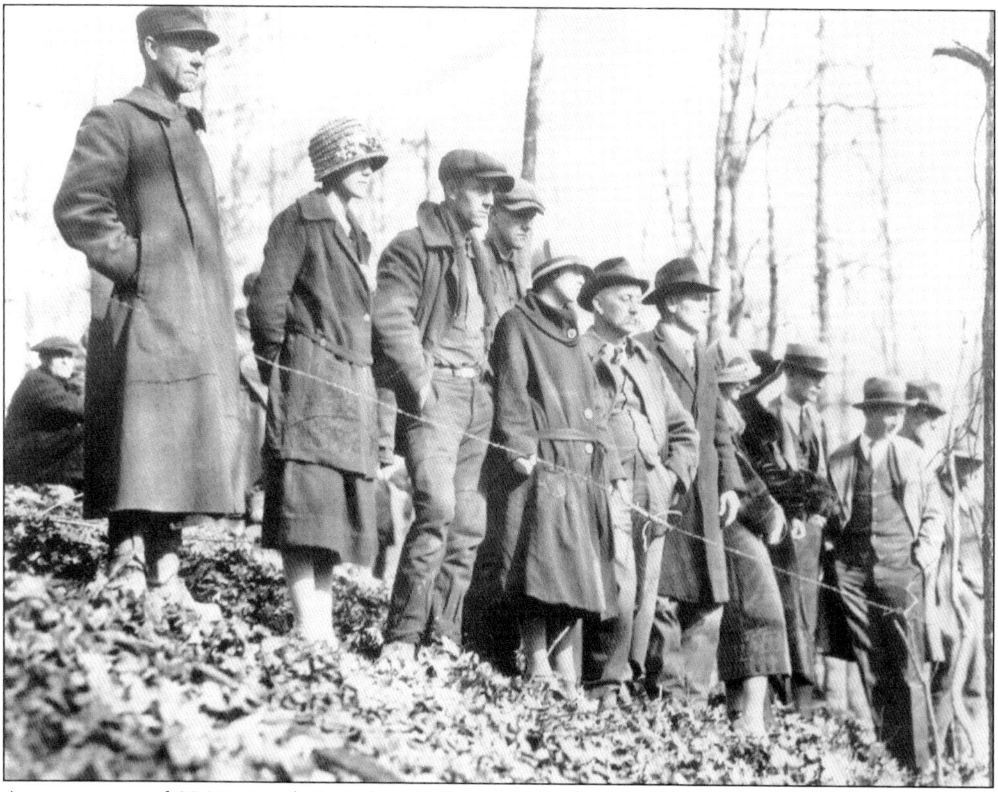

A contingent of 33 National Guardsmen from nearby Smiths Grove arrived on the scene, but they were not enough to control the large crowd, and more people kept coming. More troops were ordered to the scene from Bowling Green. (Dean Snyder Collection.)

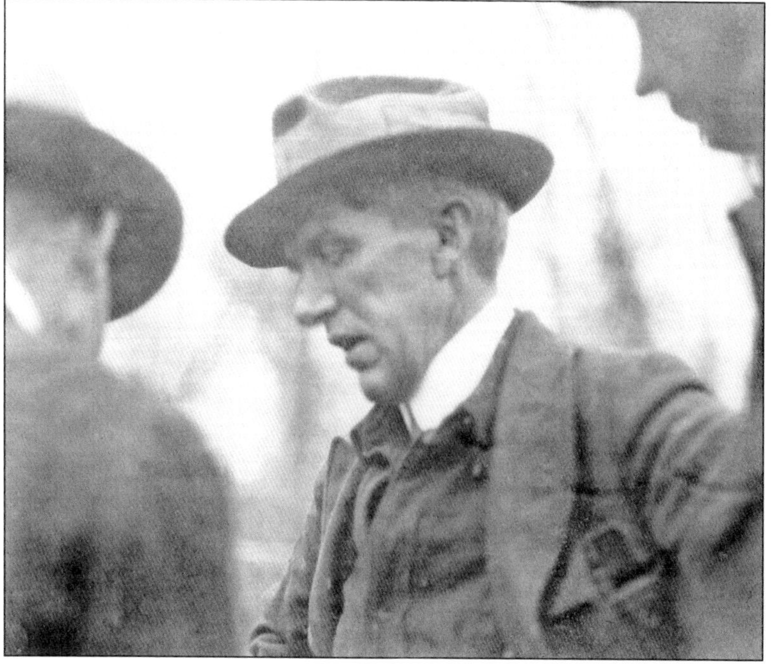

On Thursday, February 5, 1925, a plan to dig a vertical shaft to rescue Collins was discussed and started. Henry T. Carmichael, manager of the local Kyrock asphalt plant and quarry, was put in charge of the shaft. A crude but efficient hoist with a small gasoline motor was installed above the shaft to raise debris vertically. (David Jones Collection.)

Carmichael had a stout wooden railway laid from the mouth of the shaft over the edge of the valley to dump the debris coming out of the cave. He appealed for labor and materials, and companies such as the Louisville & Nashville Railroad generously responded. Crews from several colleges, such as Vanderbilt and Western Kentucky State Normal School, answered the call for labor on the shaft. (Right, Highbaugh Collection; below, National Cave Museum.)

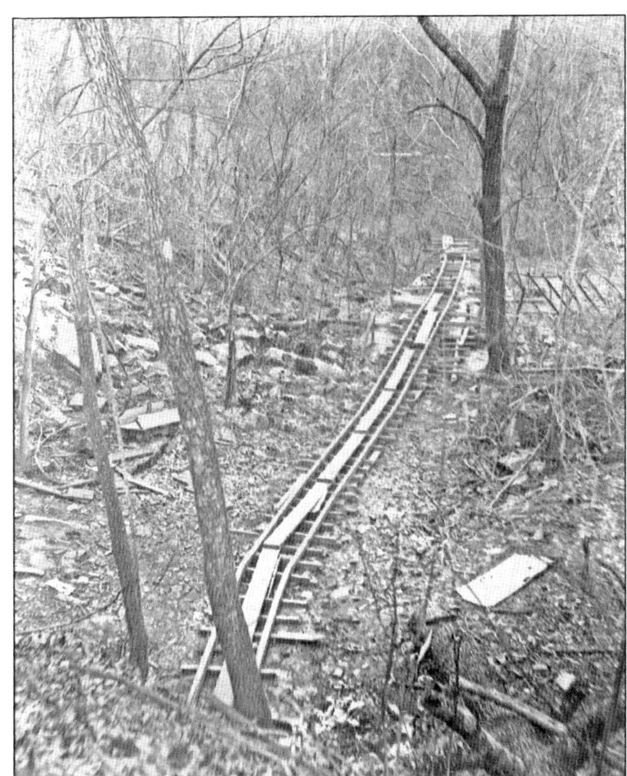

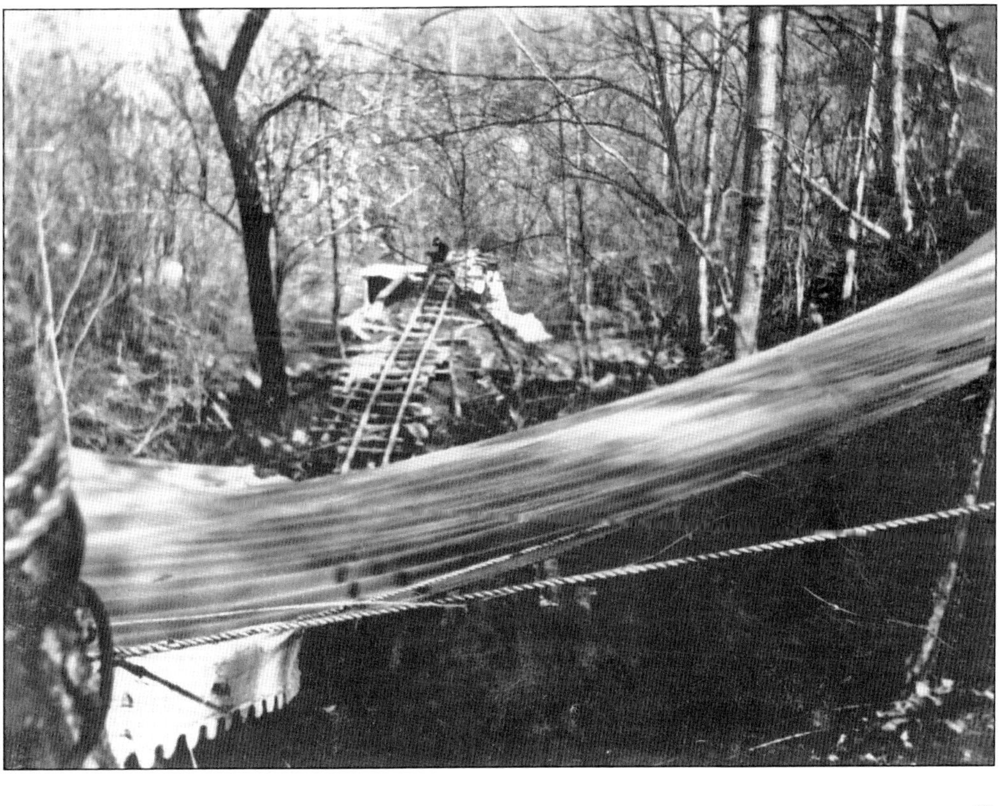

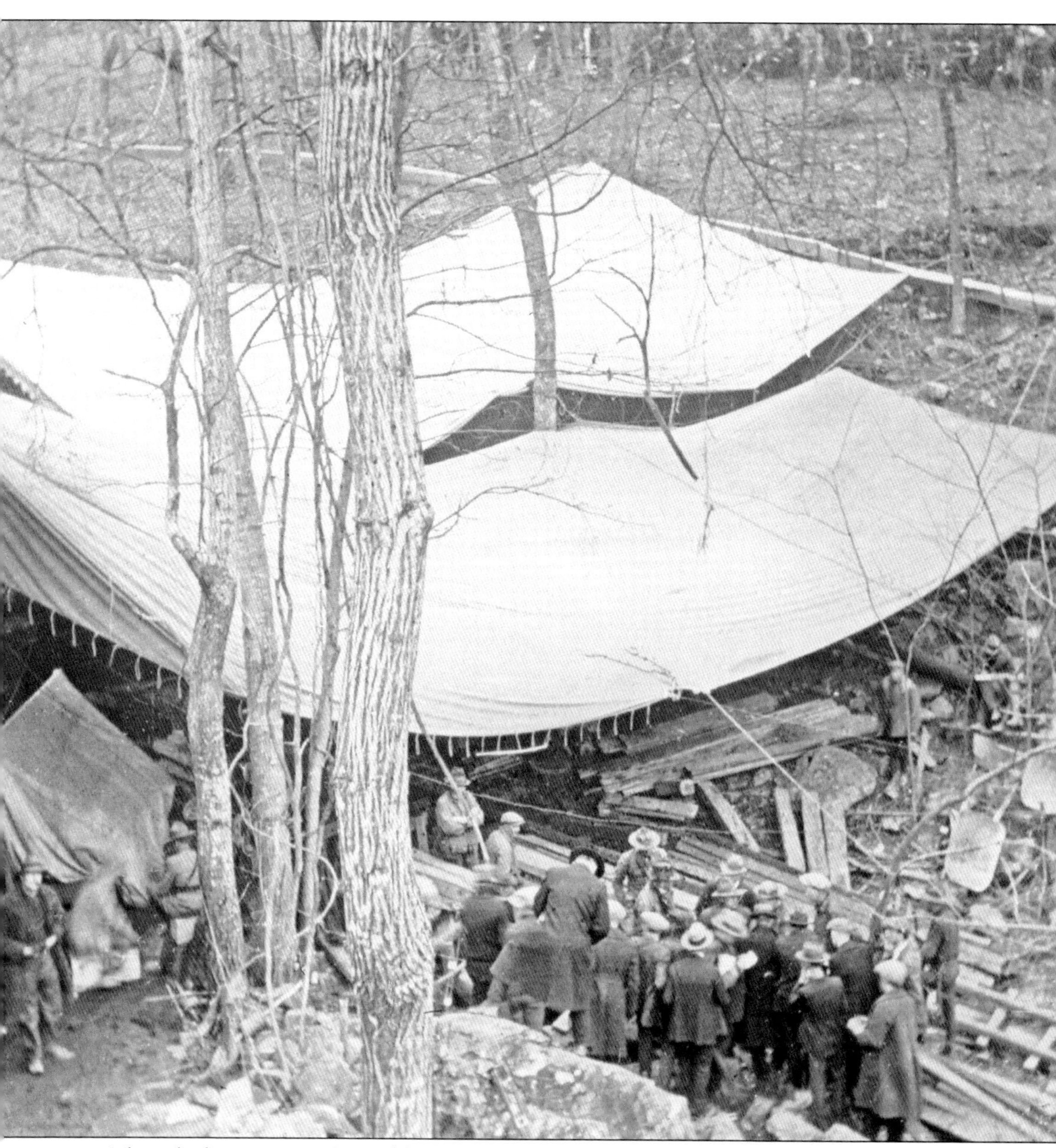

A board of strategy was formed by Henry T. Carmichael, Prof. William D. Funkhouser from the University of Kentucky, and M.E.S. Posey, secretary of the Kentucky State Highway Commission. Carmichael coined the slogan, "Dig, Dump, and Pray" with hopes of the shaft reaching Collins while he was still alive. A 2,400-square-foot canvas tarp was tented over the Sand Cave shaft by Carmichael's crews to protect themselves from the weather. (National Cave Museum.)

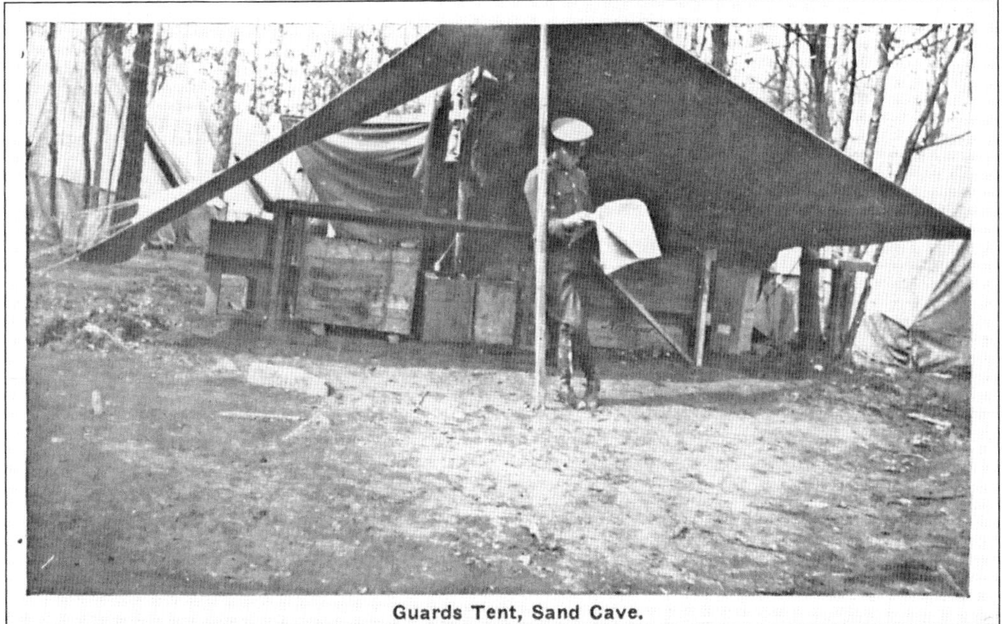

Ed Brenner, Albert Marshall, and Albert Blevins were called the "three musketeers of Carmichaels' legion," as they worked very hard digging the shaft. The State of Kentucky took over the scene. Army tents started dotting the landscape. The National Guard was there in force. Boundary areas were marked off with strands of barbed-wire fence, the yellow caution tape of its day. (National Cave Museum.)

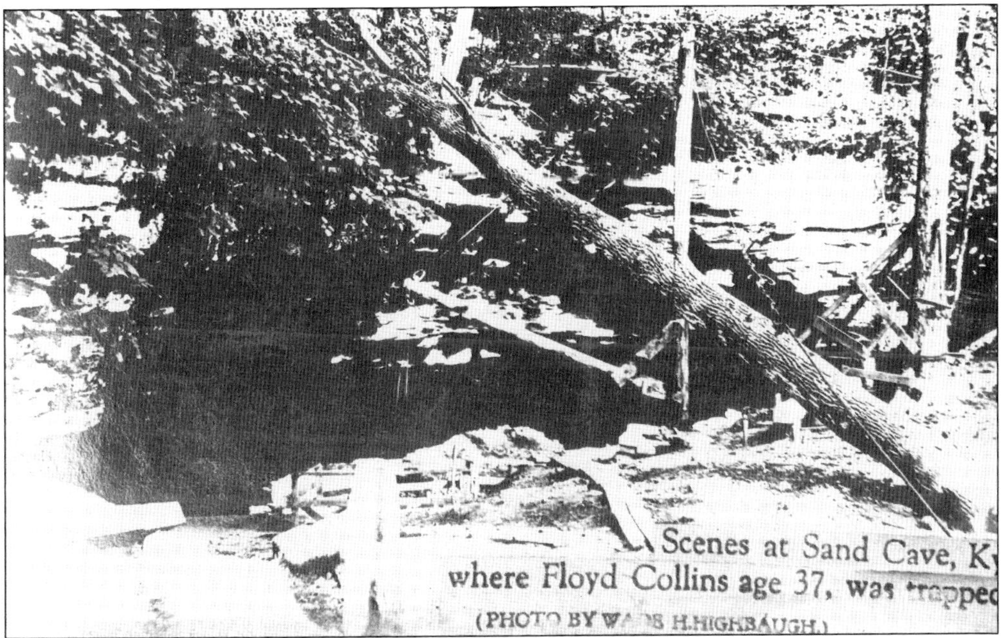

On Friday, February 6, 1925, Homer Collins went back into Sand Cave to try to reach his entrapped brother. He failed and said he "could only hope Floyd is still alive." Workmen continued boring a vertical shaft to reach Collins. Another of Collins's brothers, Andy Lee, arrived from Illinois. (National Cave Museum.)

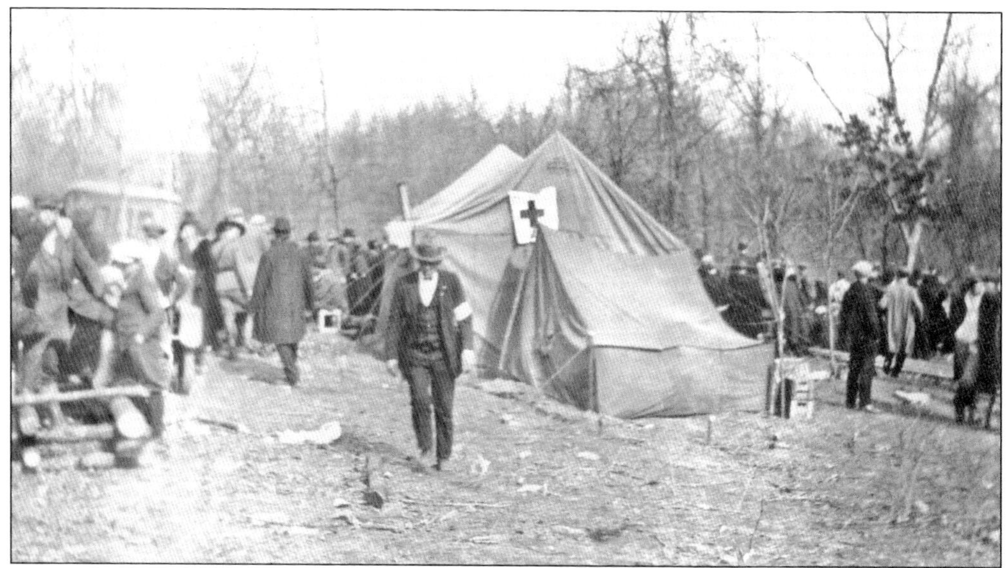

The Red Cross arrived on the scene and began making food and coffee for the workers. Over 200 meals were given at a serving. Soon, the local chapter was out of money, and the National Red Cross in Washington, DC, stepped in. Medical services, supplies and material, and manpower arrived, but progress on the shaft was slow. (National Cave Museum.)

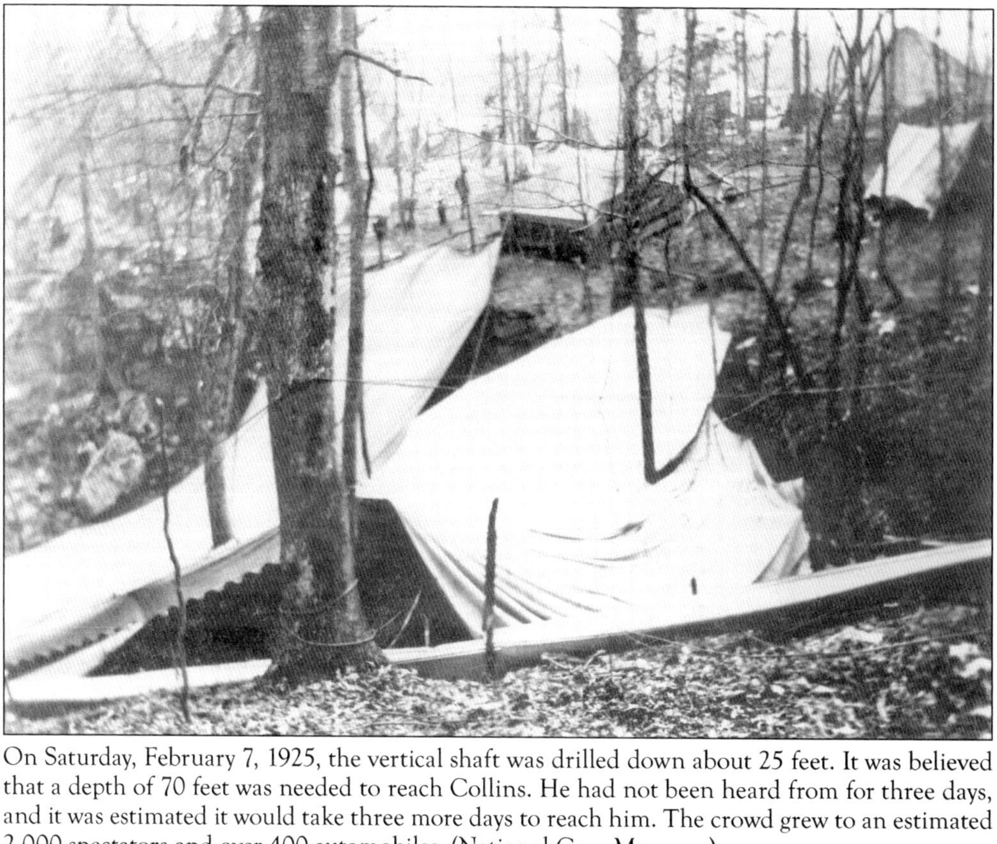

On Saturday, February 7, 1925, the vertical shaft was drilled down about 25 feet. It was believed that a depth of 70 feet was needed to reach Collins. He had not been heard from for three days, and it was estimated it would take three more days to reach him. The crowd grew to an estimated 2,000 spectators and over 400 automobiles. (National Cave Museum.)

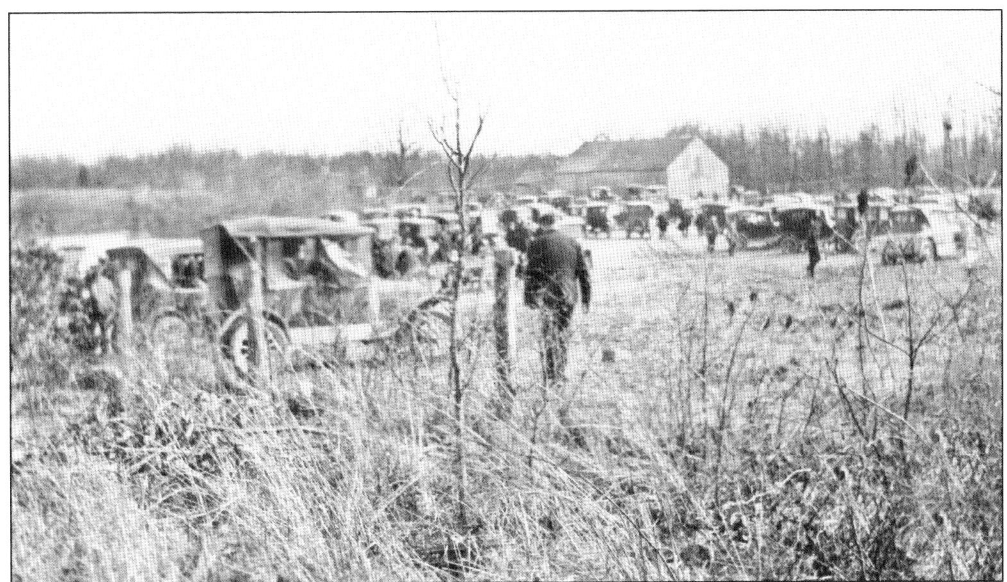

Sunday, February 8, 1925, was known as Carnival Sunday as several thousand onlookers were roaming the Sand Cave grounds. License plates from 20 states were noted in the area. Hundreds of animal-drawn conveyances were there as well. The Louisville & Nashville Railroad added several passenger coaches to its rail service. The crowds were estimated in the thousands, but no one really knew for sure. (National Cave Museum.)

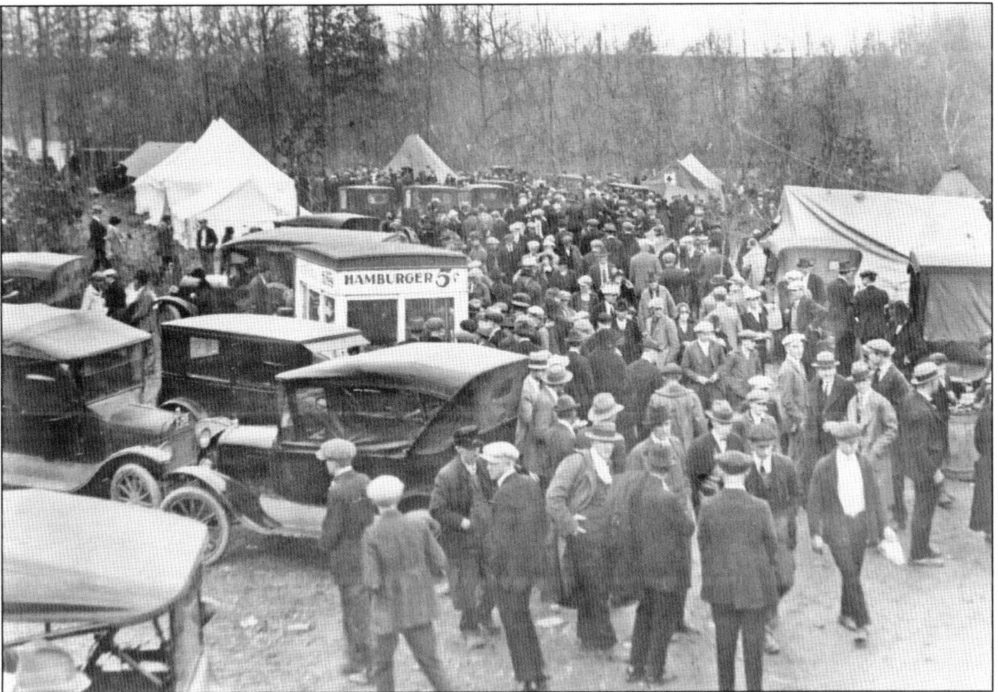

Vendors were set up to cater to the crowds, selling hamburgers, balloons, illegal moonshine, and more. Automobiles were lined up and parked for over four miles in each direction on all roads in the vicinity leading to Sand Cave. Most left disappointed, as they came expecting to be able to pass into a cave and gawk upon a fellow human being in death's agony. (National Cave Museum.)

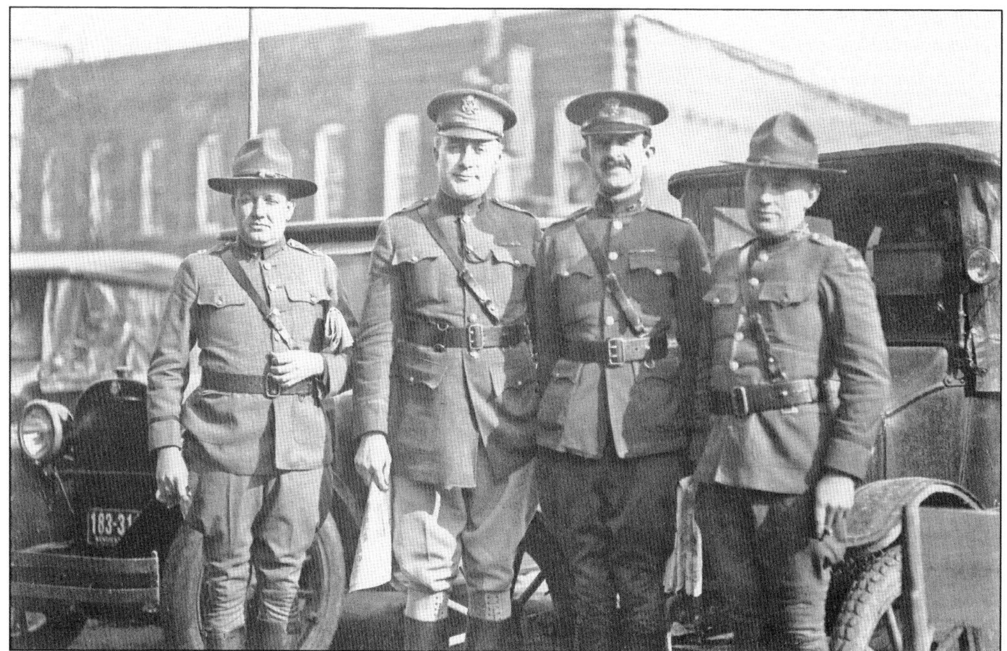

On Monday, February 9, 1925, a military inquiry was ordered by Governor Fields as chaos continued at the cave. General Denhardt and four National Guard officers met in Cave City to hear testimony. Many argued and attacked each other for not being able to free Floyd Collins. The *Louisville Courier-Journal* reporter Skeets Miller was among the first to testify. (David Jones Collection.)

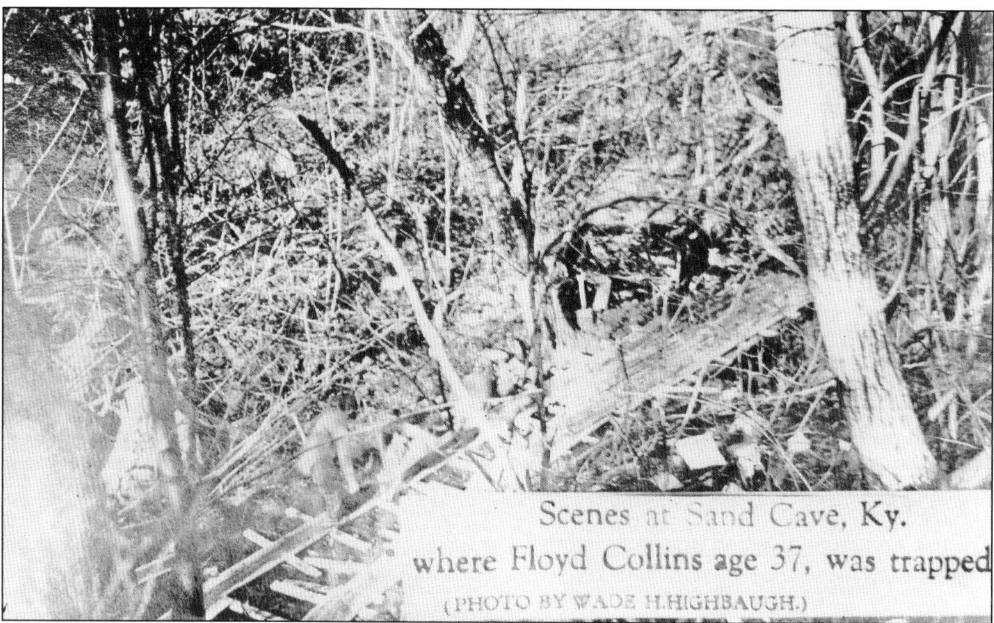

On Tuesday, February 10, 1925, the Kentucky Militia Court of Inquiry was seated in Cave City. Skeets Miller and six other witnesses testified that Collins was trapped. The military court of inquiry ordered a "bullpen" be established within full view of the shaft, in order that reporters and photographers be accommodated in an orderly manner. Miner Ed Brenner from Cincinnati testified that he was a strong worker and truthful. (National Cave Museum.)

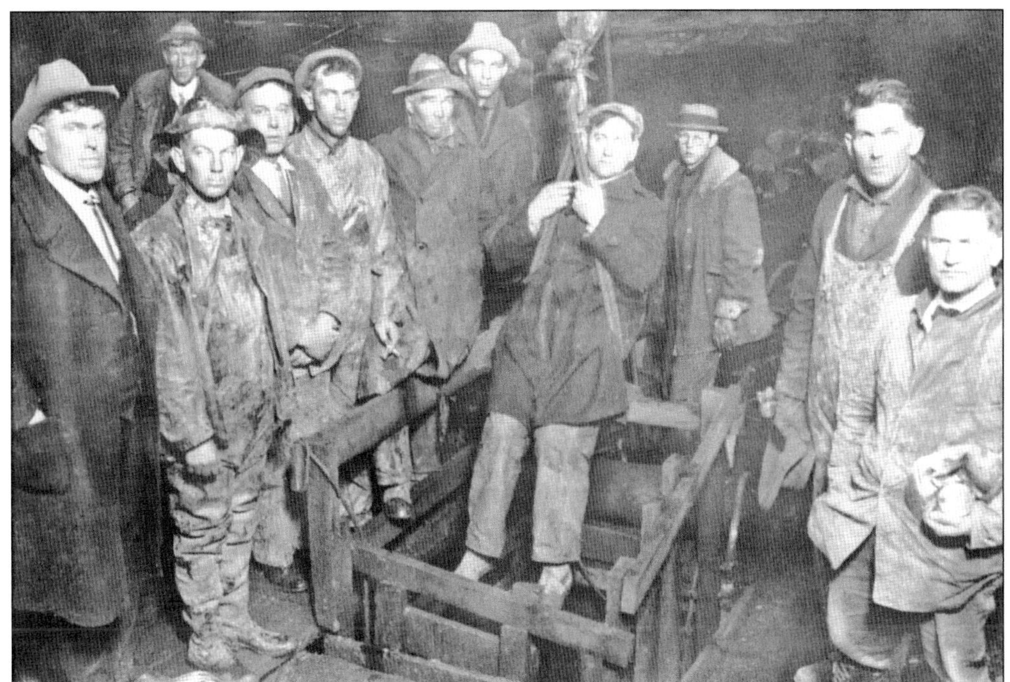

On Wednesday, February 11, 1925, the workmen sinking the vertical shaft were down about 45 feet. They believed they were within about 10 feet of their goal. The rescuers did not know if Collins was still alive, as the last time anyone had talked to him was February 4. Photographer Wade Highbaugh took this picture of some of the workers at the top of the rescue shaft. (Tim Donley Collection.)

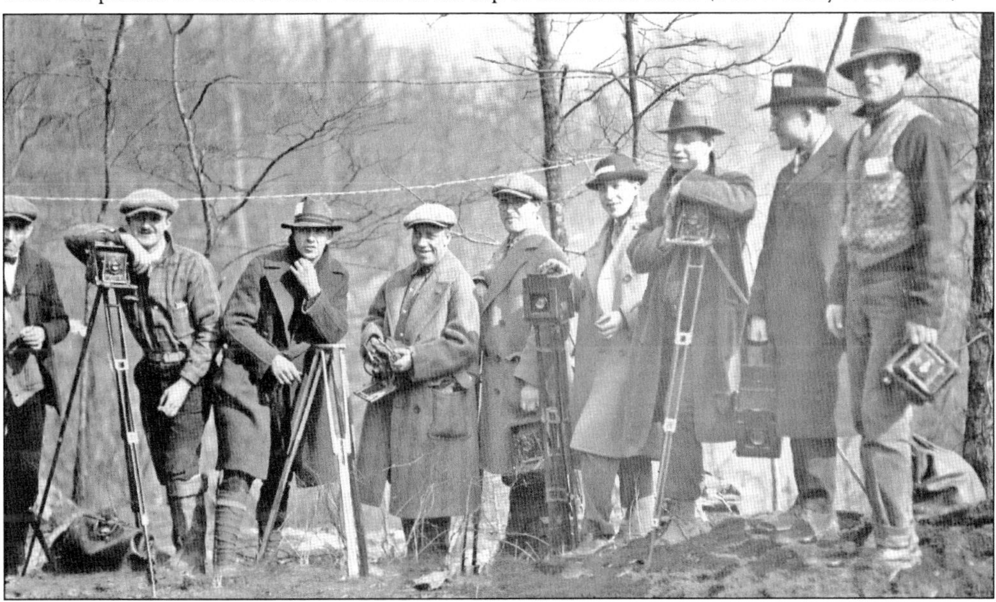

Some reporters tried to outdo others by running fake photographs, creating stories about Collins's dog waiting at the scene, or making up stories about Collins's girlfriend. One story stated that an "eight ton rock . . . holds Floyd." Other stories said that Collins had exited the cave by a back entrance. The Sunday edition of the *Louisville Herald-Post* had an erroneous headline that read, "Kentuckian Rescued from Cave." (Dean Snyder Collection.)

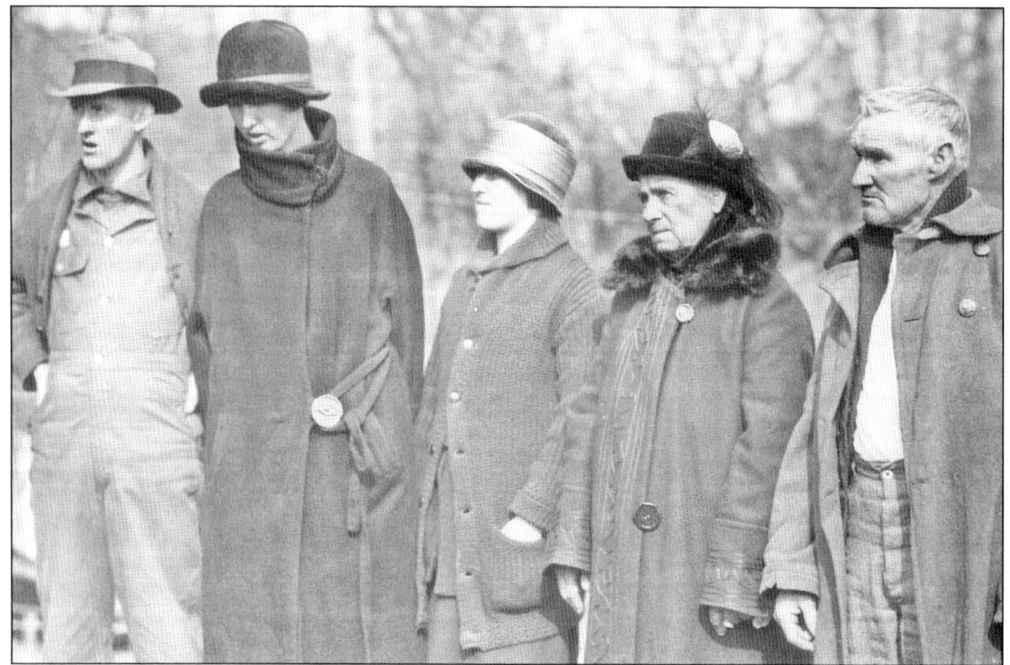

On Thursday, February 12, 1925, Floyd Collins's brother Homer told a military court of inquiry in Cave City how he had gone into Sand Cave to try to rescue his brother. Workmen continued sinking a shaft toward Collins. Members of the Collins family, from left to right, Marshall, Anna, Nellie, Jane, and Lee, are shown standing near Sand Cave waiting for an update of the rescue efforts. (David Jones Collection.)

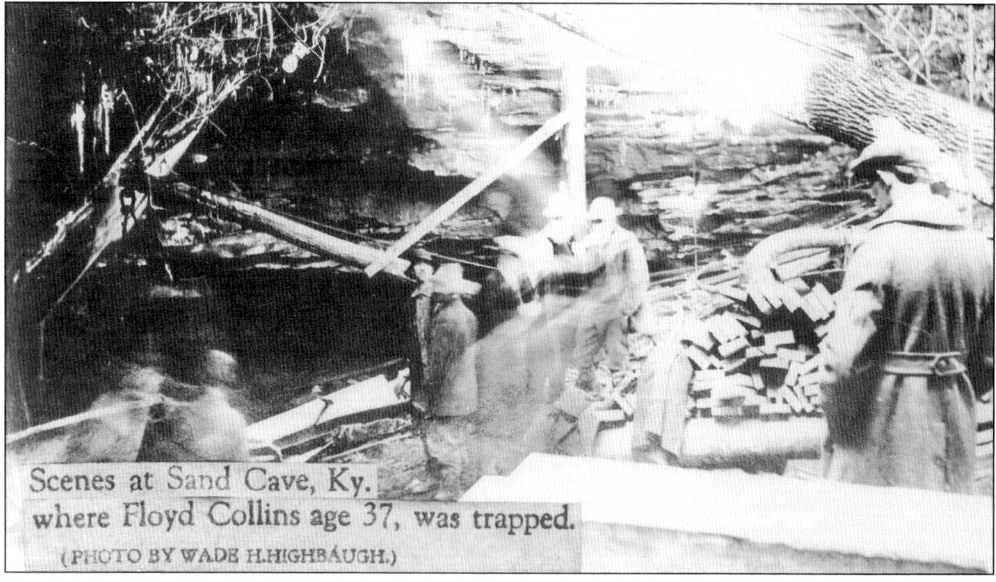

On Friday, February 13, 1925, a small cave-in near the bottom of the shaft caused a delay in operations. The shaft was now 53 feet deep, and workmen felt they were very close to reaching Collins. The court of inquiry was winding down, with newspapermen and miners testifying. The afternoon court hearings were moved to the Sand Cave site for testimony. Cave City was nearly deserted. (National Cave Museum.)

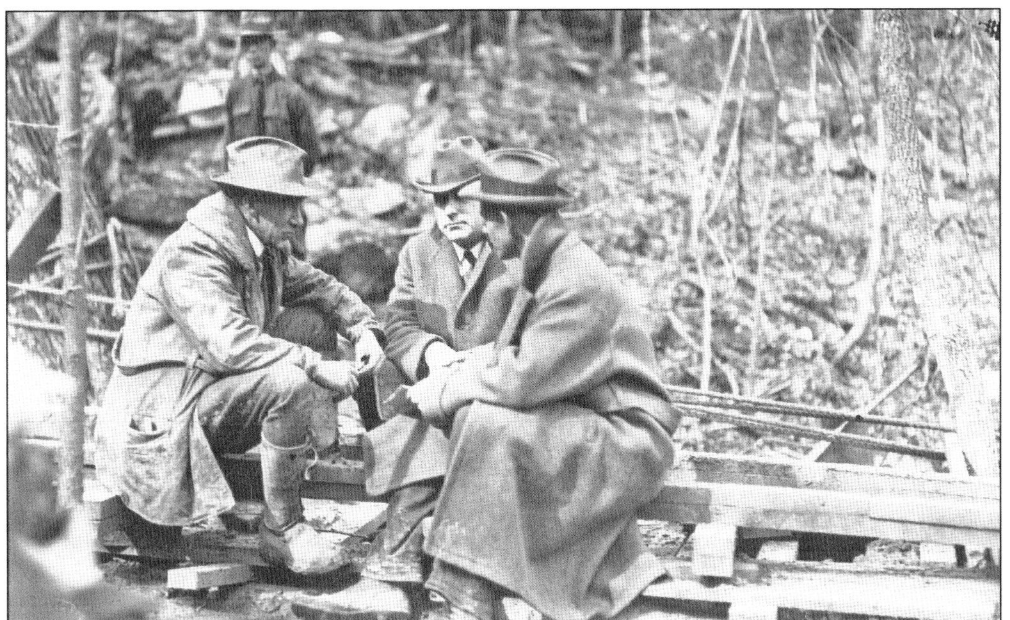

On Saturday, February 14, 1925, Henry T. Carmichael stated that the shaft was at a depth of 55 feet. Work was stopped on the vertical shaft due to cave-ins. However, a decision was made to start a lateral tunnel at the bottom of the rescue shaft in the direction of the passageway that had trapped Collins since January 30. Carmichael (left) is shown with General Denhardt (center) and Dr. Funkhouser (right). (David Jones Collection.)

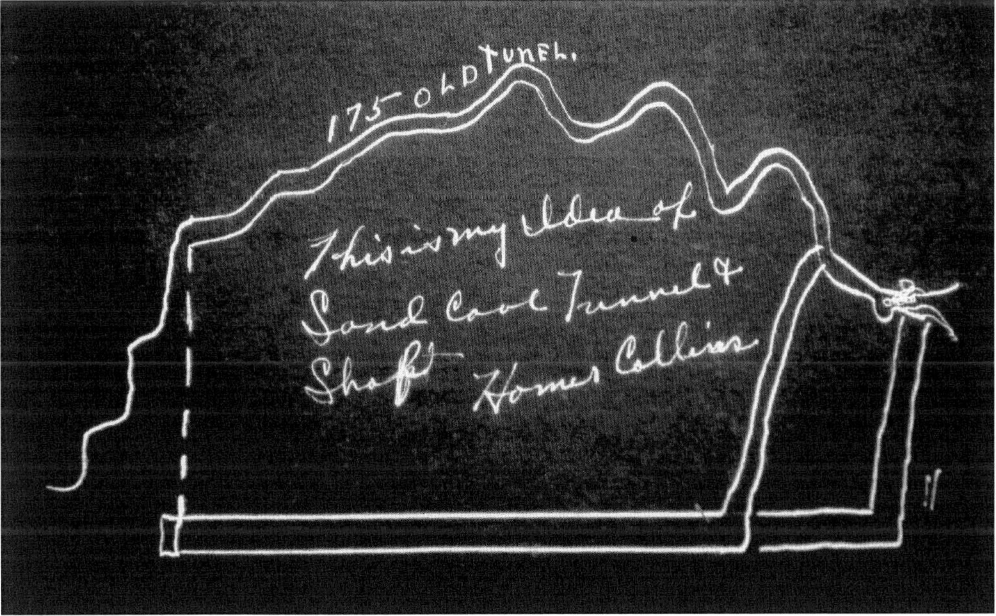

On Sunday, February 15, 1925, the workmen pushed a lateral tunnel about seven feet to where they believed Floyd Collins was trapped. This sketch, drawn by Homer Collins, shows the passageway (top) into Sand Cave where Floyd Collins was trapped, the vertical shaft (bottom), and the two horizontal lateral tunnels that were dug from the shaft to reach Collins. (Neville Collection, Cave Research Foundation.)

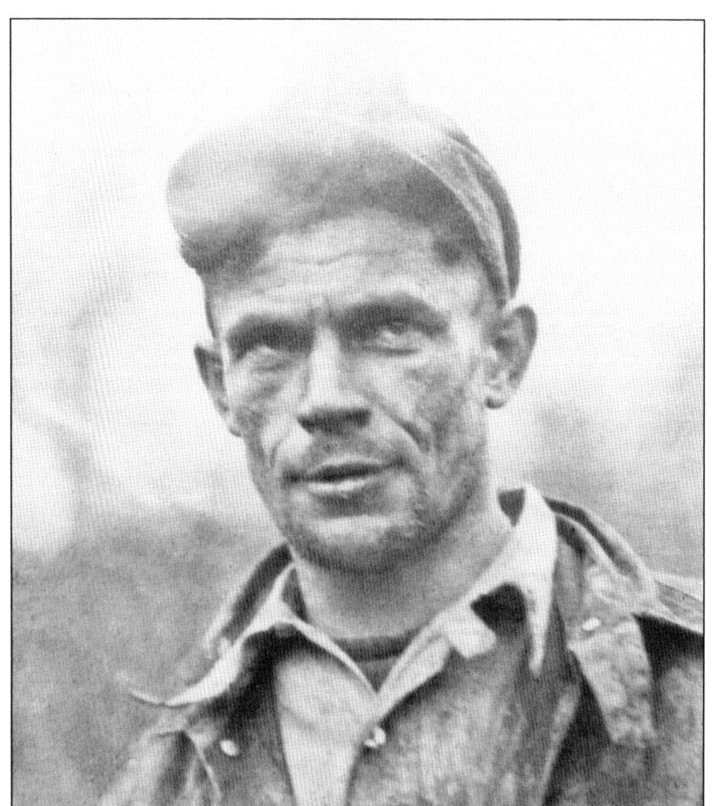

On Monday, February 16, 1925, the workers finally broke through the lateral tunnel into Sand Cave. Ed Brenner (pictured) was the first man in to discover that Collins was "cold and apparently dead." Johnny Gerald was permitted to go into the tunnel and positively identify the body of his friend. Dr. William Hazlett went into the shaft and said Collins had been dead between three and five days. (David Jones Collection.)

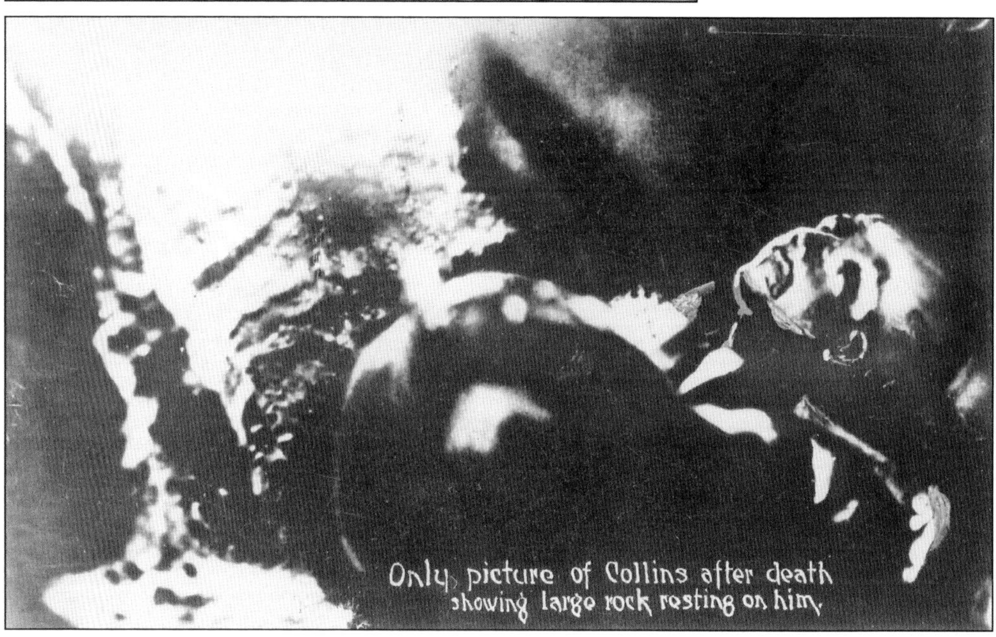

To show proof that Floyd Collins was trapped in Sand Cave, on February 17 it was decided by the press that one Chicago photographer would go down into the shaft and take a picture of the body, and then they all would share it. The negative was flown to Chicago but was found to be blank. Soon after, this picture materialized, but it was found to be a fake. (National Cave Museum.)

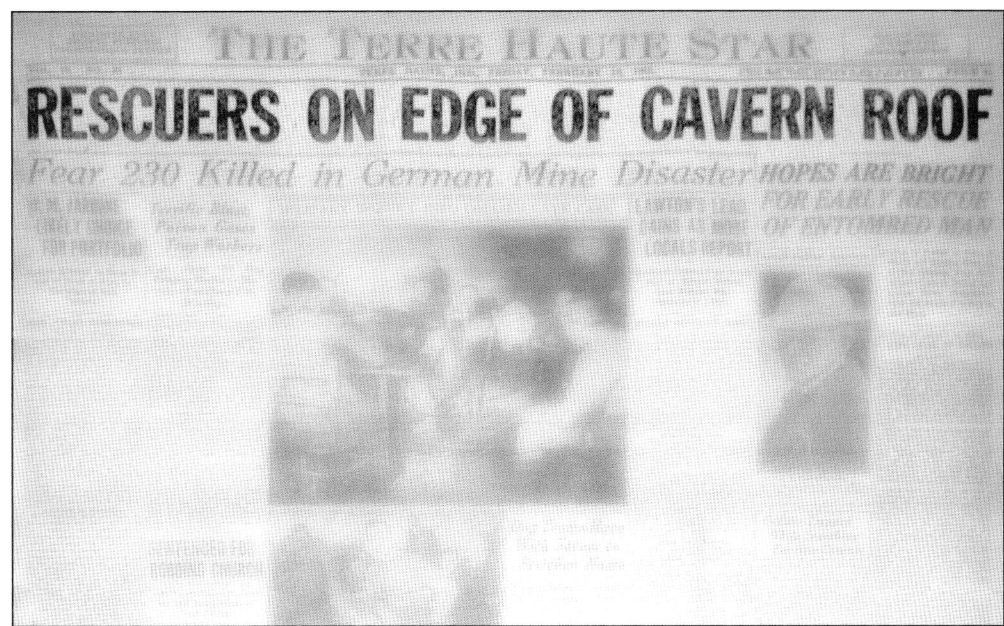
THE TERRE HAUTE STAR

RESCUERS ON EDGE OF CAVERN ROOF

Fear 230 Killed in German Mine Disaster

HOPES ARE BRIGHT FOR EARLY RESCUE OF ENTOMBED MAN

Using daily newspaper headlines, here is an excerpt of the official bulletin of the finding of Floyd Collins's body as read to the press by Dr. William D. Funkhouser from the University of Kentucky: "At 1:30 o'clock the lateral (tunnel) heading at a distance of twelve feet from the shaft, as measured circularly, broke through into a natural cave, just below the breakdown, which was found completely closed." (National Cave Museum.)

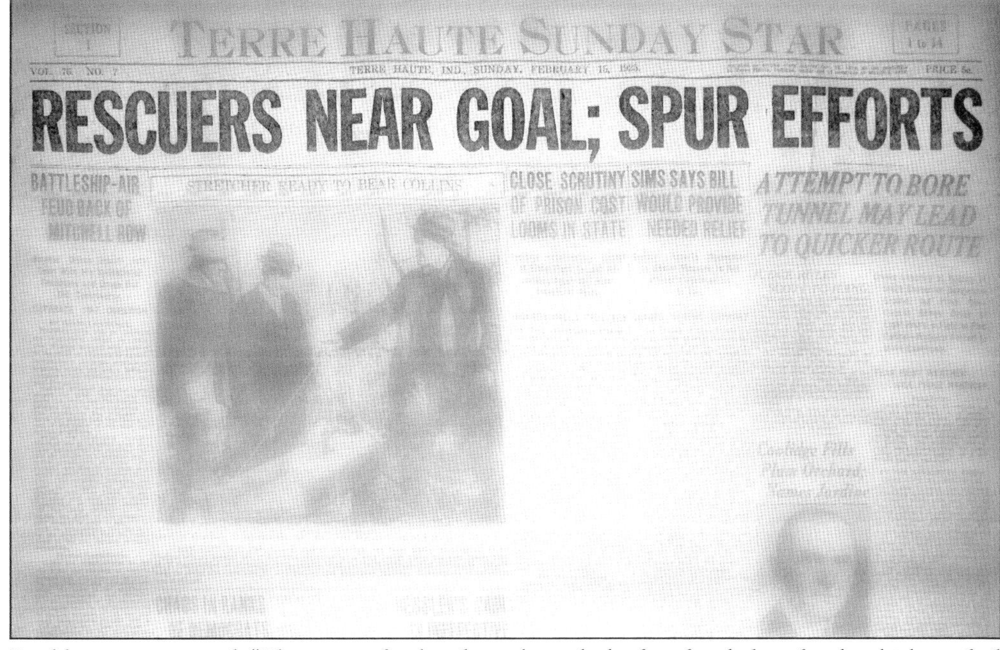
TERRE HAUTE SUNDAY STAR

TERRE HAUTE, IND., SUNDAY, FEBRUARY 15, 1925.

RESCUERS NEAR GOAL; SPUR EFFORTS

BATTLESHIP-AIR FEUD BACK OF MITCHELL ROW

STRETCHER READY TO BEAR COLLINS

CLOSE SCRUTINY OF PRISON COST LOOMS IN STATE

SIMS SAYS BILL WOULD PROVIDE NEEDED RELIEF

ATTEMPT TO BORE TUNNEL MAY LEAD TO QUICKER ROUTE

Funkhouser continued, "This came after breaking through the four-foot ledge of rock, which verified the predictions to an inch. The distance from the entrance to Collins head is six feet. The location of Collins is at the elevation originally estimated and within a few feet of the position detected by the first survey." (National Cave Museum.)

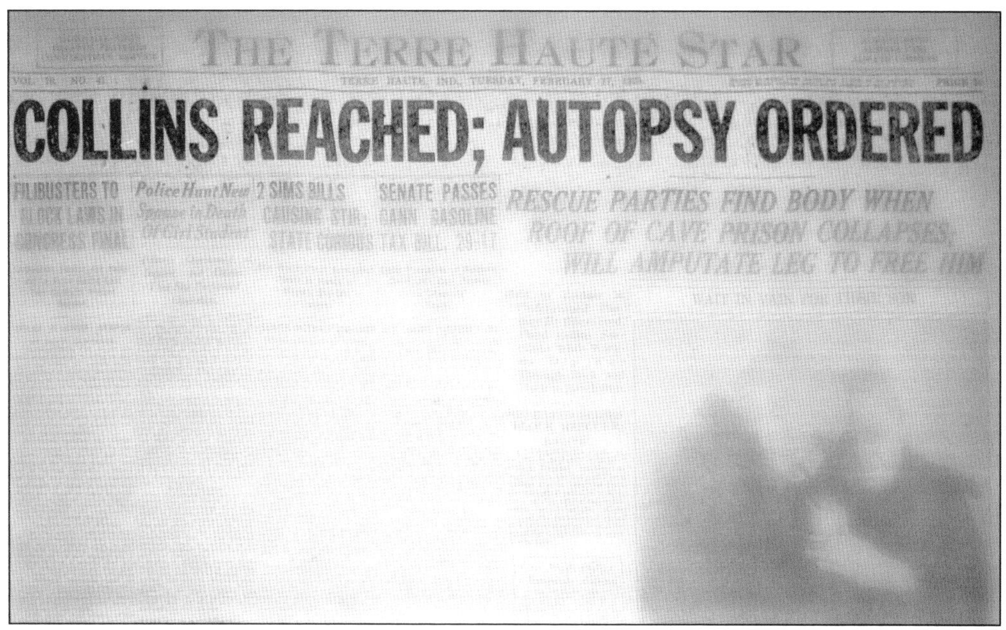
THE TERRE HAUTE STAR

COLLINS REACHED; AUTOPSY ORDERED

FILIBUSTERS TO BLOCK LAWS IN CONGRESS FINAL

2 SIMS BILLS CAUSING STIR STATE CORRIDORS

SENATE PASSES

RESCUE PARTIES FIND BODY WHEN ROOF OF CAVE PRISON COLLAPSES; WILL AMPUTATE LEG TO FREE HIM

Funkhouser stated, "Meanwhile, Albert Marshall, showing the same splendid courage so manifest throughout the shaft work from surface to foundation, propped the loosely hanging, dangerous boulders and let himself down into the pit feet foremost, the opening being too small on account of his large stature, for him to go in head first. He touched with his feet what he thought to be the blanket around Collins." (National Cave Museum.)

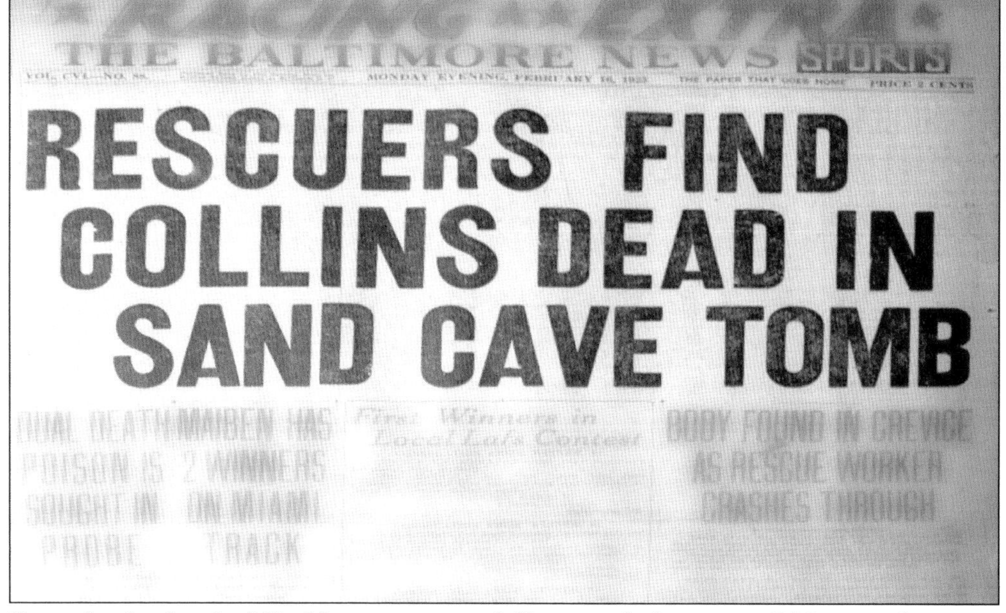
RACING EXTRA

THE BALTIMORE NEWS SPORTS

MONDAY EVENING, FEBRUARY 16, 1925 — THE PAPER THAT GOES HOME — PRICE 2 CENTS

RESCUERS FIND COLLINS DEAD IN SAND CAVE TOMB

DUAL DEATH POISON IS SOUGHT IN PROBE

MAIDEN HAS 2 WINNERS ON MIAMI TRACK

BODY FOUND IN CREVICE AS RESCUE WORKER CRASHES THROUGH

"Immediately after this," Funkhouser continued, "his game little partner, Ed Brenner, by reason of his comparatively small stature, great strength, agility, and iron nerve, went down into the hazardous pit. With a light he closely examined face and position of the man we believe to be Floyd Collins, and called up to Mr. Carmichael, five feet above him, that the man was cold and apparently dead." (National Cave Museum.)

The official cause of Floyd Collins's death was "exposure and exhaustion." Removing the body at the time would probably have required amputation. Having decided it was too dangerous to tunnel any more, the vertical shaft was partially filled with logs and cement, and the body left in Sand Cave. (National Cave Museum.)

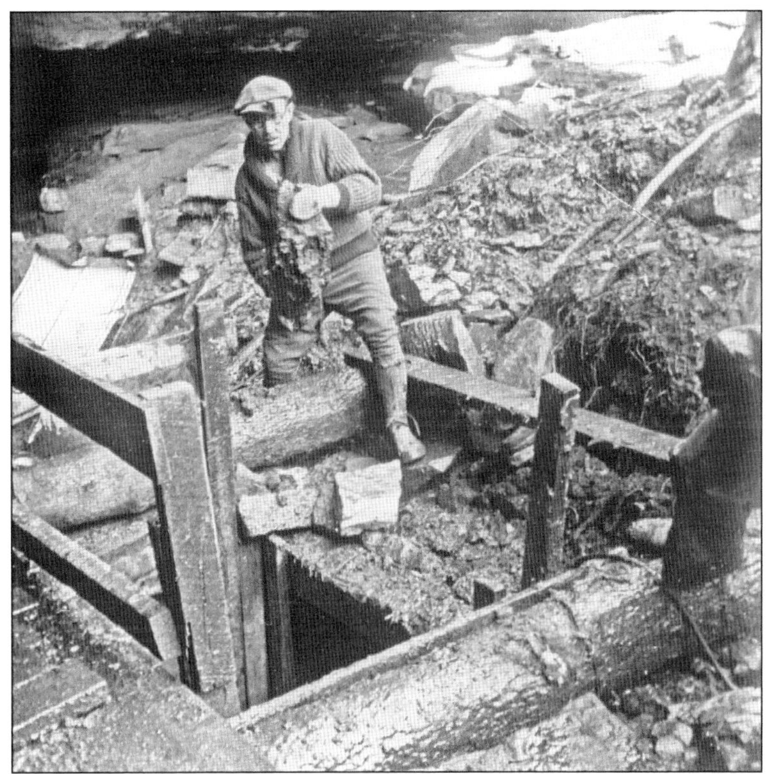

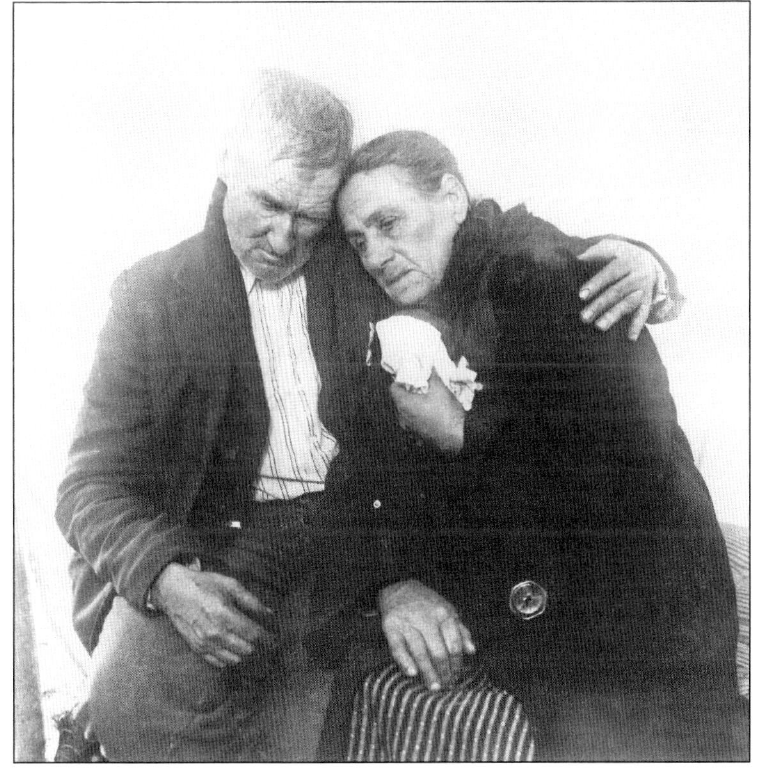

Funeral services were held on Tuesday, February 17, 1925, for Floyd Collins on the hillside above Sand Cave. About 150 people attended the service. Governor Fields extended his sympathy to the Collins family (pictured). This was considered Collins's first burial. General Denhardt reconvened the military court of inquiry for the final time. He declared the court's work finished; the body had been found. (David Jones Collection.)

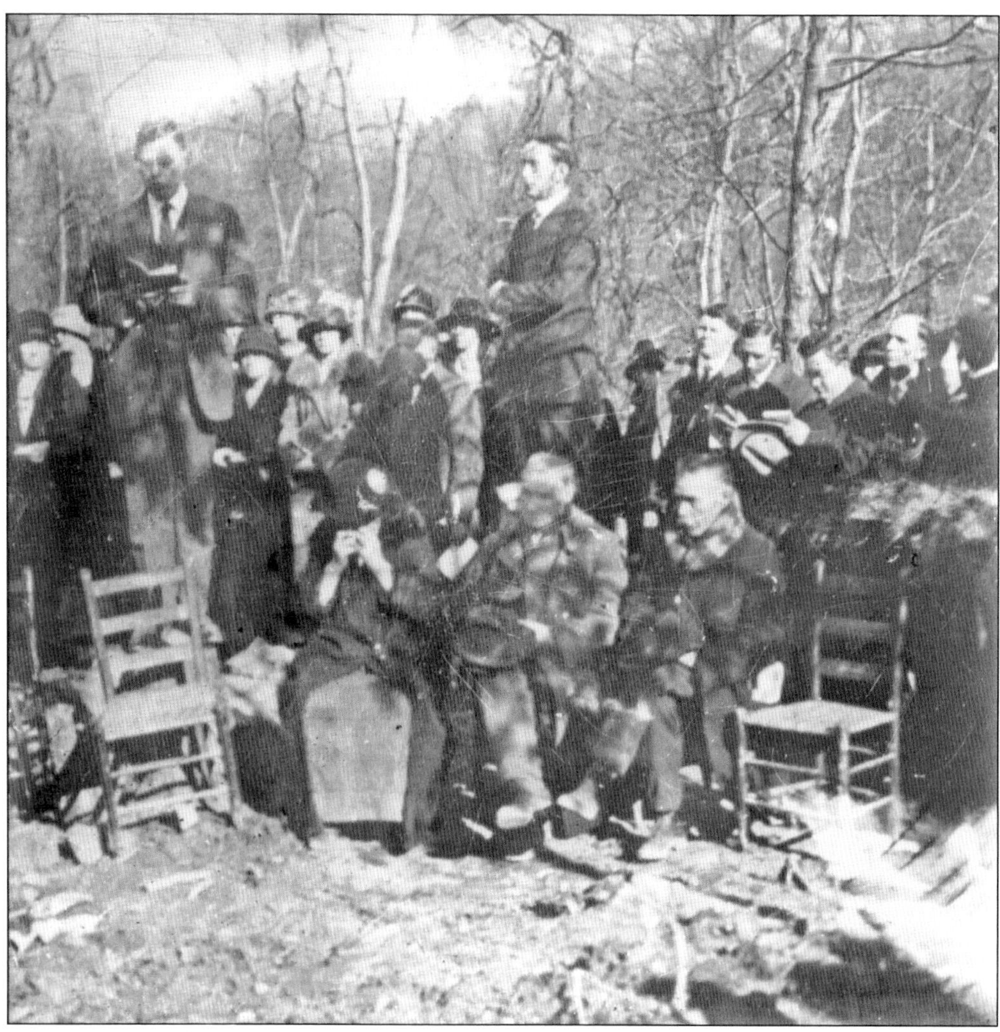

The funeral for Floyd Collins had no casket, corpse, grave, or marker. The service at Sand Cave began as the Rev. Roy H. Biser (left, standing on a tree stump), minister of the First Christian Church in Glasgow, gave a 55-minute funeral service with the help of the Rev. Charles K. Dickey (right, standing), pastor of the Horse Cave Methodist Church in Horse Cave, who said a prayer. Reverend Dickey spoke briefly on Collins's adventurous life as a cave explorer. A choir of eight women from Cave City sang three hymns. Floyd Collins's father, Lee; stepmother Jane; and Lee's brother William (all seated) were the only family members at this funeral. Nearby, to show their sympathy, were neighbors, friends, and the volunteers who struggled but failed to save Collins. (National Cave Museum.)

Five

Recovery from Sand Cave

Disorder, Distrust, and Death

PRINCESS THEATRE

The Inside Story of

FLOYD COLLINS

And the Kentucky Cave told by his Brother

HOMER COLLINS

IN PERSON

Exclusive Motion Pictures of One of the Most Interesting Incidents in History

Wednesday, Nov. 25

—ALSO—

"Stage Struck"

FEATURING

Gloria Swanson

COMEDY:-"Change the Needle"

ADMISSION 15c and 30c

Even though Floyd Collins was found dead in Sand Cave on February 16, 1925, he was not brought to the surface until April 23 because of the instability of the cave. An effort was made by Homer Collins to raise money for Floyd's removal by doing shows around the country. Here is a vaudeville poster bill from a show Homer did in 1925. (National Cave Museum.)

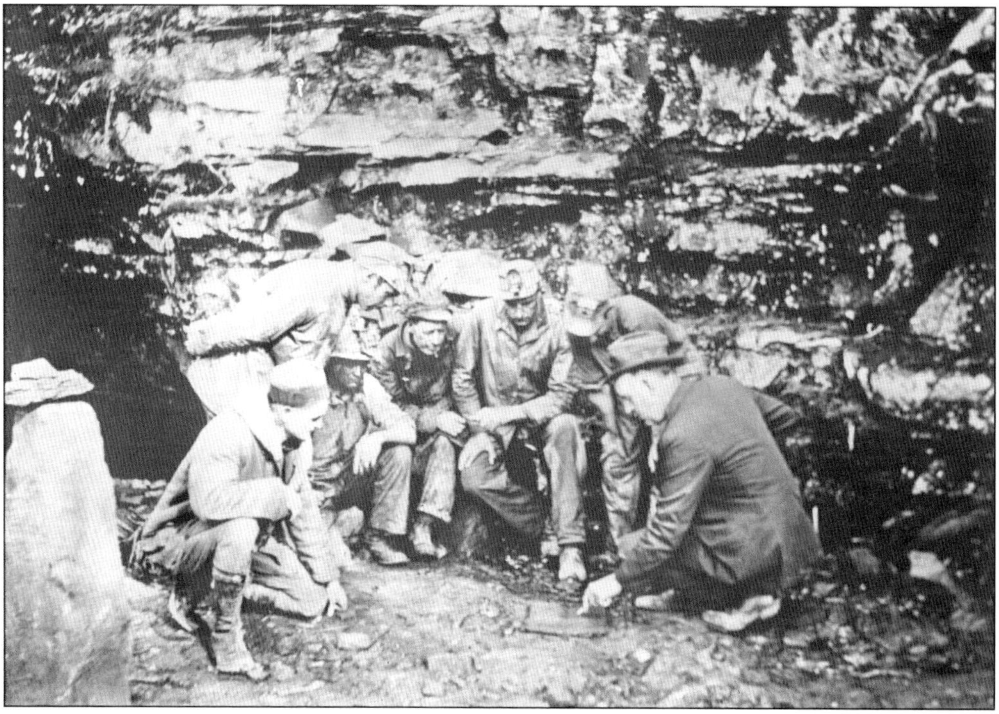

On April 4, 1925, a contract was signed by Homer Collins and William Howard Hunt, a state mining engineer from Central City, Kentucky, to remove Floyd Collins's body from Sand Cave. William H. Hunt (right) is shown here with his six-man work crew drawing up plans to reopen the shaft to remove the body of Floyd Collins from Sand Cave. (Wade Highbaugh Collection.)

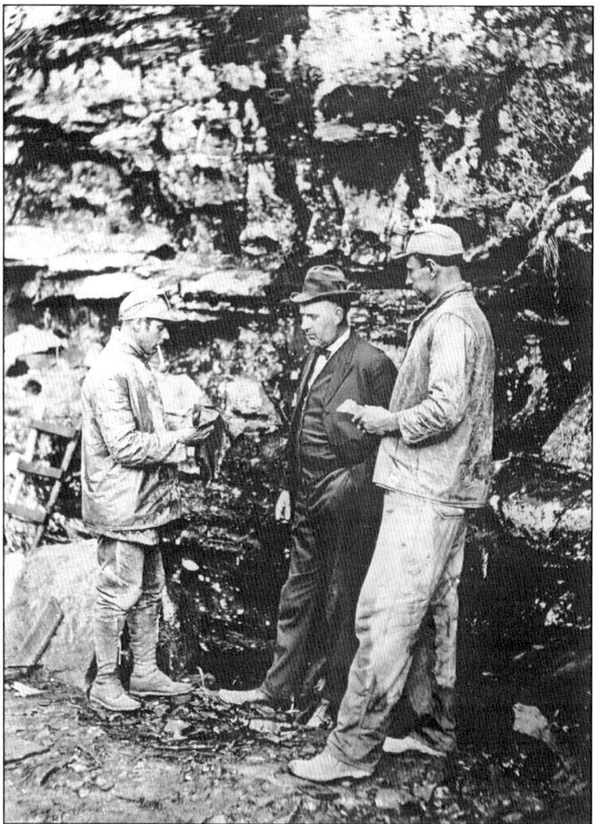

Rescuing the body of Floyd Collins was a dangerous feat and a cave-in was always a possibility. According to Hunt, conditions in the cave were the worst he had ever encountered underground in 30 years of mining. Elmer Hays, one of the miners, became trapped himself for one hour by shifting rocks while going through the original lateral tunnel to Collins. (Wade Highbaugh Collection.)

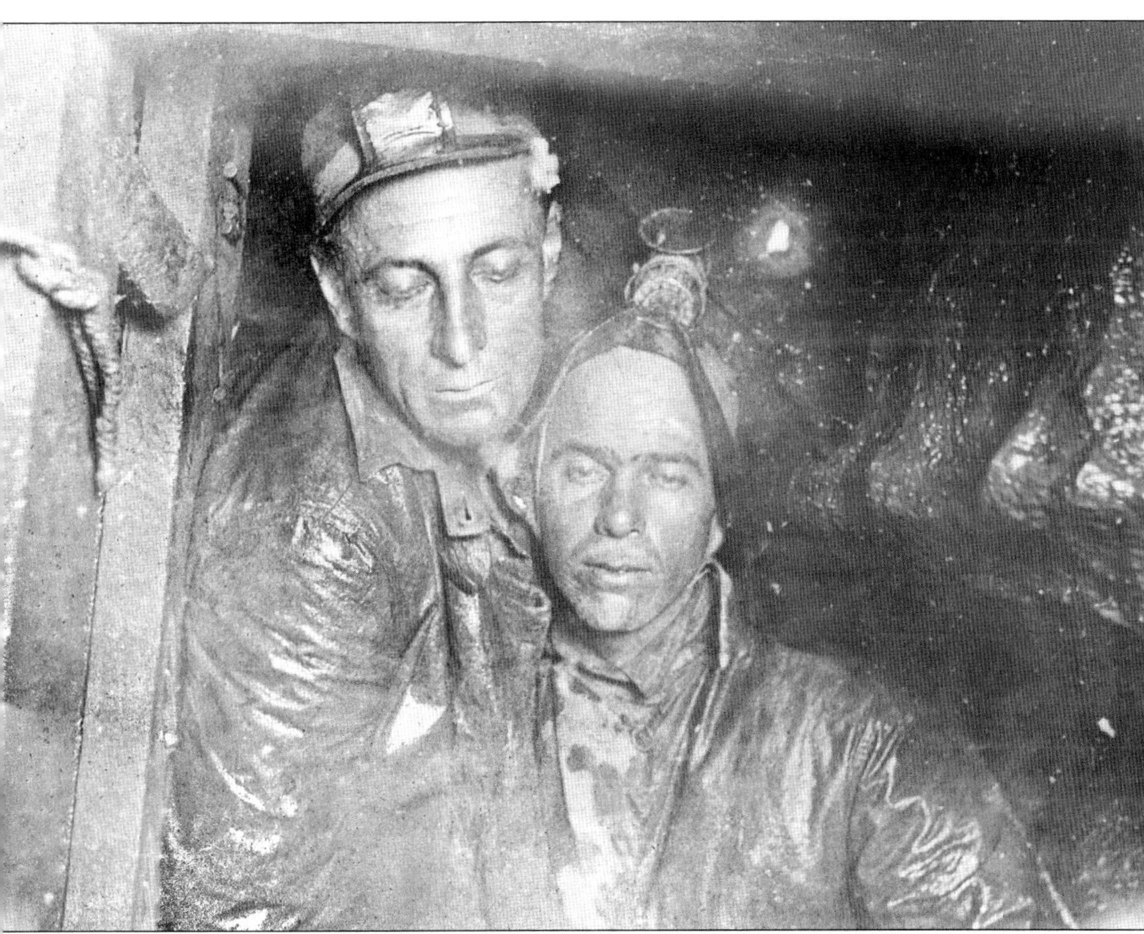

On April 8, 1925, rescue operations were started by William H. Hunt and his crew. Hunt's effort to recover the body consisted of cleaning out the original 55-foot rescue shaft and then digging down into the shaft another 15 feet because of the collapse of the original lateral tunnel. A new 20-foot lateral tunnel was dug to reach Collins. Two of the mud-covered rescue workers are shown here in the vertical shaft. (Wade Highbaugh Collection.)

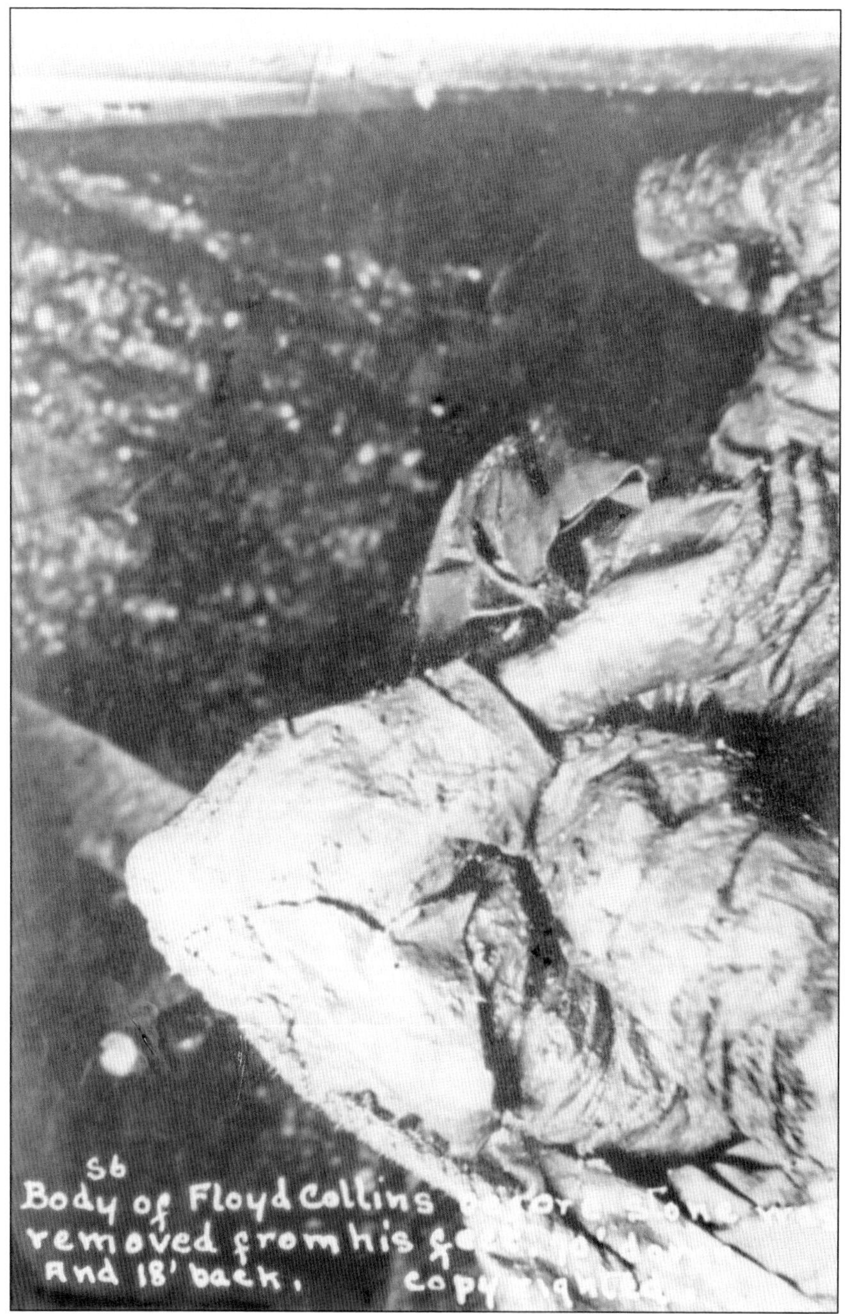

The body of Floyd Collins was reached on the morning of April 22, 1925. By evening, the body was pulled from the cave into the shaft. Collins was trapped at the very edge of a large pit in Sand Cave when William H. Hunt and two of his workers loosened the rock that held Collins's left leg. The edge of the pit began to crumble away as the body was removed. The body was found in a sitting position in the narrow passage leading from the pit. This photograph shows the mud-caked body of Floyd Collins just before he was removed from the shaft on April 23. The body was wrapped in cotton to prevent its exposure to the surface air just before it was hoisted to the top of the shaft. (Library Special Collections, WKU.)

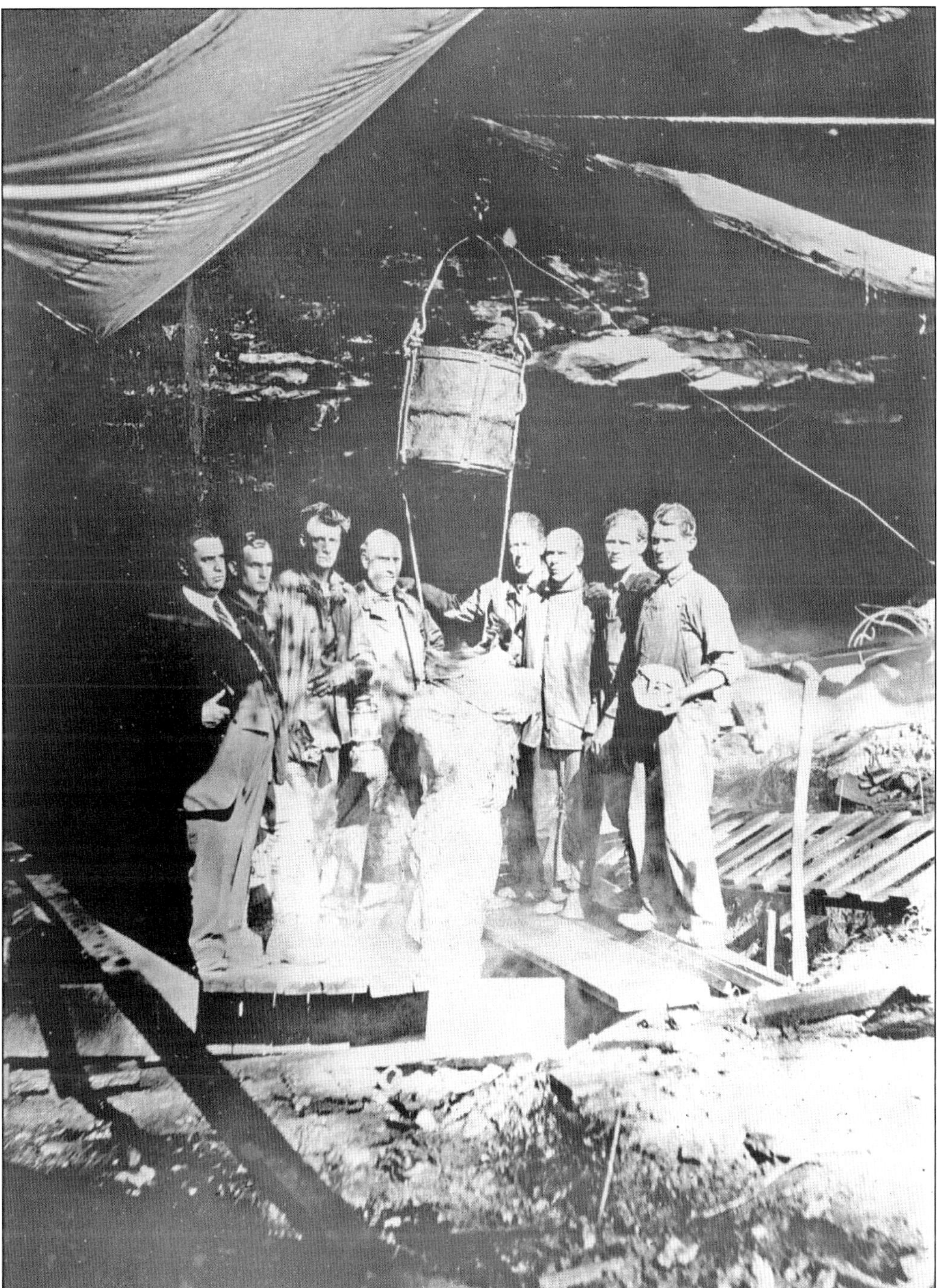

On April 23, 1925, the body of Floyd Collins was removed from Sand Cave. Not a tear was shed the morning Collins's body was hauled up from the cave trap where he died two months before. The nation that poured out sympathy earlier had already forgotten. About 100 persons, practically all of them from the immediate neighborhood, witnessed the removal of Floyd Collins from Sand Cave. The Collins family was not present the day the body was brought out. (Wade Highbaugh Collection.)

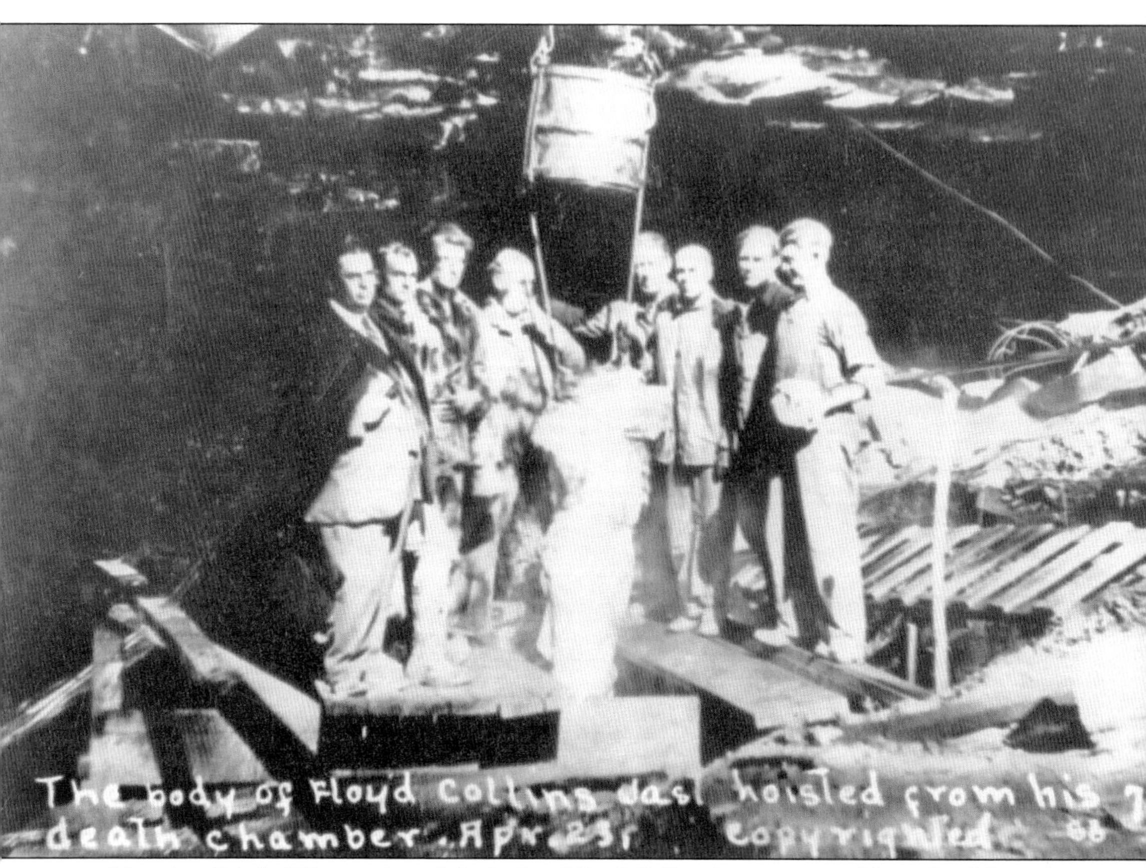

Here is a slightly different view of the body of Floyd Collins being removed from Sand Cave. It was wrapped in a dirty cloth like a mummy and hanged from a rope and raised to the top of the 70-foot rescue shaft by a derrick. There the body hung until a picture was taken by Wade Highbaugh, a local photographer who lived only a mile away from Sand Cave. (Library Special Collections, WKU.)

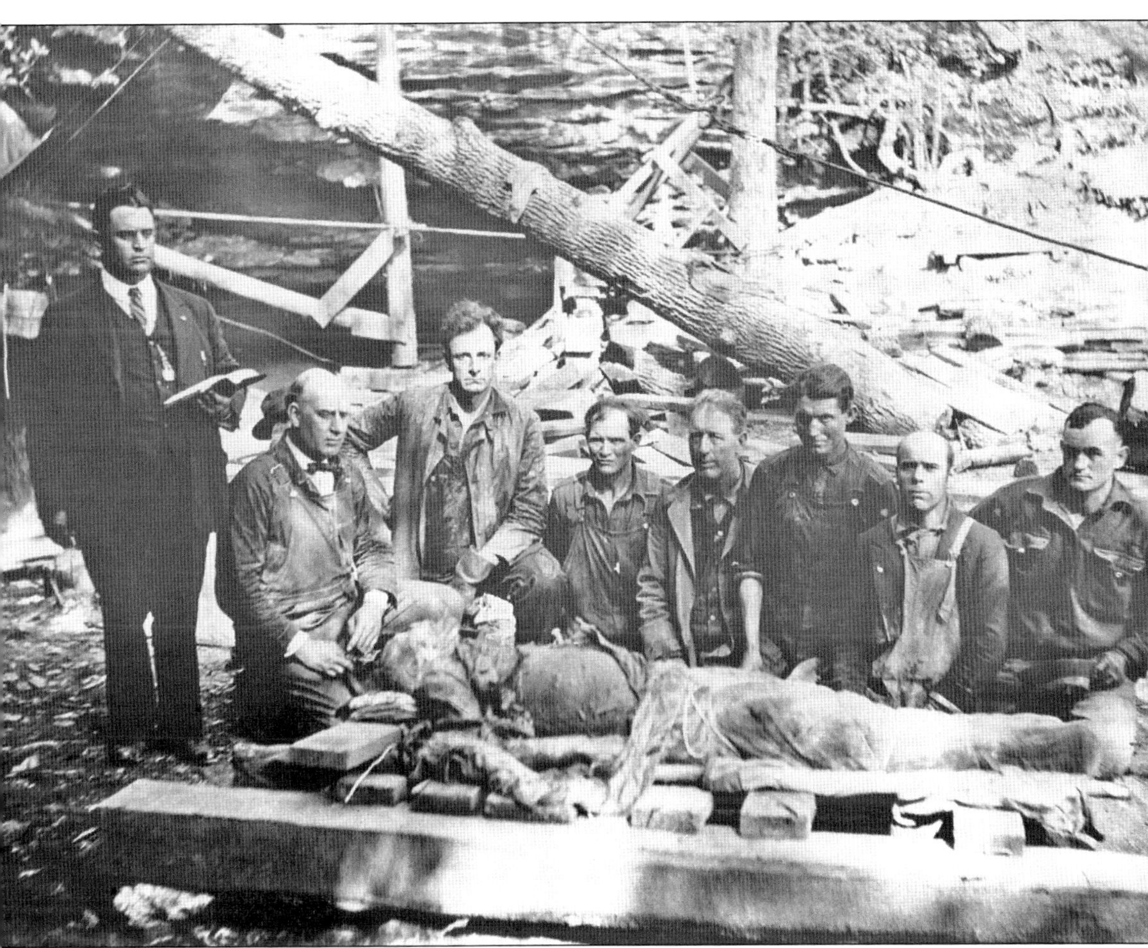

After the picture was taken, Floyd Collins's body was unfastened from the derrick and put on a stretcher made of two poles run through the sleeves of the miner's blue denim coats. William H. Hunt wanted to show proof to all who were present that the body they just recovered was Floyd Collins. Pen knives were used to cut away the rags from Collins's head and chest. (Bill Napper Collection.)

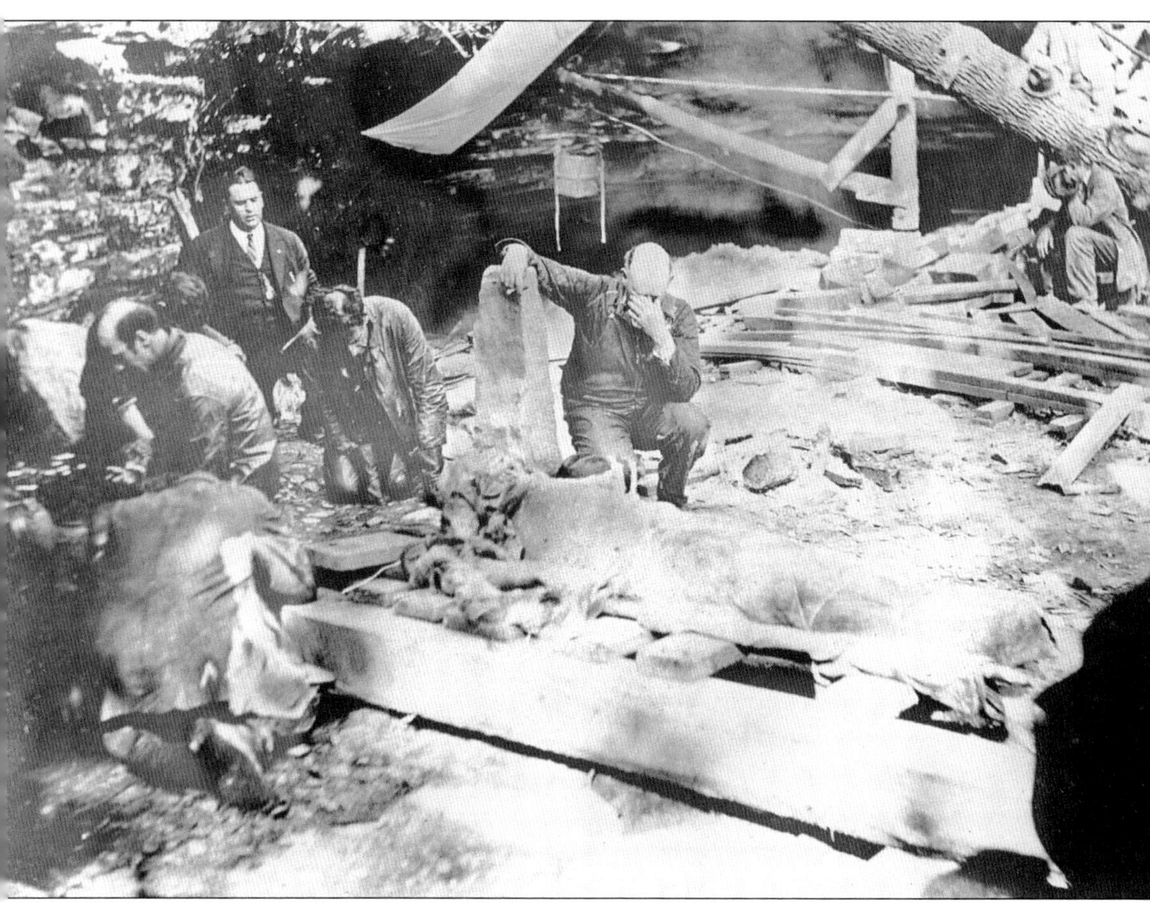

A few people said that while the face had passed recognition, Collins's gold tooth offered enough proof. One of the miners asked permission to speak a minute. He said the work crew had never entered the shaft without bowing in prayer, and he asked for Rev. Rufus Burch Neel of Bowling Green (pictured here with Bible) to lead them in prayer for the success of their efforts. (Wade Highbaugh Collection.)

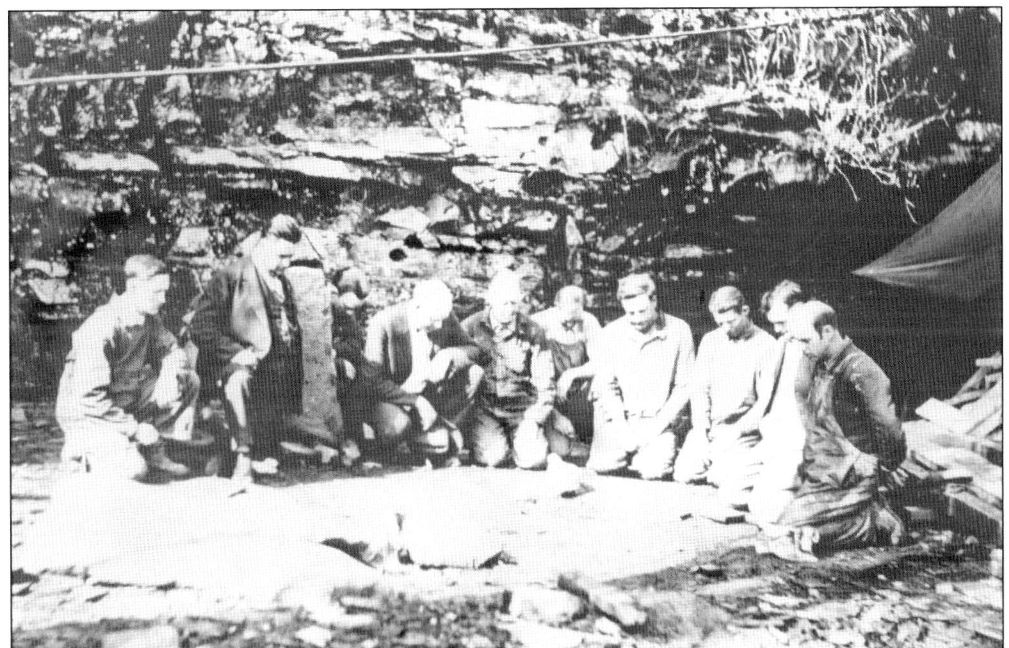

The work crew, including William H. Hunt, all knelt with Reverend Neel in a semicircle around the body. After the prayer, the onlookers were requested to pass single file past the body to convince them that Collins had at last been freed. Men, women, and children embraced the opportunity. Lifelong friends of the victim were positive in their identification. (Wade Highbaugh Collection.)

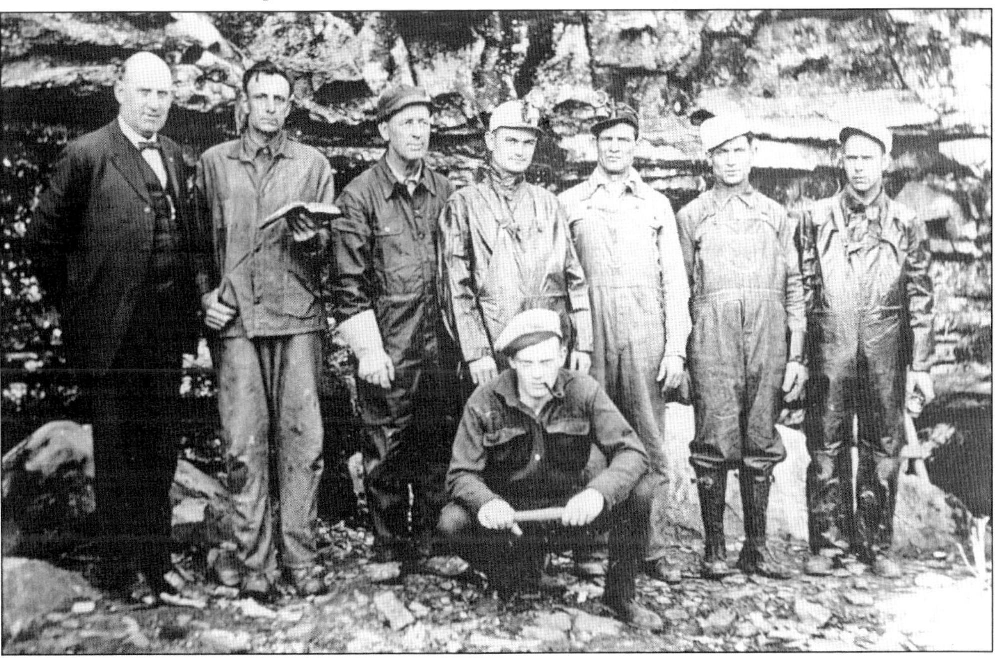

William H. Hunt, his six-man work crew, and Hunt's son are shown posing for photographer Wade Highbaugh. From left to right are (kneeling) Thurston Hunt; (standing) William H. Hunt, Rev. James Samuel Smith (with Bible), Harden T. Weaver, Oscar Roy Logsdon, Benjamin E. Cook, Clinton E. Goodley, and Elman Shepherd Hays. (Wade Highbaugh Collection.)

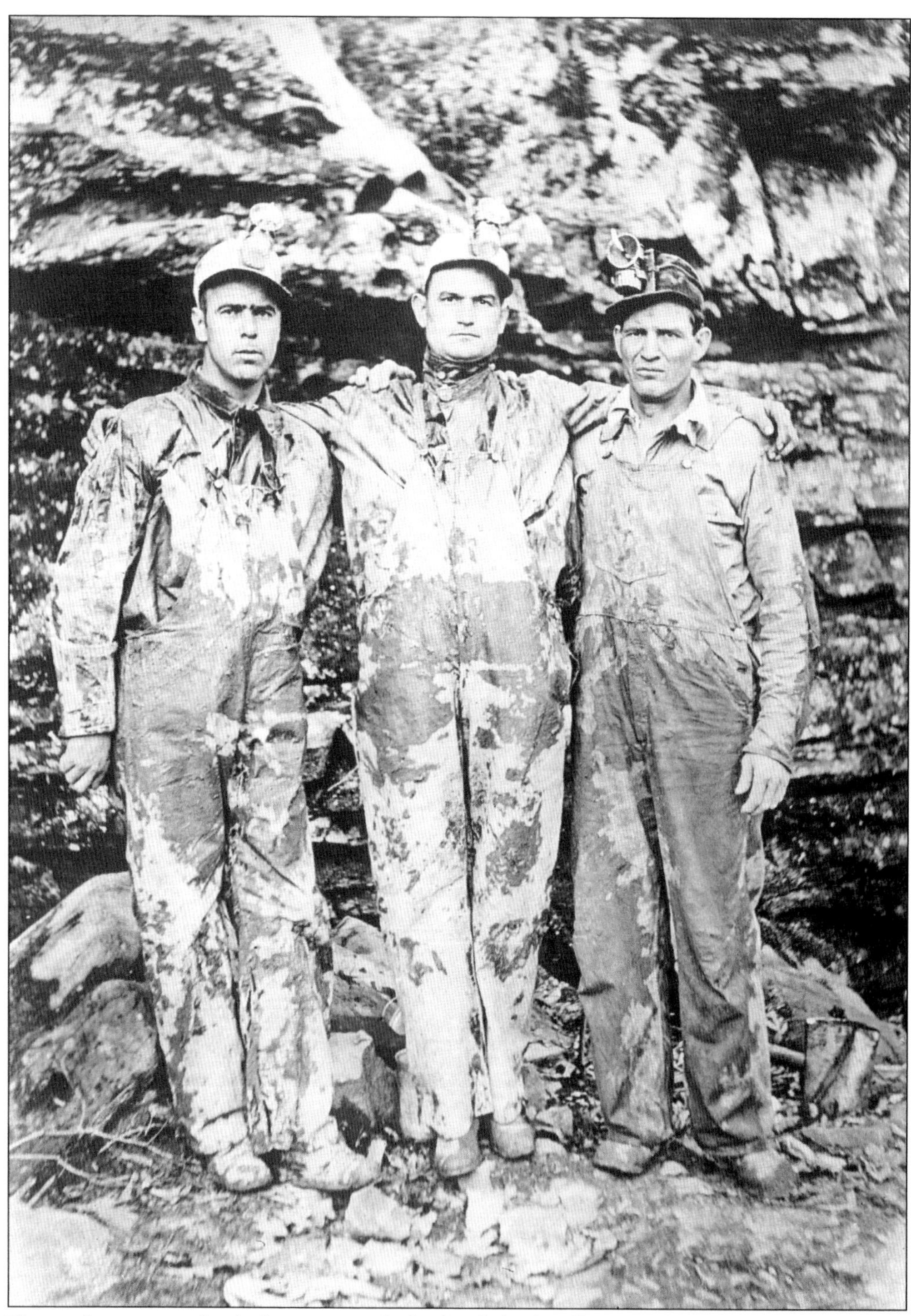

The work to reopen the shaft to remove the body of Floyd Collins was done from April 8 to April 23, except for on Sundays and two days of rain. The Kentucky State Board of Health gave the miners until May 1 to remove the body from the cave. Three of the work crew are shown posing in front of the entrance to Sand Cave on April 23. (Wade Highbaugh Collection.)

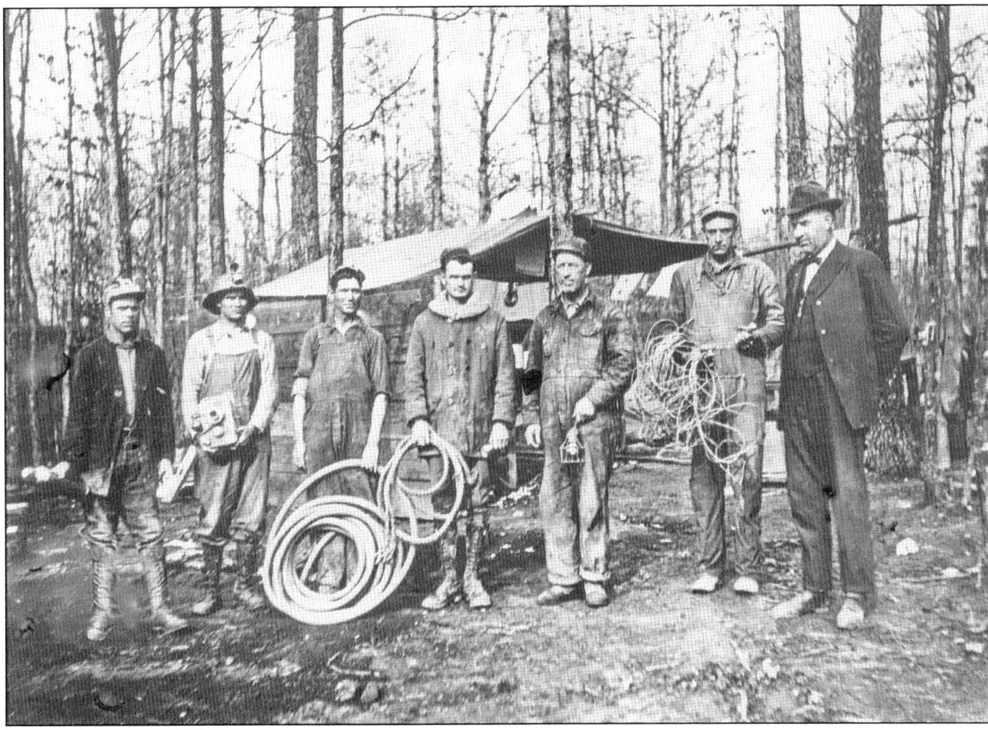

Compared to the hundreds of automobiles crowding all parking spaces near the cave during the first rescue effort in February, there were barely 25 cars as Collins's body was brought out of the cave on April 23. Only one bore the license tag of an outside state. The work crew is shown with the items that were found in the cave and brought out. (Wade Highbaugh Collection.)

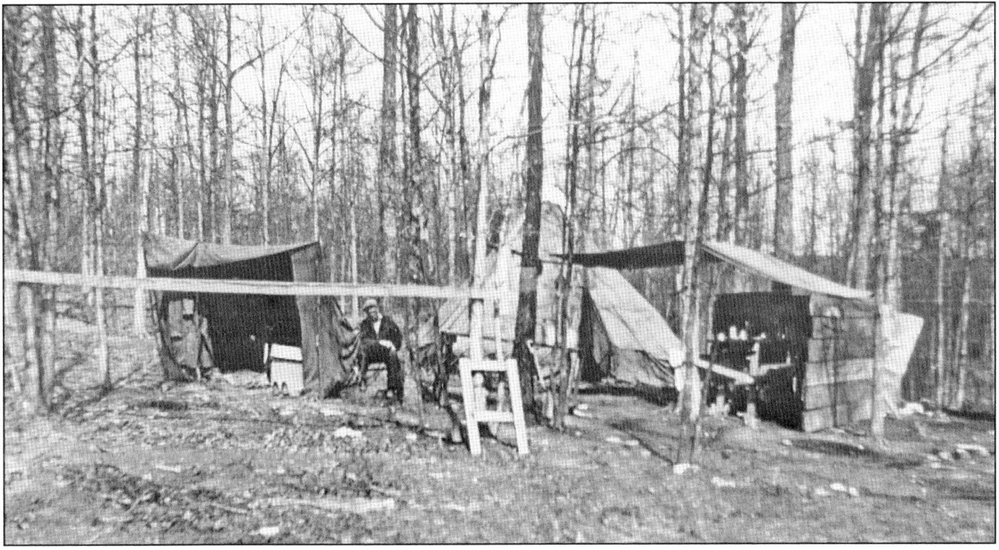

The rescue men, all experienced miners who had volunteered their services, were living above Sand Cave in tents. The recovery of Floyd Collins's body in April drew little interest in comparison to February, when hopes were high the explorer might be saved alive and the area was crowded with tourists and newspapermen. This is the campsite that was used by the workers. (Wade Highbaugh Collection.)

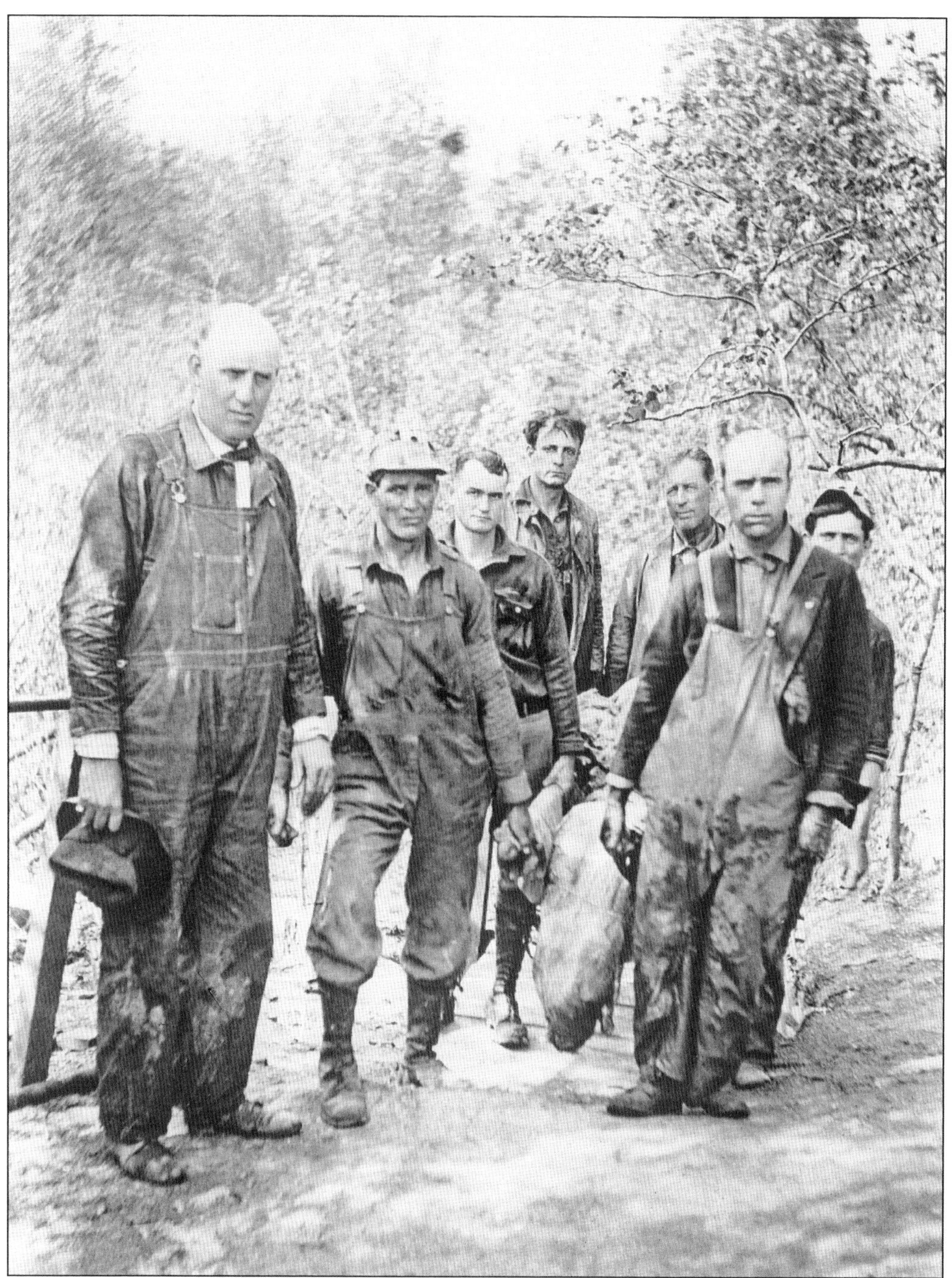

The body of Floyd Collins is carried to the hearse after being recovered from Sand Cave on April 23, 1925. The body was placed in a wicker basket and was then taken to the undertakers in Cave City for embalming. William H. Hunt banned all photographers at the cave the morning Floyd Collins's body was brought out except for Wade Highbaugh, who was employed by Hunt. Even the tourist's small cameras were forbidden. Newspapermen were closely watched. Hunt intended to use Highbaugh's pictures for his own purposes. Two motion picture cameramen were also ordered off the lot as Hunt wanted his own pictures to be exclusive. (Wade Highbaugh Collection.)

Six

The Funeral

A Final Resting Place?

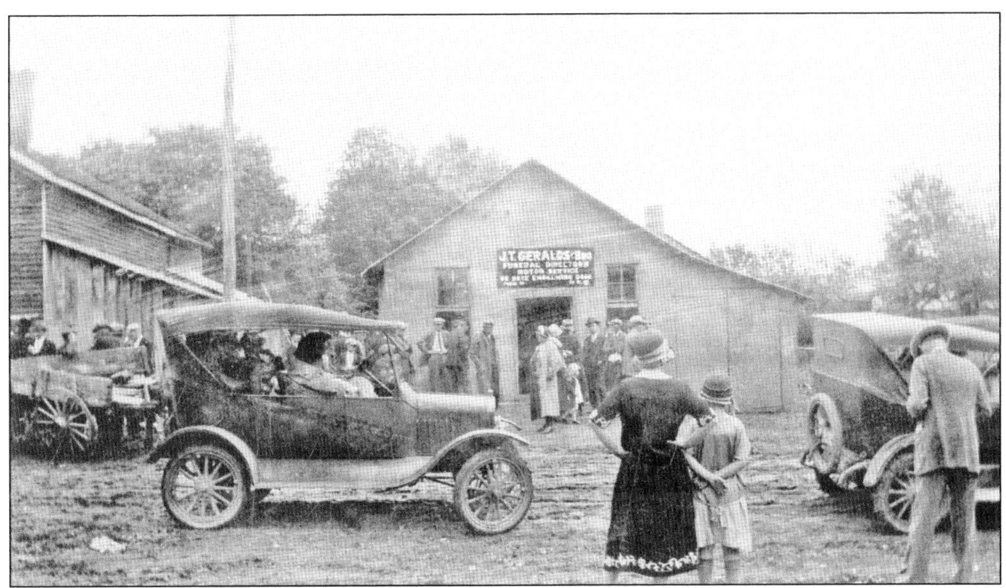

On April 23, 1925, the body of Floyd Collins was brought to Cave City for embalming at J.T. Geralds and Brothers undertakers. According to William H. Hunt, the body was still in good condition considering the time that had passed since he died. Collins's body had been preserved remarkably well by the constant temperature in the cave. (William R. Reynolds Jr., Library Special Collections, WKU.)

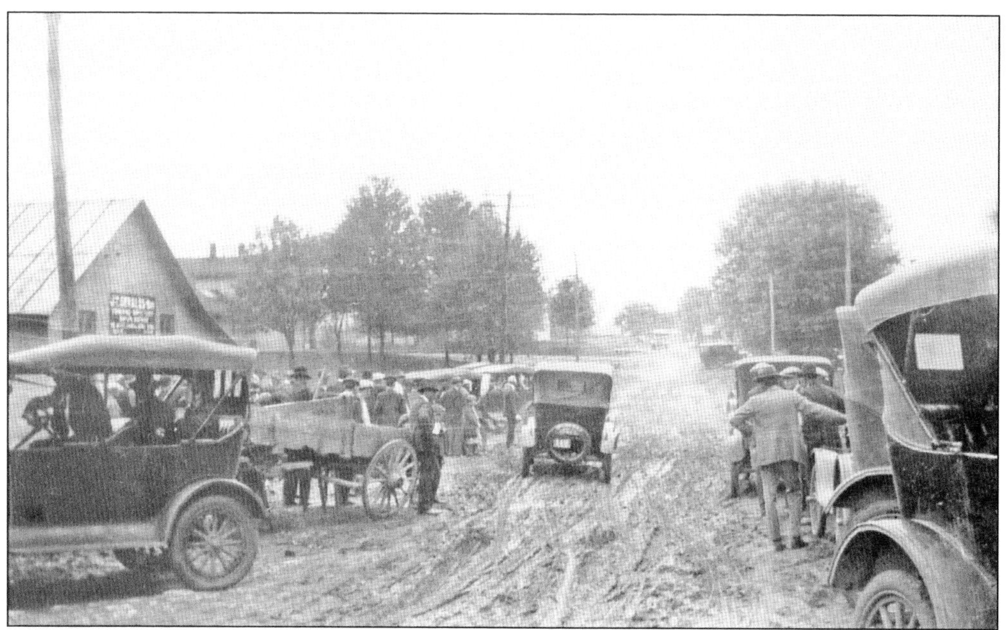

J.T. Geralds and Brothers Funeral Home was located in Cave City about 10 miles from the Sand Cave scene. The funeral home is visible at left behind the cars. (William R. Reynolds Jr., Library Special Collections, WKU.)

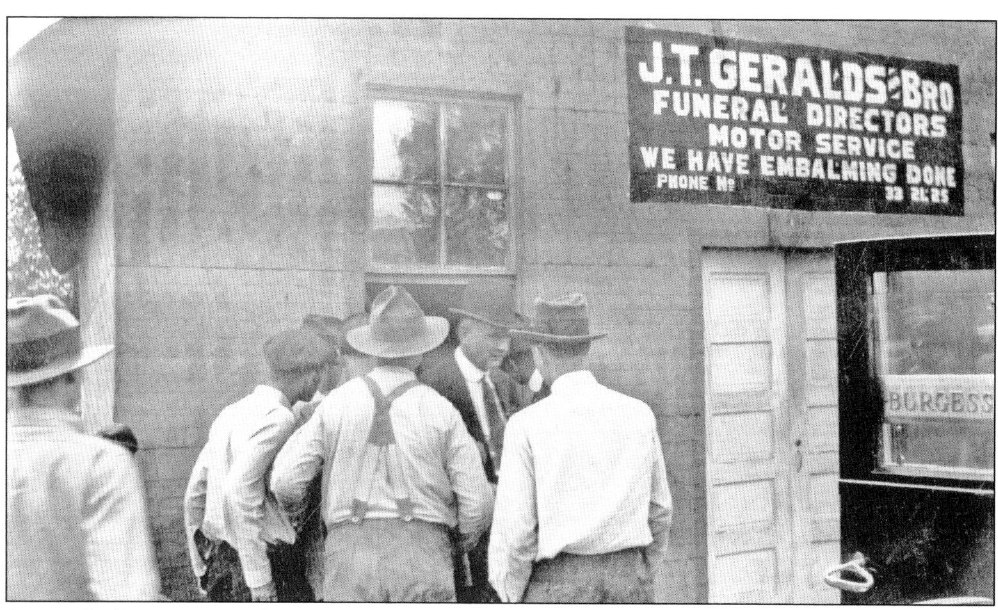

A crowd of spectators gather around the front of J.T. Geralds and Brothers Funeral Home as the body of Floyd Collins was taken inside to be embalmed. A deposit book was found in a breast pocket of Collins's overalls. He had $1,900 saved up at the bank in Cave City. The money was used to buy a casket and a large steel vault. (William R. Reynolds Jr., Library Special Collections, WKU.)

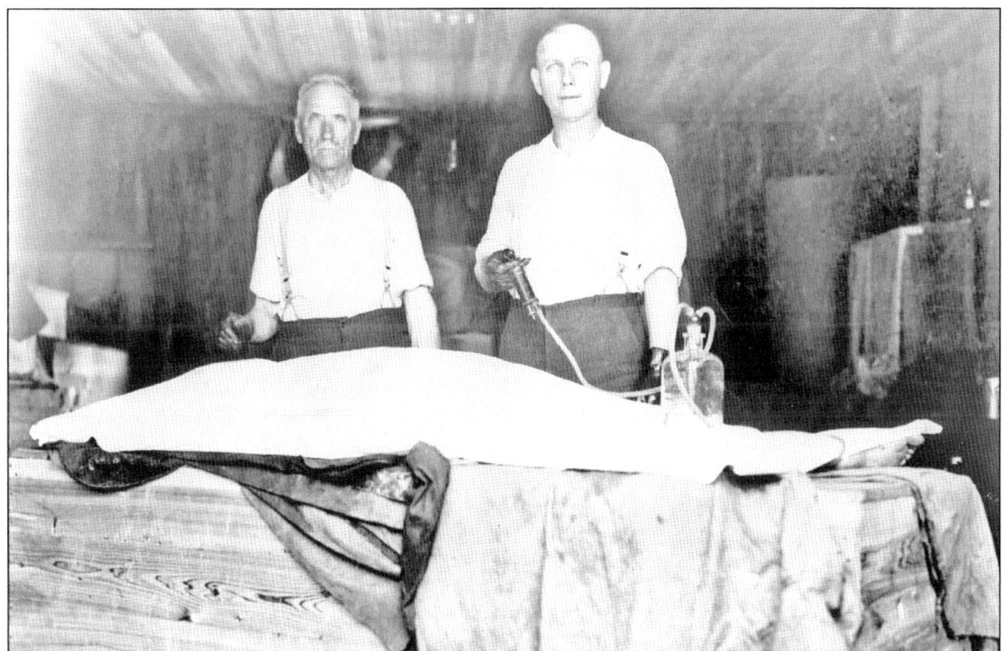

James Thomas Gerald, undertaker (left), and Orval O. Burgess, embalmer (right), are shown inside the J.T. Geralds and Brothers Funeral Home with the covered remains of Floyd Collins on April 24. Restoration on the body included the replacement of the destroyed facial features—the eyes, nose, and mouth. The body showed bruises on the left leg and a dislocated right shoulder. (Dean Snyder Collection.)

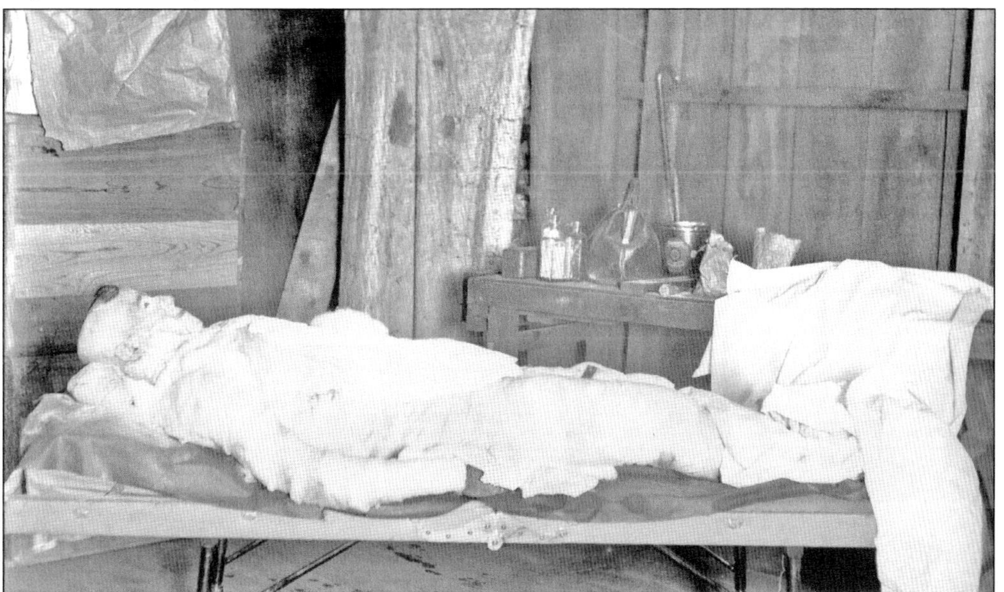

Floyd Collins's body is lying in the undertaker's parlor at Cave City after being embalmed on April 24. Cave crickets had eaten away parts of the face and ears, which had to be replaced with plaster. Orval O. Burgess had to embalm each limb and then the trunk separately. Collins's hair, scraped from the front of the head, was replaced with hair from the back. (Neville Collection, Cave Research Foundation.)

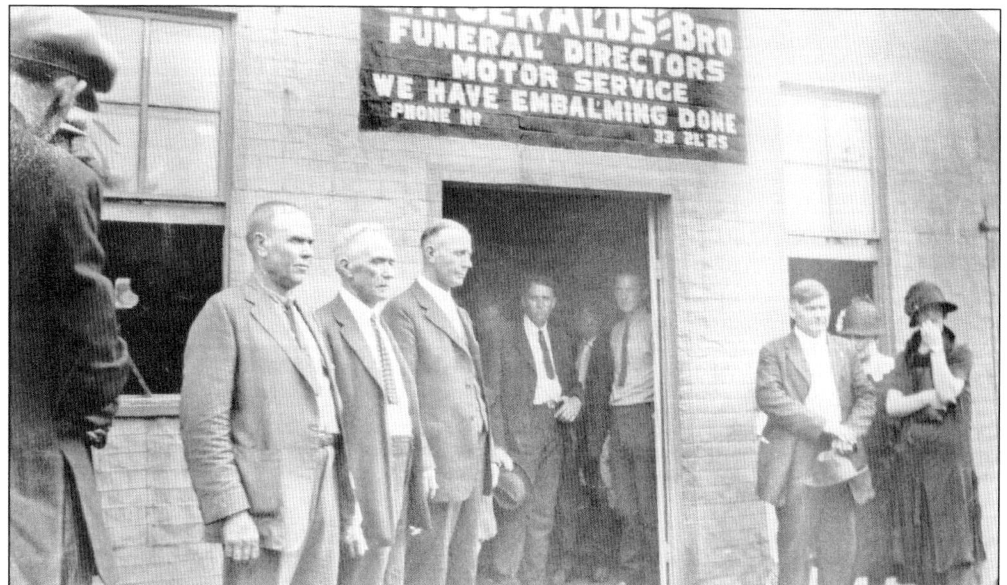

Relatives, neighbors, and friends of Floyd Collins passed by the casket inside of J.T. Geralds and Brothers undertaking chapel on April 24 and 25. James T. Gerald (second from left) and Orval Burgess (right of Gerald) are standing just outside the funeral home waiting for the body of Floyd Collins to be brought out by the six pallbearers on April 26. (William R. Reynolds Jr., Library Special Collections, WKU.)

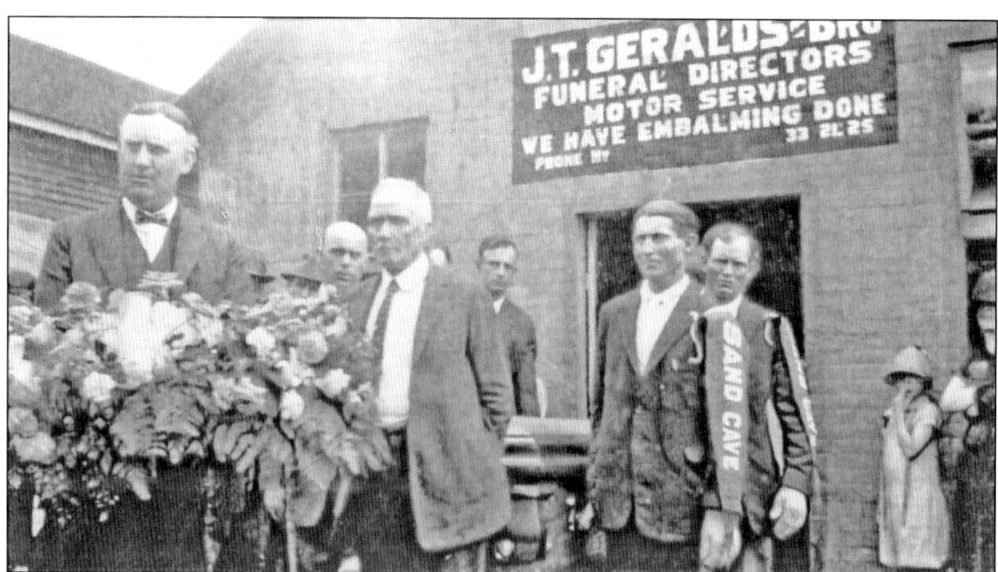

On April 26, 1925, the casket containing the body of Floyd Collins was carried out of the funeral home by six pallbearers with pennant arm bands that read "Sand Cave." The pallbearers were the six workers who pulled the body of Collins out of Sand Cave. Collins's body was carried to the hearse for the trip to the Collins homestead for burial. (William R. Reynolds Jr., Library Special Collections, WKU.)

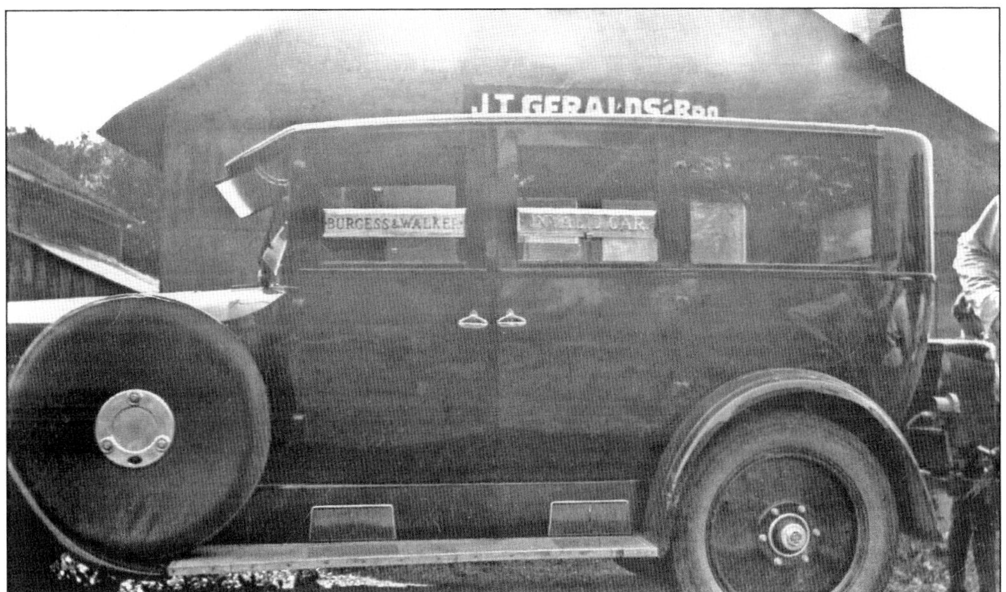

This was the funeral car that was used to transport the body of Floyd Collins from Sand Cave to Cave City and from Cave City to the Collins homestead after the two-day visitation at the funeral home. The Burgess-Walker funeral car was brought to Cave City from the Burgess Funeral Home in Bowling Green. (William R. Reynolds Jr., Library Special Collections, WKU.)

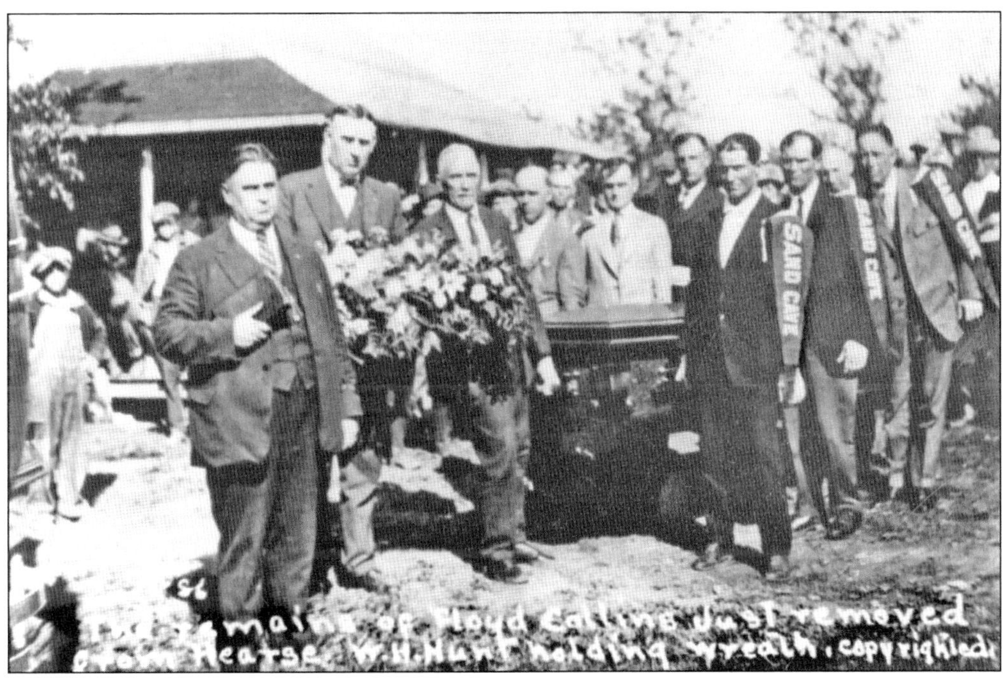

The casket of Floyd Collins has just been removed from the hearse and is being taken to his resting place on the Collins homestead on April 26. Pictured are, from left to right, Reverend Neel, William H. Hunt, James T. Gerald, and the six work crew who served as pallbearers. (National Cave Museum.)

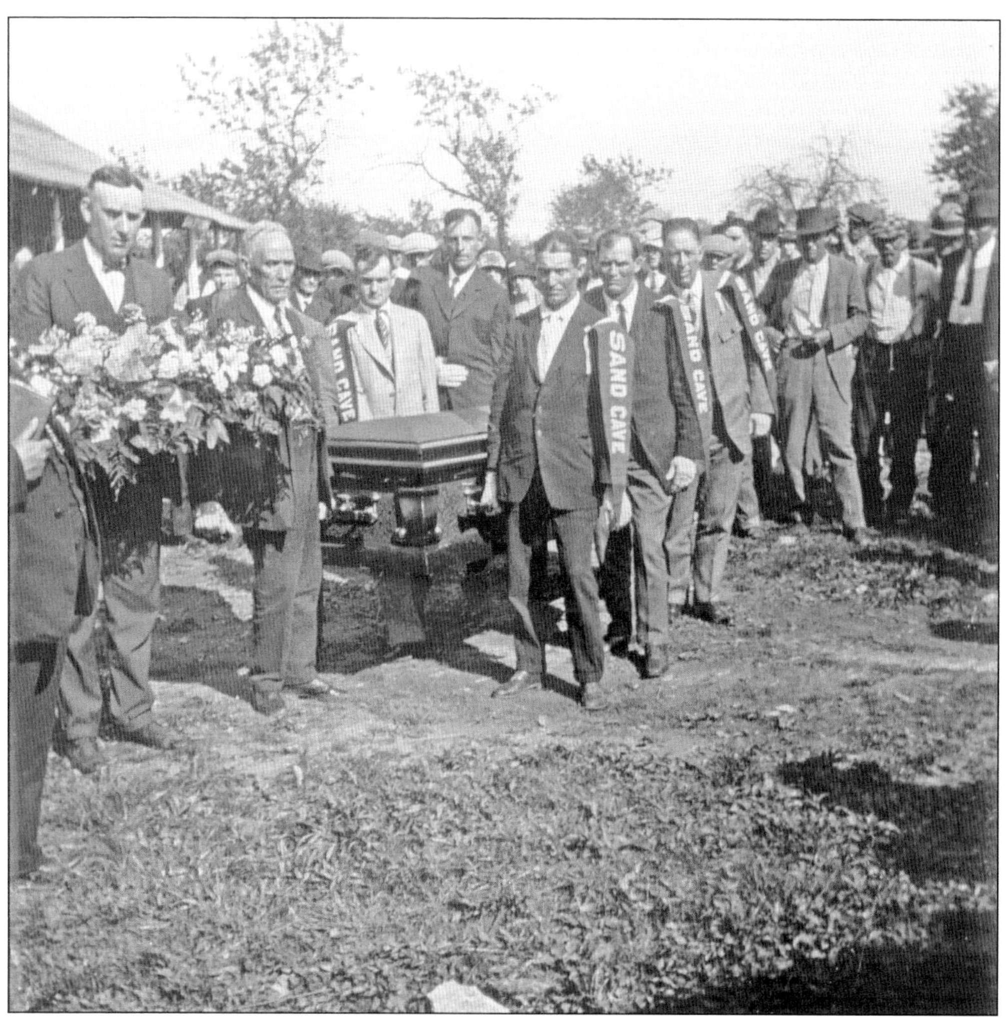

Another photograph shows the casket of Floyd Collins just being removed from the hearse and taken to his resting place on the Collins homestead on April 26. From left to right are William H. Hunt, James T. Gerald, and the six work crew who served as pallbearers. The work crew included James Samuel Smith, Harden T. Weaver, Oscar Roy Logsdon, Benjamin E. Cook, Clinton E. Goodley, and Elman Shepherd Hays. (National Cave Museum.)

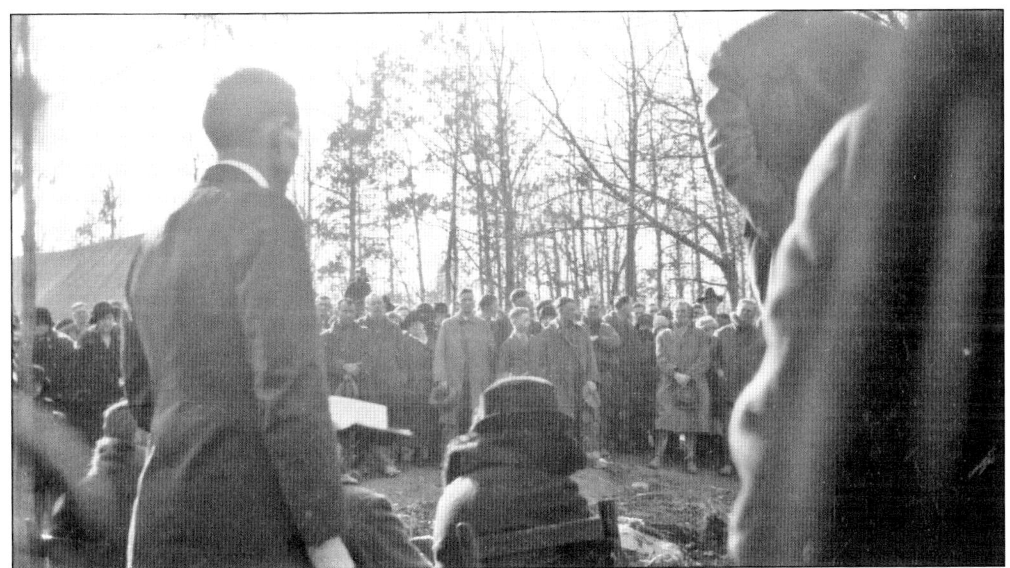

Rev. Charles Kirk Dickey is giving a service to a crowd of approximately 150 people, mostly locals, at Sand Cave during the first funeral for Floyd Collins on February 17, 1925. (William R. Reynolds Jr., Library Special Collections, WKU.)

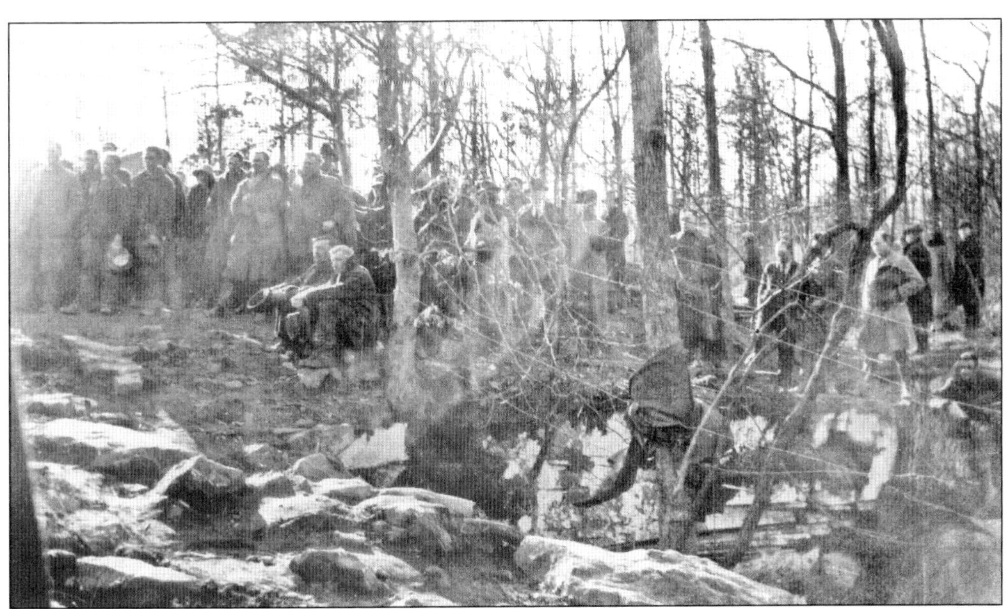

Pictured here on the hillside just above the entrance to Sand Cave is part of the crowd at Floyd Collins's first funeral. (William R. Reynolds Jr., Library Special Collections, WKU.)

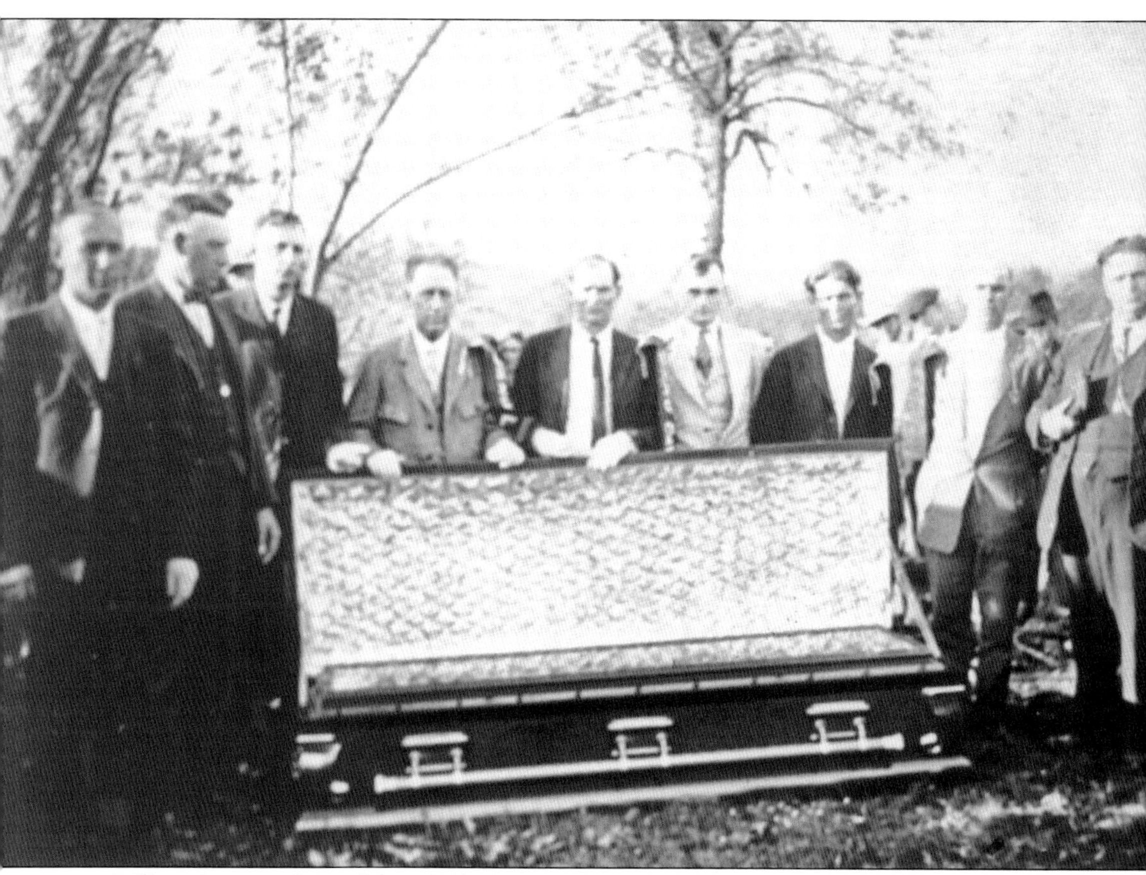

William H. Hunt (second from left), the six-man work crew, and Reverend Neel (right, with Bible) are shown standing by the open casket of Floyd Collins at his second funeral on April 26. Funeral services lasted for an hour and were conducted by the Rev. James S. Smith of Central City and Reverend Neel of Bowling Green. (Wade Highbaugh Collection.)

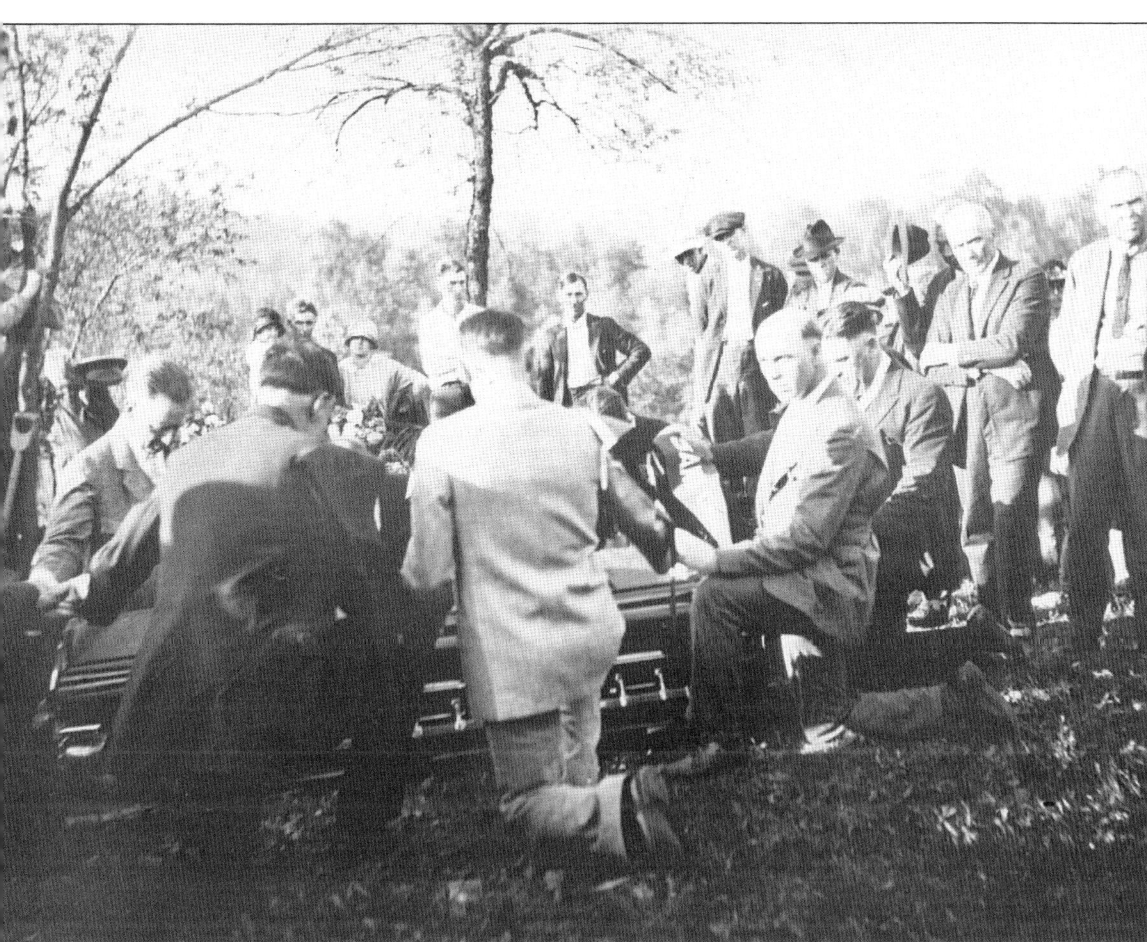

William H. Hunt and his crew are shown kneeling in prayer around the casket of Floyd Collins on April 26. No other incident within memory had brought so many prayers from the brotherhood of man for one fellow human trapped underground. (Wade Highbaugh Collection.)

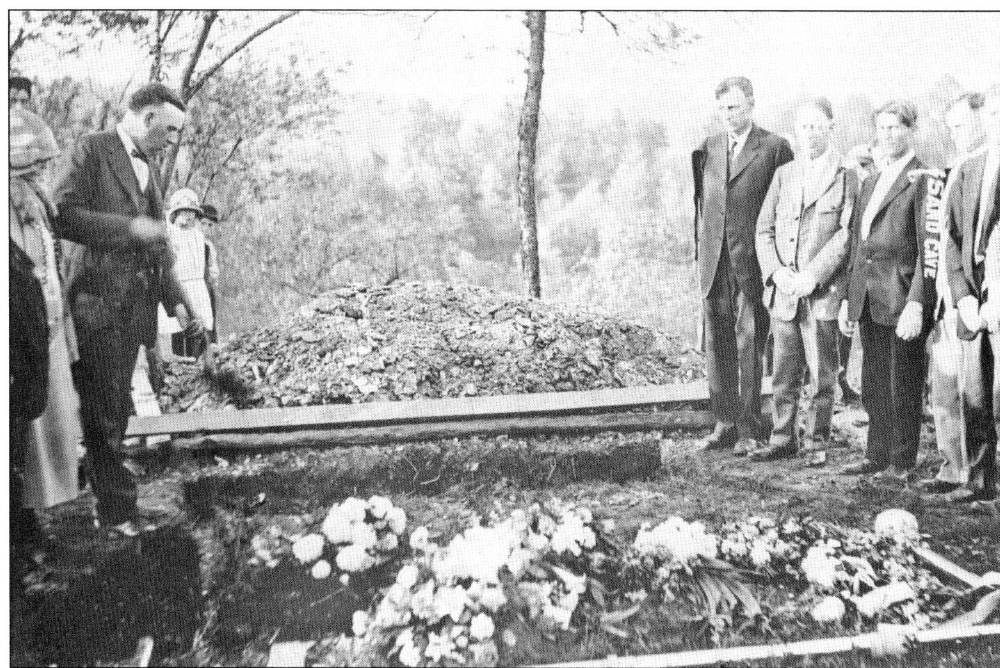

William H. Hunt (left) is placing the first dirt on the remains of Floyd Collins on April 26. A tribute was given to Collins by those who were part of his life. (Wade Highbaugh Collection.)

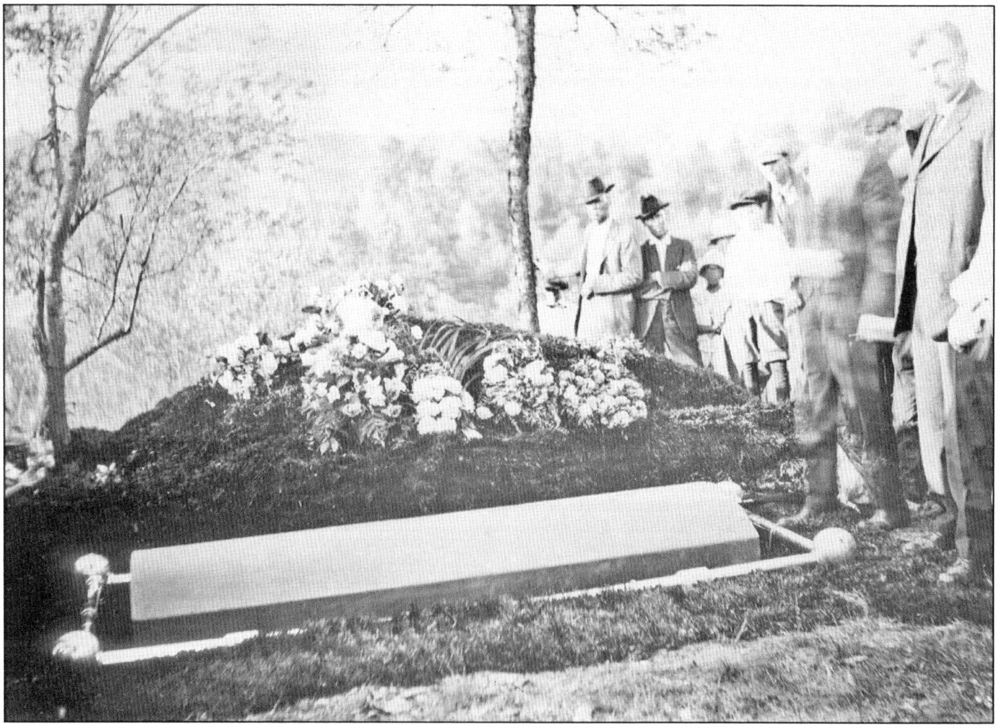

The gravesite of Floyd Collins is shown on the farm where he lived. The record of Floyd Collins as a cave explorer was unsurpassed for bravery. His discoveries were his contribution to the world of science. (Wade Highbaugh Collection.)

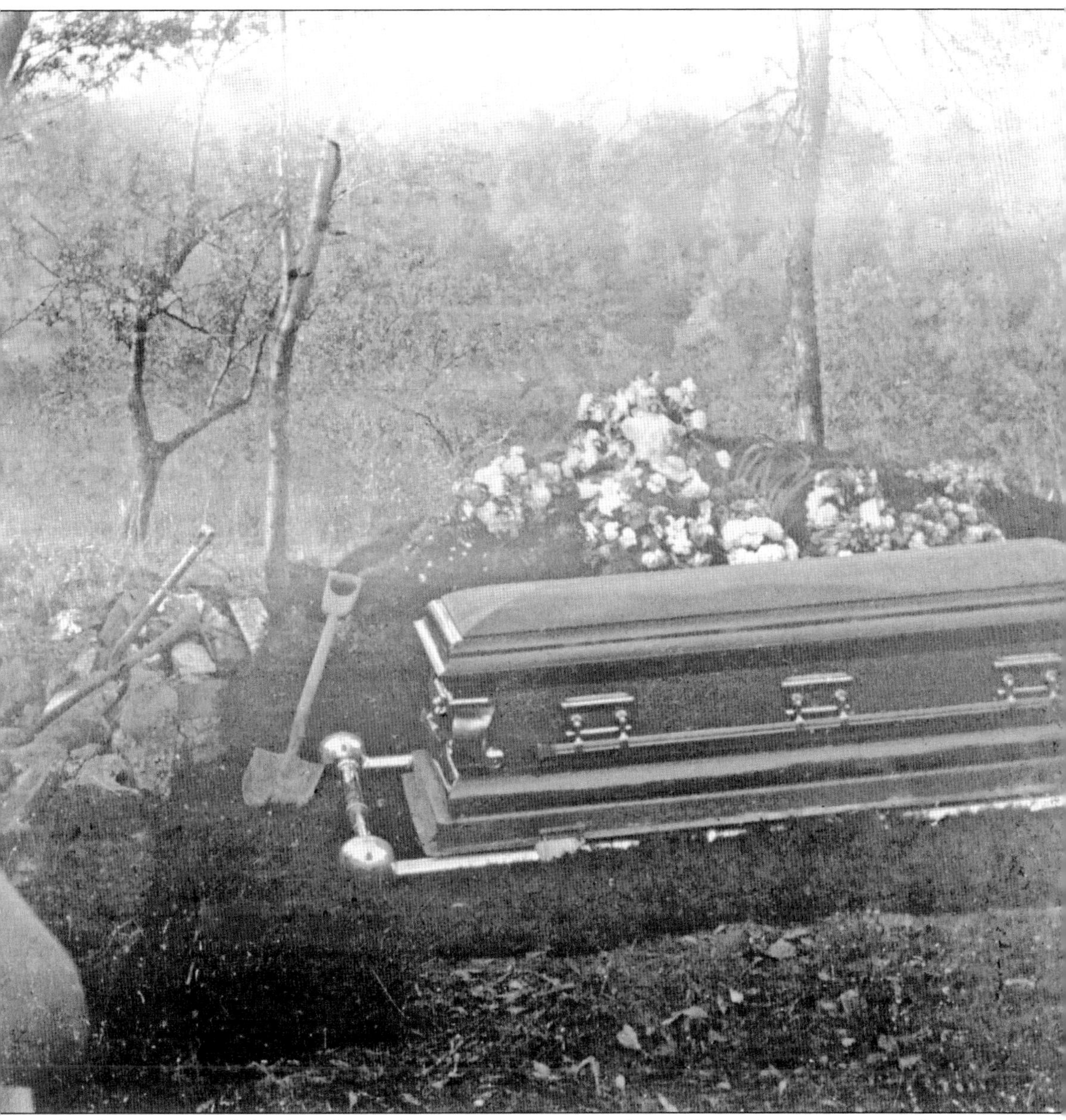

The closed casket of Floyd Collins is shown just before it was lowered into the ground in the large steel vault on the hillside near the Collins family homestead, close to the path to Great Crystal Cave. Shovels and different flower arrangements can be seen. After 82 days in Sand Cave, the body of Floyd Collins was laid to rest on April 26, 1925. This was the second burial location for Floyd Collins. Approximately 400 people attended Collins's second funeral. A much larger crowd was expected, but an all-day rain kept many away. (National Cave Museum.)

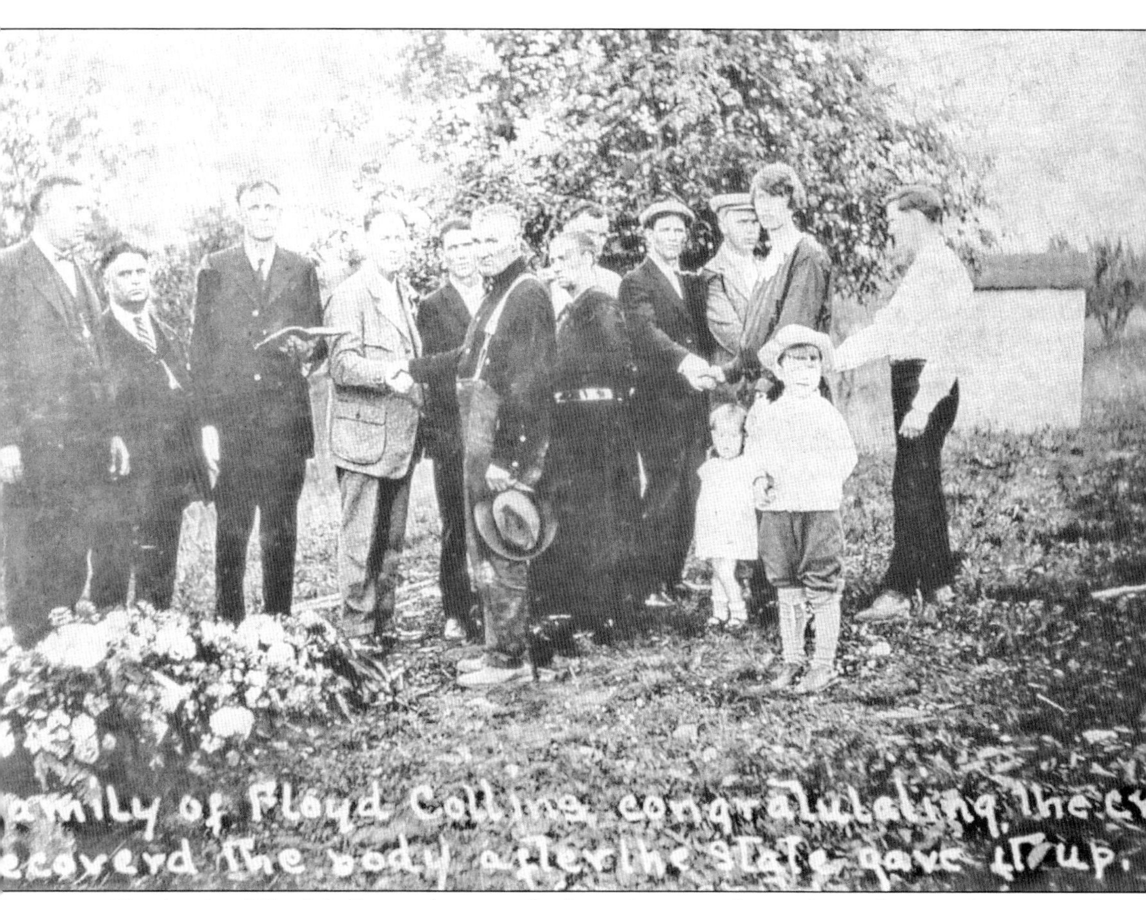

The family of Floyd Collins is shown at the funeral congratulating the work crew who recovered the body of Collins from Sand Cave. From left to right are William H. Hunt, Reverend Neel, Reverend Smith, five work crew members, Lee and Jane Collins, and Anna and Marshall Collins and their two children, Gordon and Cleona. (Library Special Collections, WKU.)

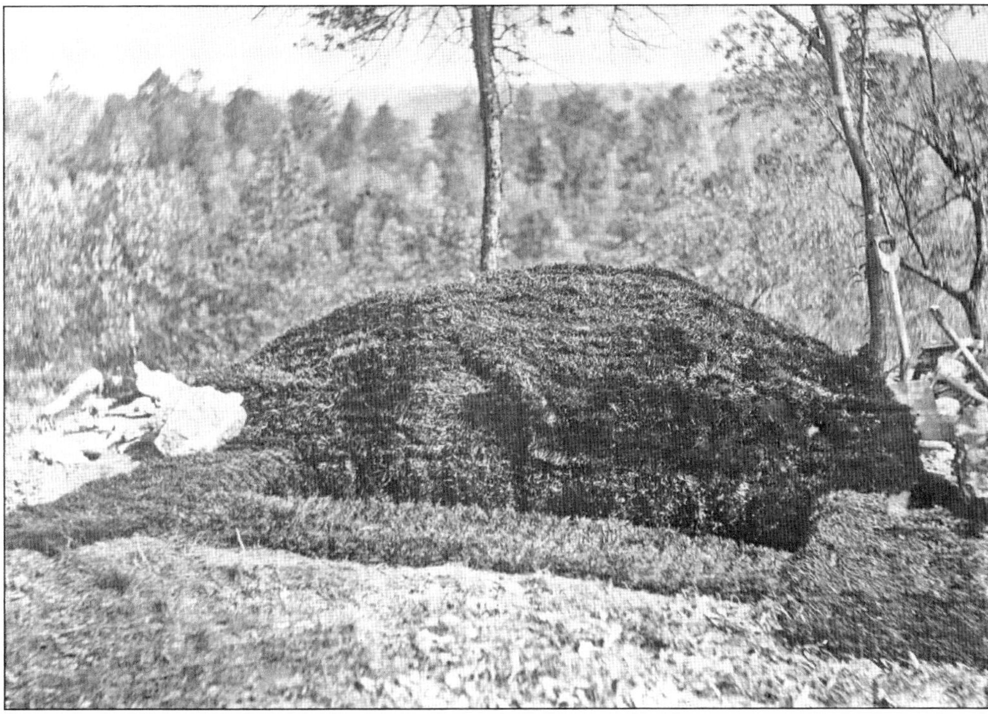

This photograph shows Floyd Collins's grave above the Great Crystal Cave entrance. Collins was not religious as a boy or as a young man, but found faith as he was trapped in Sand Cave. He prayed for assistance and deliverance but realized his escape was not assured and prayed, "But if my death in Sand Cave be Thy will, Thy will be done." (Wade Highbaugh Collection.)

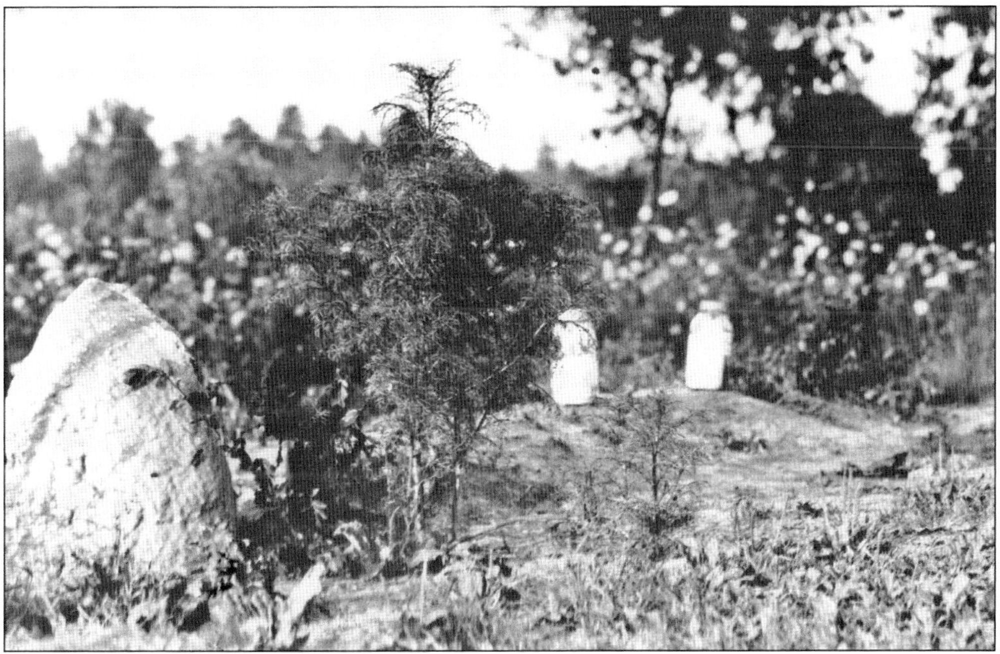

Floyd Collins's grave on the Collins homestead was marked by a huge stalagmite until a pink granite headstone replaced it in 1926. (Neville Collection, Cave Research Foundation.)

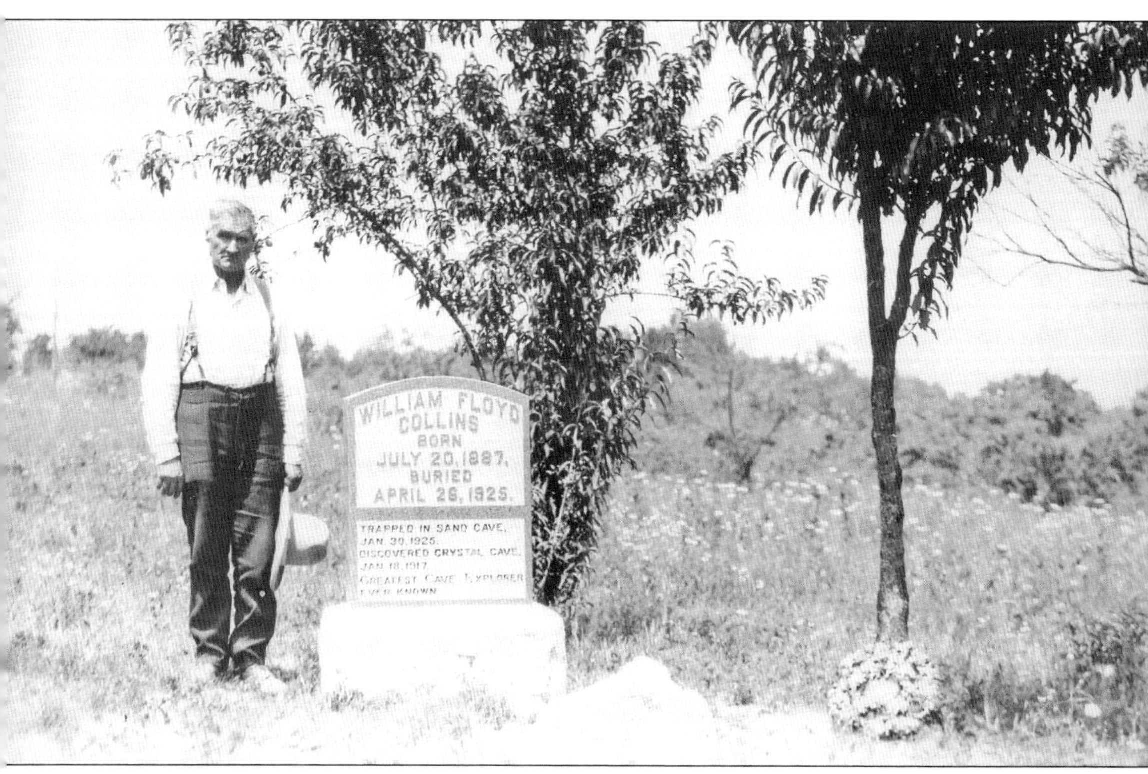

Lee Collins is standing by his son's grave in 1926. The inscription from the headstone of Floyd Collins reads, "William Floyd Collins, Born July 20, 1887, Buried April 26, 1925, Trapped in Sand Cave, Jan. 30, 1925, Discovered Crystal Cave, Jan. 18, 1917, Greatest Cave Explorer Ever Known." (Neville Collection, Cave Research Foundation.)

Seven

Sand Cave Aftermath

Floyd Collins Becomes a Tourist Attraction

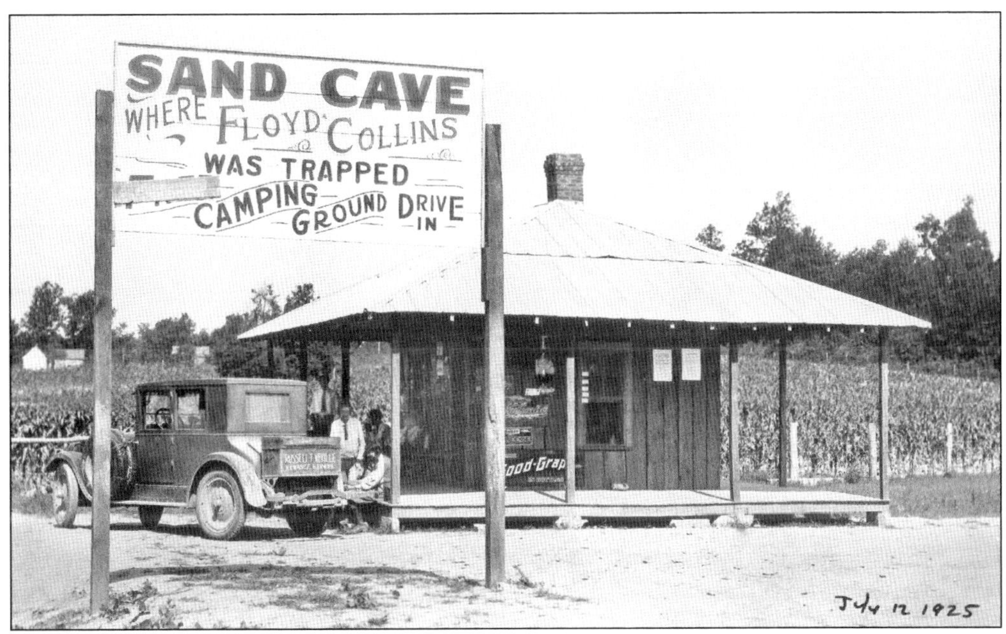

Soon after Floyd Collins's body was found and left in Sand Cave in February 1925, Bee Doyel, the owner of the cave, started charging 25¢ admission for "country" people and 50¢ for "foreigners." Doyel built a one-room office with a circled veranda on the highway near Sand Cave. A large sign was built to lure tourists. (Neville Collection, Cave Research Foundation.)

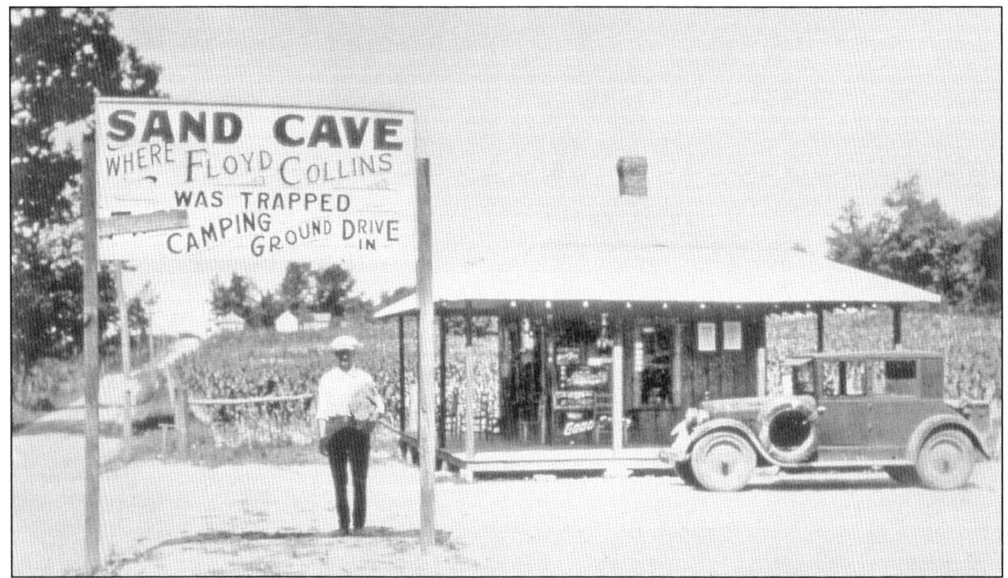

After Floyd Collins was brought out of Sand Cave in April 1925, Bee Doyel continued to operate Sand Cave as a tourist attraction to show where Collins had been trapped. Note the word "free" is covered on the sign; evidently Doyel found out he could make money by charging for campers. Doyel is shown holding the 27-pound rock that pinned Floyd Collins. (Neville Collection, Cave Research Foundation.)

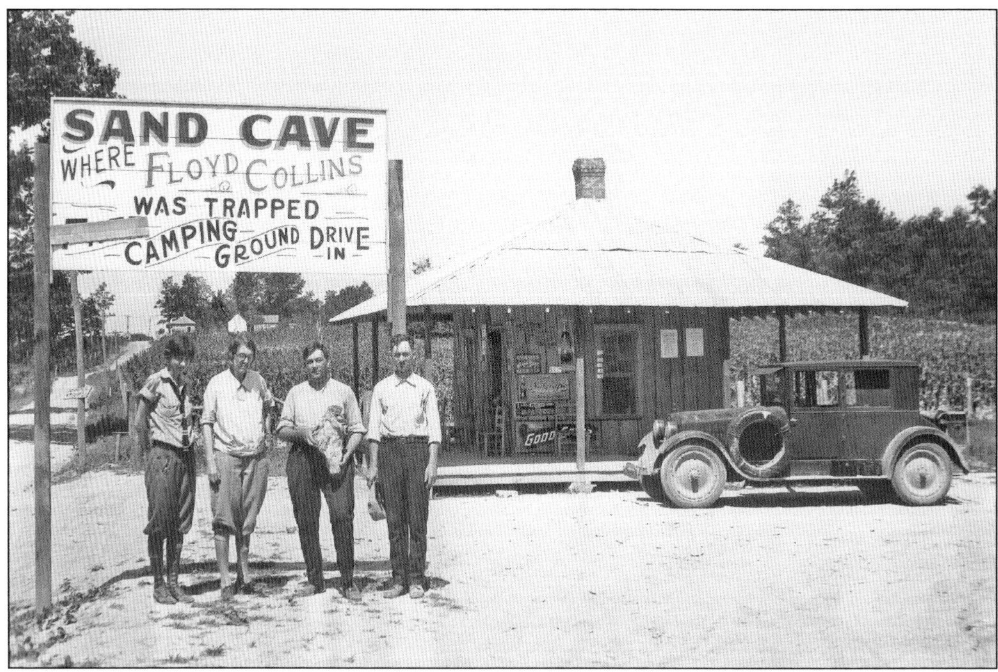

Bee Doyel sold many of photographer Wade Highbaugh's postcards of Sand Cave at his ticket office/souvenir stand. Photographer Russell T. Neville (second from right), his sister Hazel (second from left), and daughter Julia (left) visited the cave area often during their summer vacations. Neville took a number of pictures during his July 1925 visit. (Neville Collection, Cave Research Foundation.)

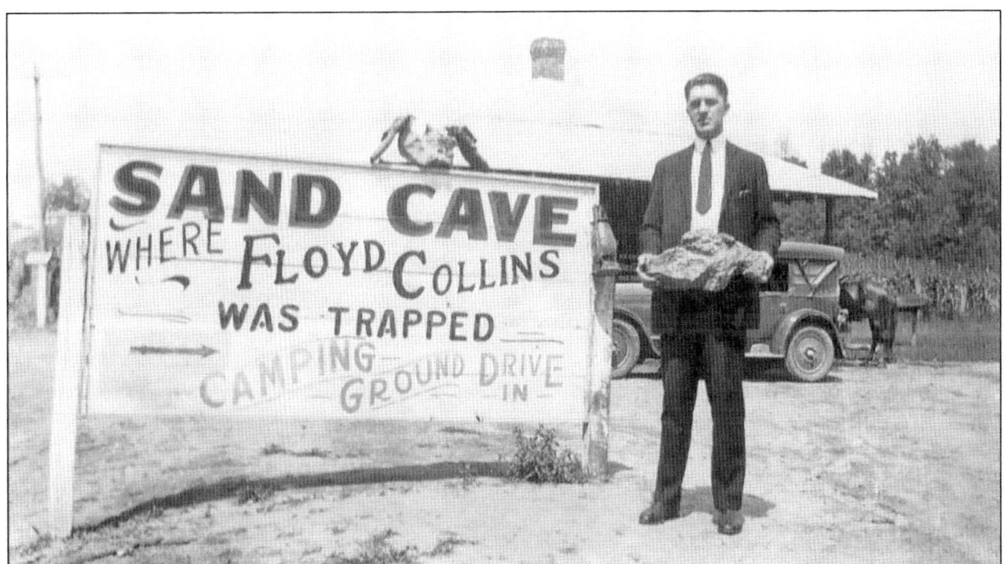

It was common to have tourists pose for pictures with the 27-pound rock that trapped Floyd Collins. Over the years, the rock has been felt and held by hundreds of those who wanted to "touch" a piece of history. The rock is now worn smooth from years of being handled, and has initials carved into one side. (Dean Snyder Collection.)

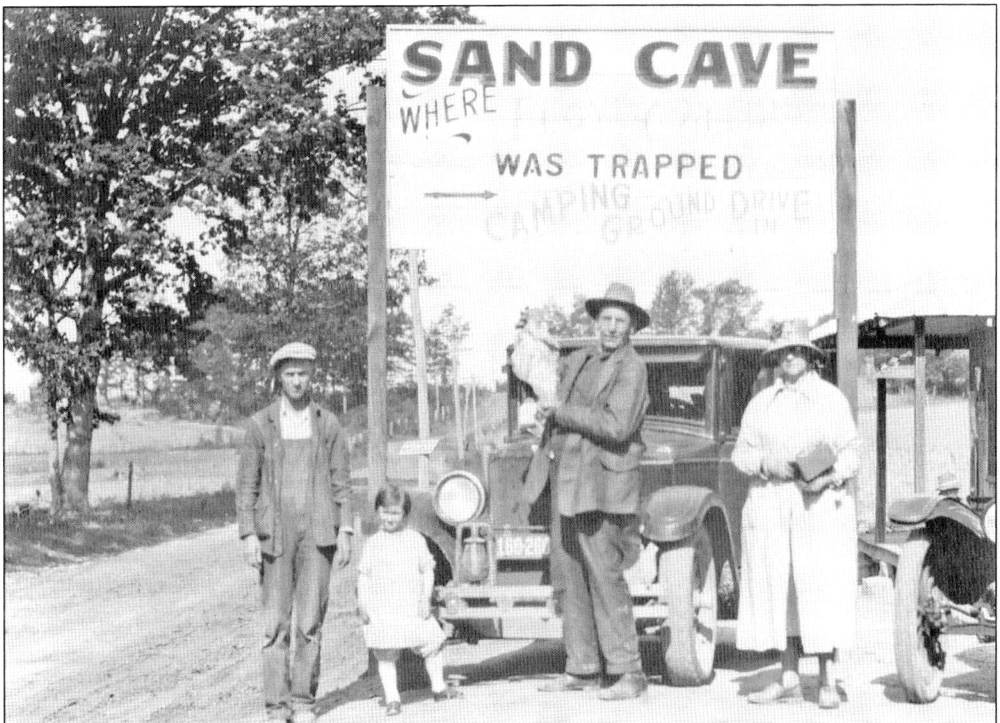

To make more money, rocks were frequently sold to tourists led to believe that they were buying the original 27-pound rock that trapped Floyd Collins. As each rock was sold, a new one was taken from under the table and placed on the shelf to sell. (Dean Snyder Collection.)

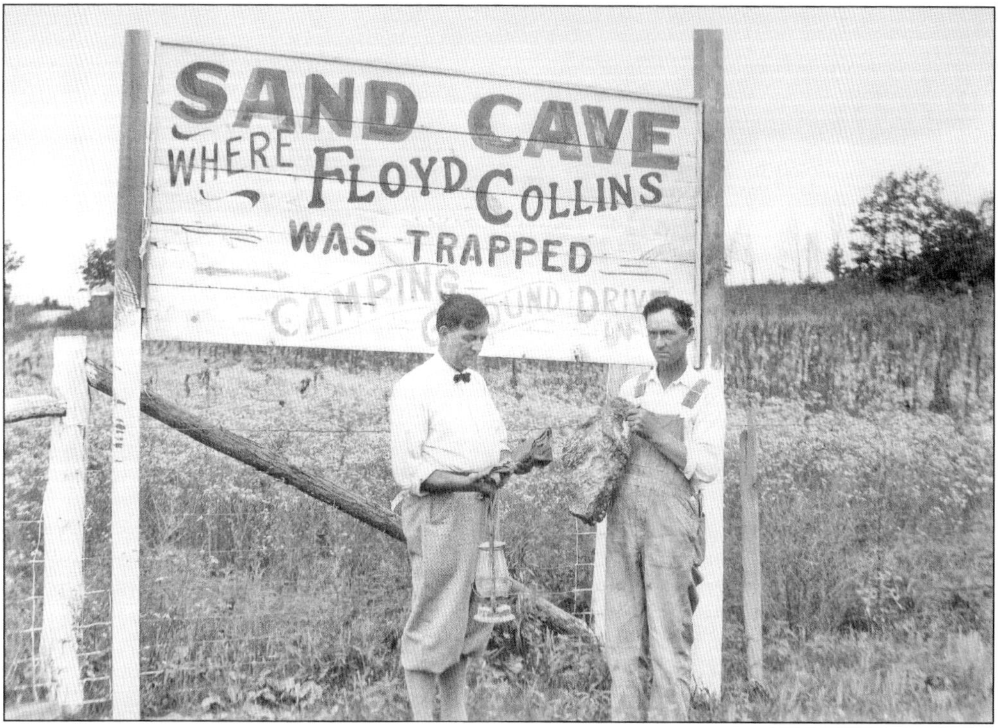

Photographer Russell T. Neville (left) and Sand Cave owner Bee Doyel (right) hold items belonging to Floyd Collins and found in Sand Cave including a lantern and the 27-pound rock that trapped Collins. (National Cave Museum.)

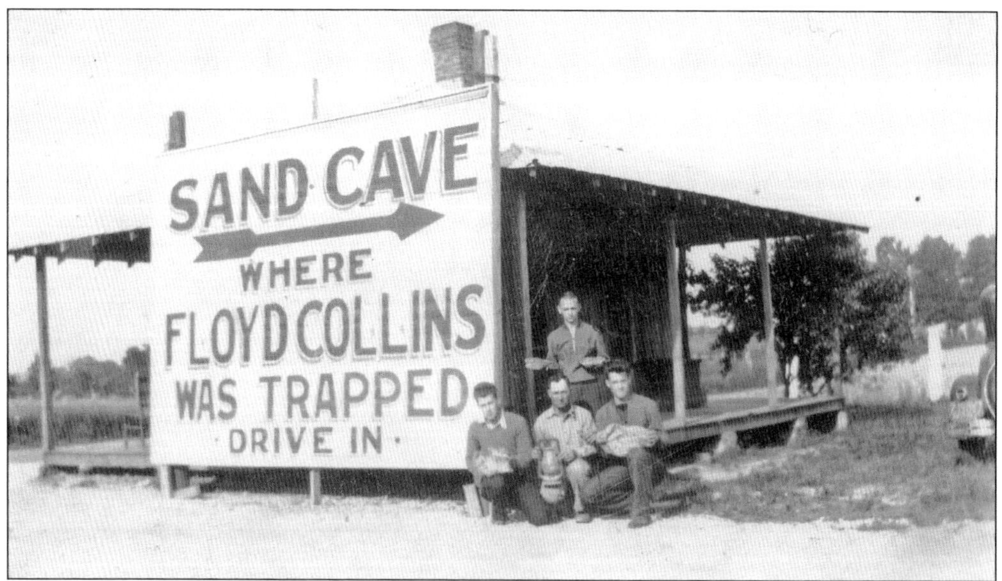

The Sand Cave ticket office was used by Bee Doyel to sell tickets to the Sand Cave attraction. Each day, the 27-pound rock that trapped Collins was brought out of the ticket office for tourists to hold and pose with. Even though Sand Cave is within the boundaries of Mammoth Cave National Park, the ticket office is outside the park and has been renovated as a private residence. (National Cave Museum.)

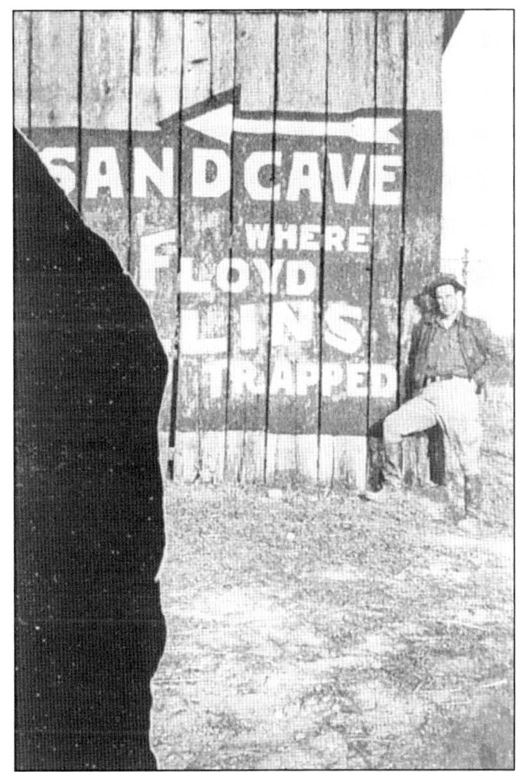

Bee Doyel (holding the 27-pound rock that trapped Floyd Collins) used the side of this barn to advertise Sand Cave as a tourist attraction. The sign reads, "Sand Cave Where Floyd Collins was Trapped." To draw attention to the attraction, Doyel could be seen flagging down cars on the main road going to Mammoth Cave. (Right, Richard Hobart Collection; below, National Cave Museum.)

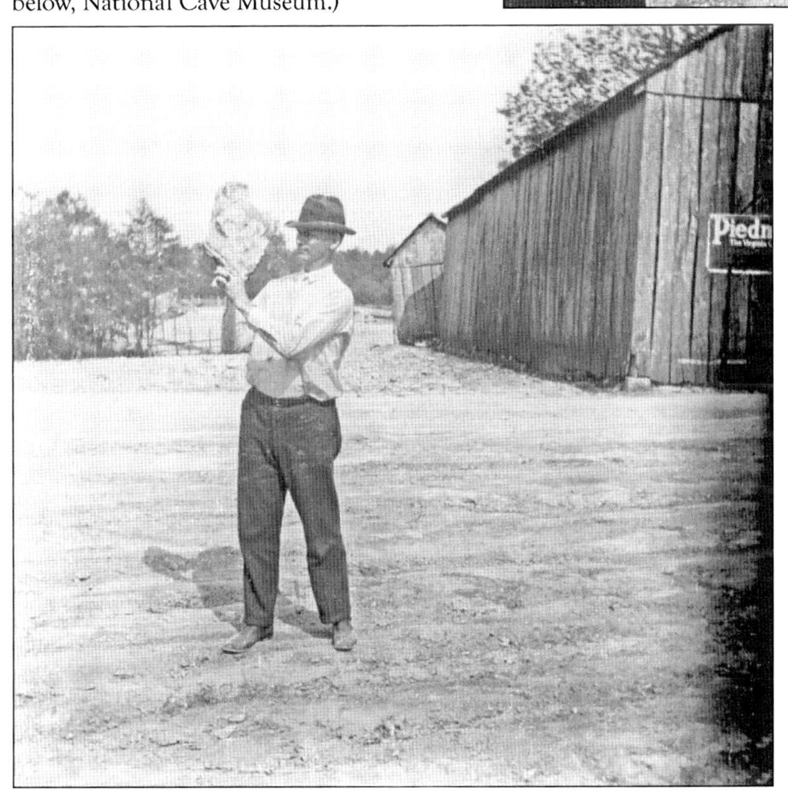

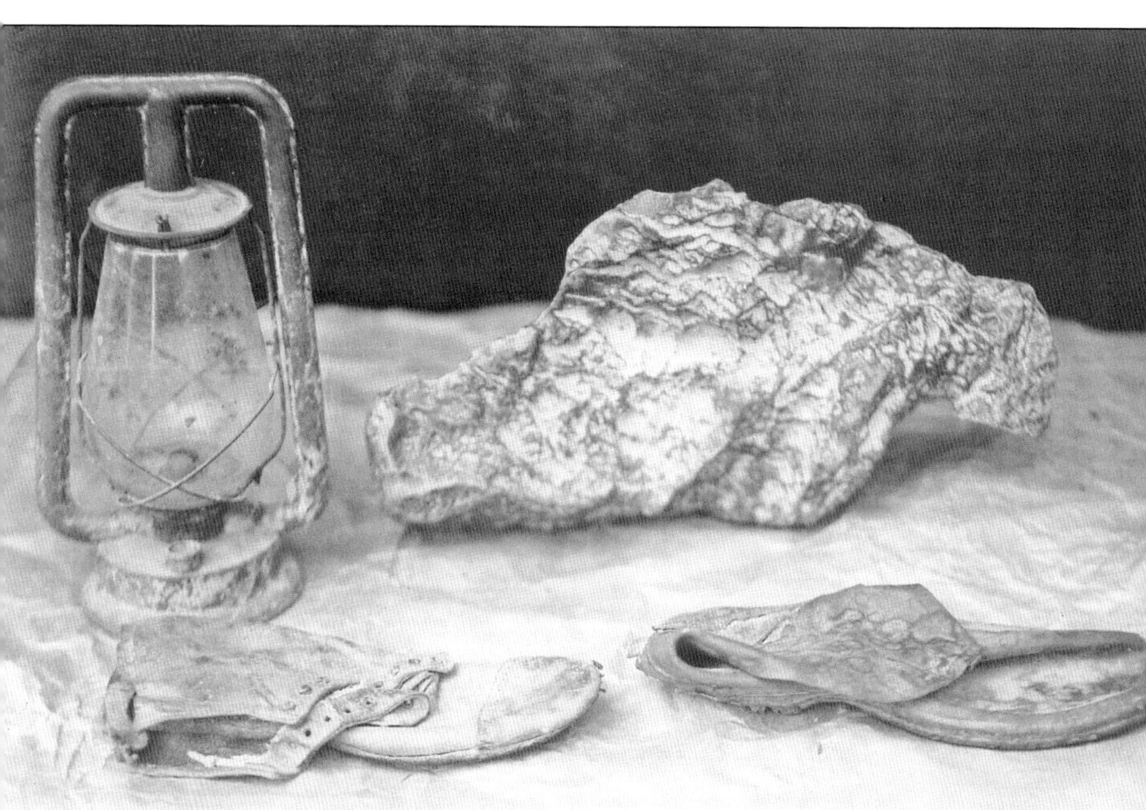

Part of the attraction to tourists at Sand Cave was the chance to see these historical items belonging to Floyd Collins. Pictured are Collins's lantern, boots, and the 27-pound rock that trapped him. The rock that trapped Collins's left ankle was shaped like a leg of lamb. (Neville Collection, Cave Research Foundation.)

SAND CAVE

When visiting the cave region do not fail to spend a few minutes viewing the only spot made famous by the late Floyd Collins and take Kodak Pictures of this beautiful spot.

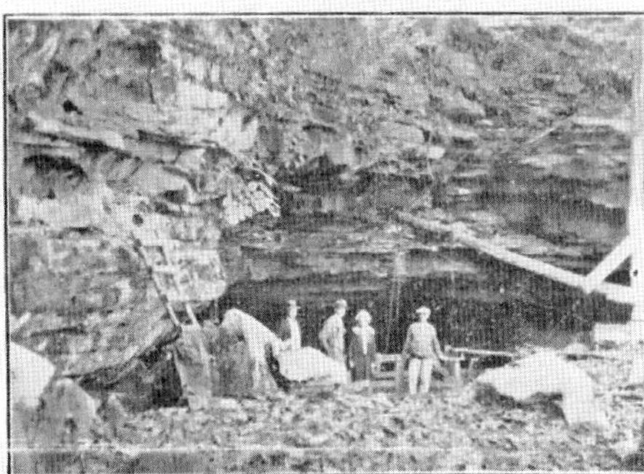

Who was given more newspaper space than any other person until exceeded by the success of Colonel Chas. Lindbergh. Lindy's efforts were crowned with success, Floyd's efforts met a tragic end.

THE ONLY SPOT MADE FAMOUS BY FLOYD COLLINS
Located on the state mantained highway 6 miles west of Dixie Highway U. S. 31 at Cave City Ky. On the direct road to Mammoth Cave.

Many tourist travel to foreign lands to visit spots made famous by ancient martyrs and now only designated by a metal marker or tablet. Here you can see the cave, shaft, tunnel and equipment of explorers.

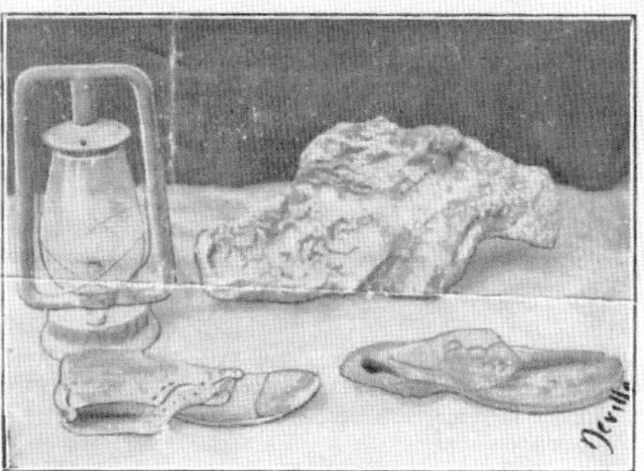

Floyd's Lantern, Shoes and Rock That Held His Foot

Full exhibitiion fee only 50 cents BEE DOYLE, Owner

Bee Doyel printed a one-sided promotional flyer of Sand Cave to help advertise his attraction. The brochure mentions that Sand Cave was "the only spot made famous by Floyd Collins," and "Here you can see the cave, shaft, tunnel, and equipment of explorers." Admission tickets of 25¢ were also printed for the short-lived attraction. The large Sand Cave sign along the main road did draw the attention of travelers going to Mammoth Cave, but very few stopped. (Both, National Cave Museum.)

696

SAND CAVE, Bee Doyle Prop.
ADMIT ONE
Admission--23c
Tax--2c
25c

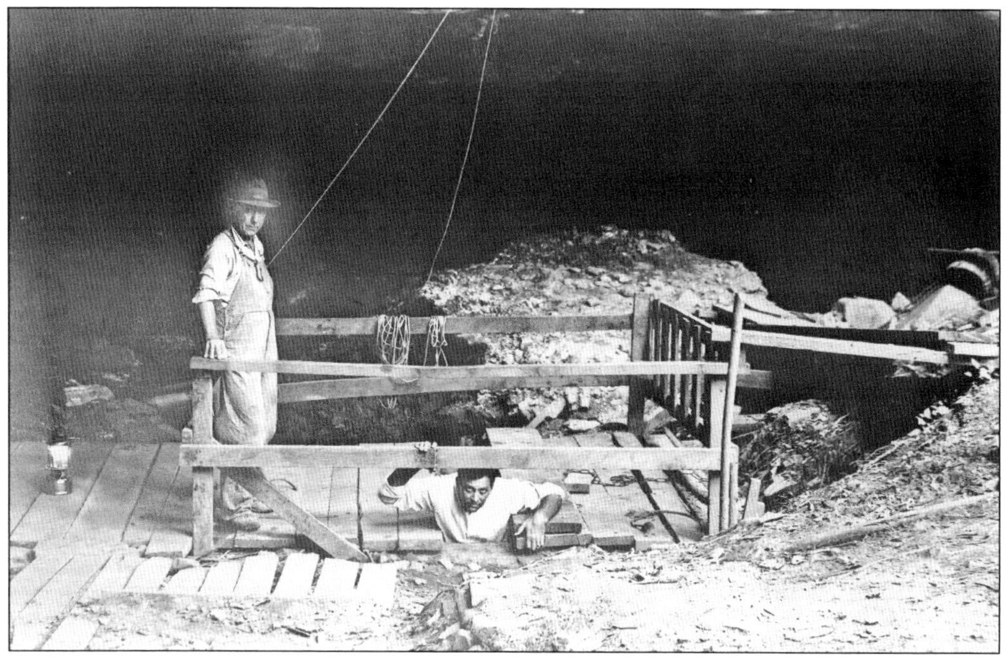

Two points of interest were shown at the Sand Cave attraction. One was the entrance where Floyd Collins entered the cave. The other was the vertical shaft that was dug down to rescue him. Photographer Russell T. Neville is shown in July 1925 at the top of the shaft after the removal of Collins's body from Sand Cave. (Neville Collection, Cave Research Foundation.)

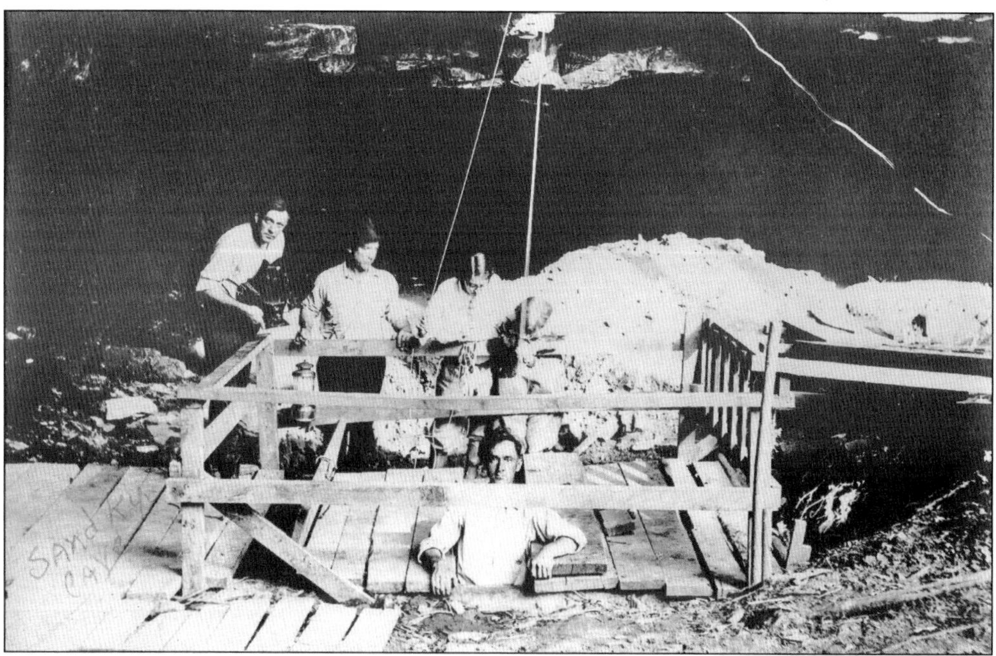

Bee Doyel is shown at the top of the shaft after the removal of Floyd Collins's body from Sand Cave. Posing for a picture at the top of the shaft where Collins was brought out was a hard-to-pass-up opportunity for tourists, who were looking for a special memory to take home about the event that captured a nation for 17 days. (National Cave Museum.)

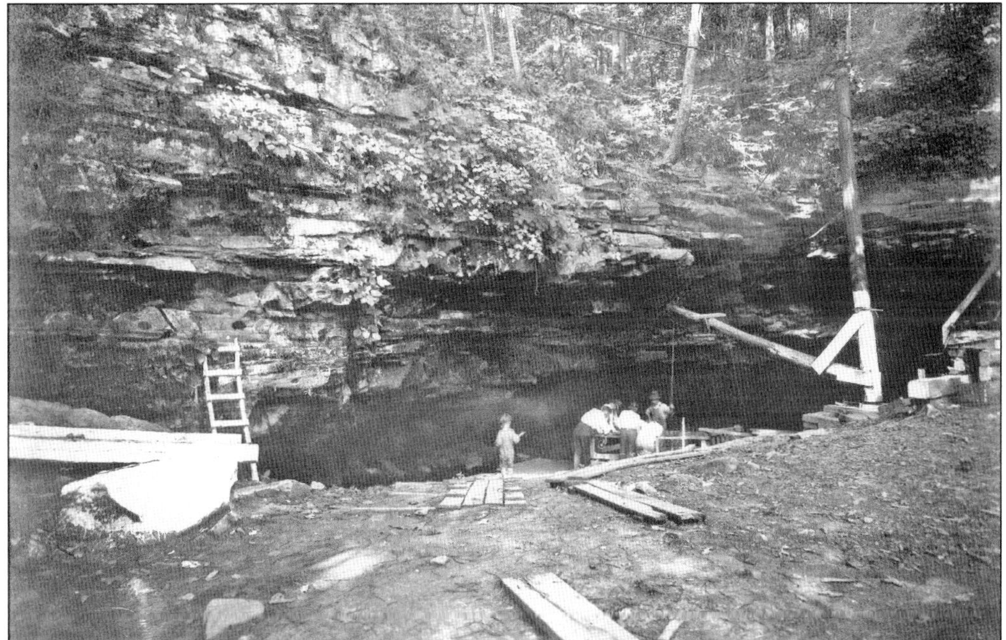

The entrance to Sand Cave was shown as part of the tourist attraction. The only part of the cave actually open to visitors was just inside the cave entrance, which was dug out by Bee Doyel. Much of the equipment seen here was used in the Collins rescue attempt and was still on-site in July 1925 during photographer Russell T. Neville's visit. (National Cave Museum.)

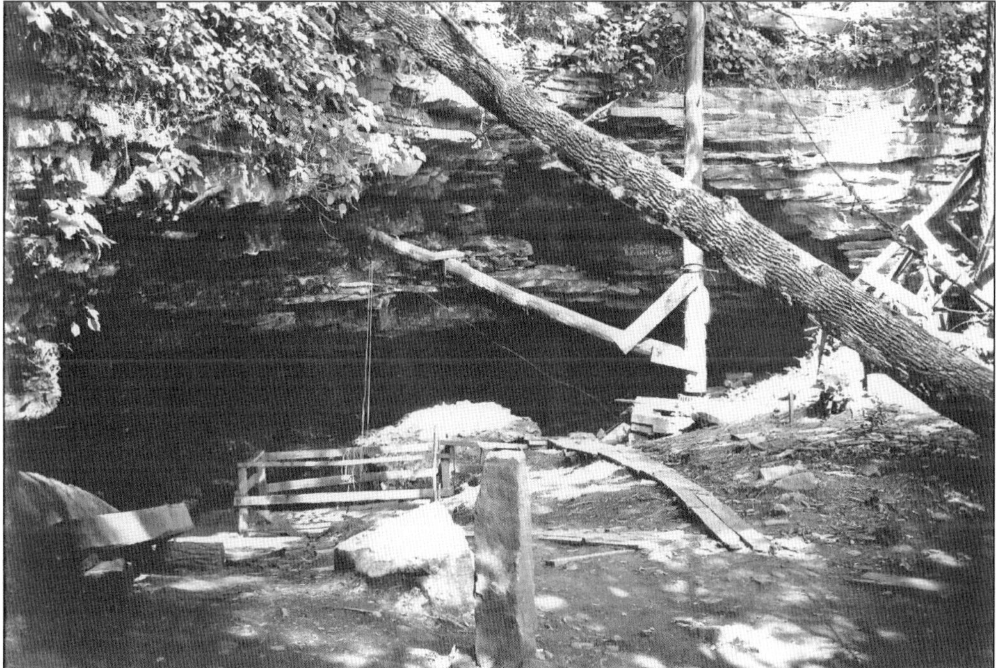

Bee Doyel instructed the workers not to fill the vertical shaft after Floyd Collins's body was taken out of Sand Cave so tourists could see where Collins was trapped. The upright rock shown in the foreground was known as the altar stone. (Neville Collection, Cave Research Foundation.)

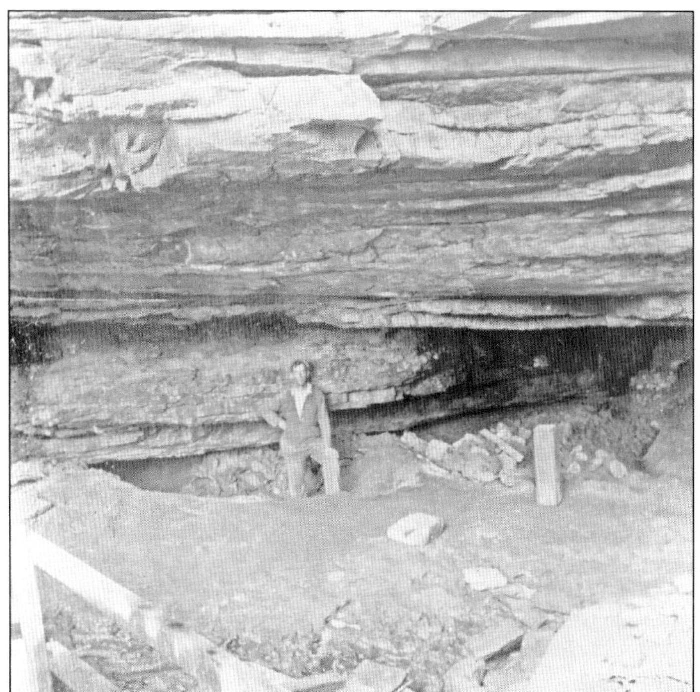

Bee Doyel is standing just under the rock overhang at the entrance to Sand Cave. When the cave was opened as a tourist attraction, visitors could go down into the entrance and into the cave's first room to see the passageway where Floyd Collins had been trapped. (National Cave Museum.)

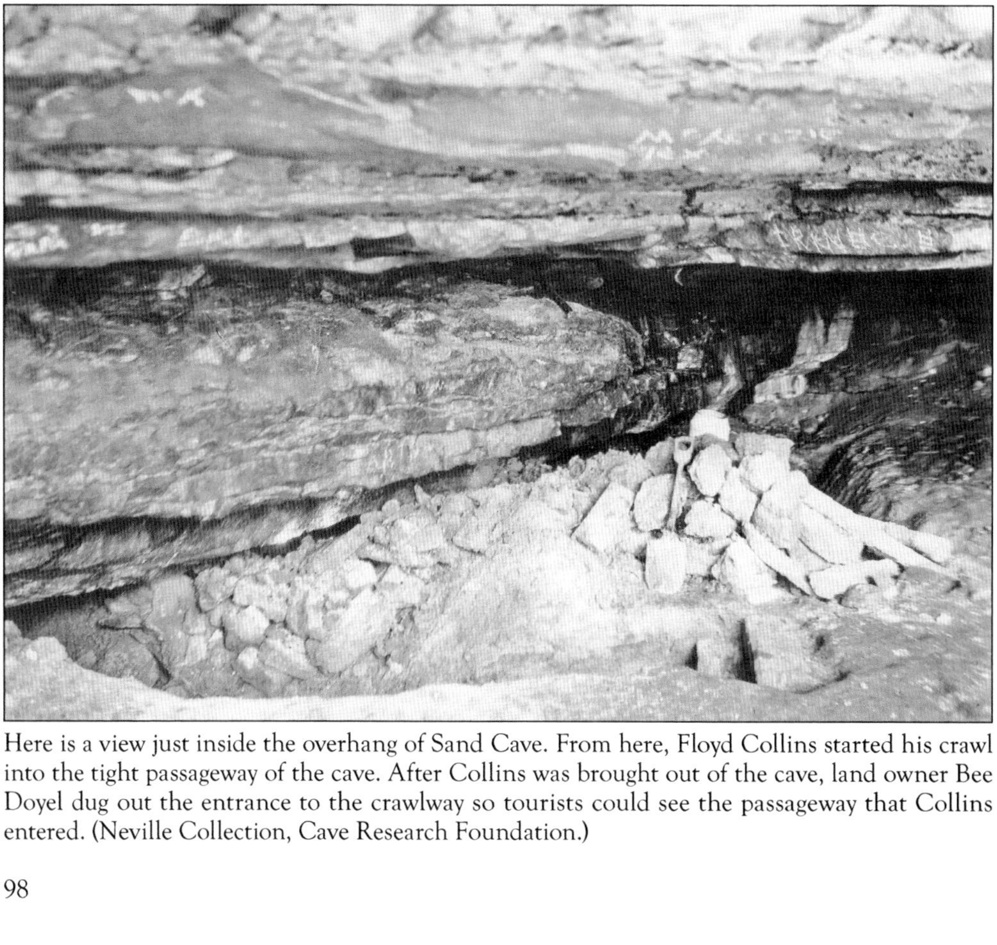

Here is a view just inside the overhang of Sand Cave. From here, Floyd Collins started his crawl into the tight passageway of the cave. After Collins was brought out of the cave, land owner Bee Doyel dug out the entrance to the crawlway so tourists could see the passageway that Collins entered. (Neville Collection, Cave Research Foundation.)

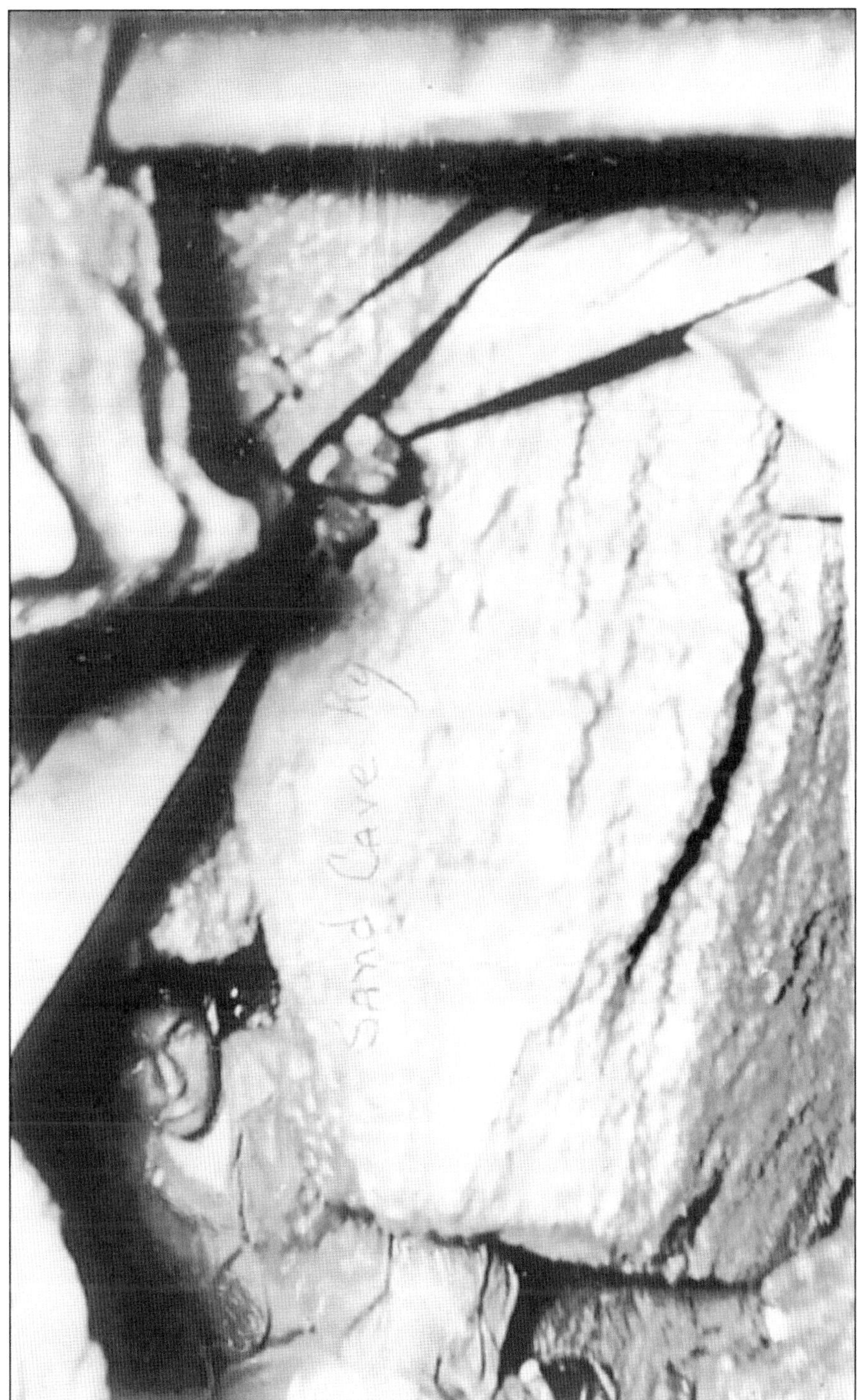

Bee Doyel is shown in the rocky slot in the shaft of Sand Cave to demonstrate the position of Floyd Collins as he was trapped. This photograph was taken in July 1925 by photographer Russell T. Neville after the Collins entrapment in Sand Cave. Two weeks after this picture was taken, the planks and timber shown gave way and closed the hole. (National Cave Museum.)

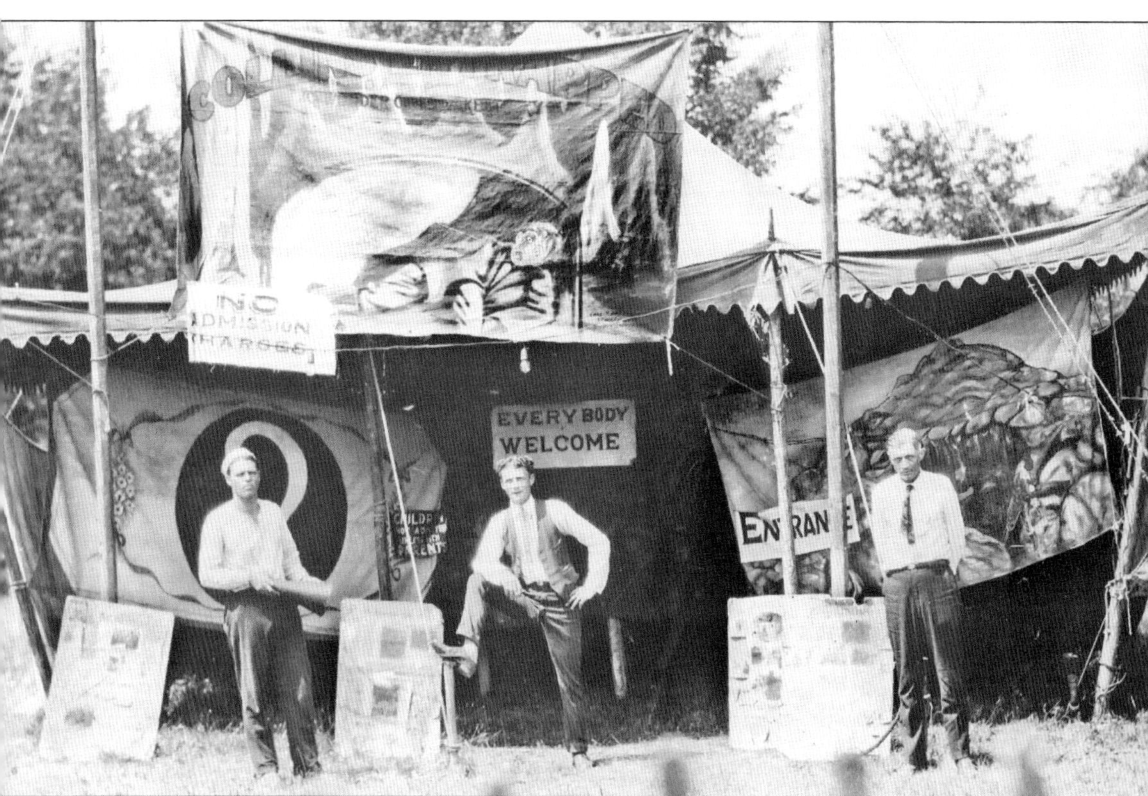

A sideshow tent was set up at the Indiana State Fair in Indianapolis, Indiana, in September 1925 to show the Collins entrapment. Lee Collins, Floyd's father, showed an exhibition of pictures of the entrapment in this tent and received a fee of $200 a week. A crude painting of the Collins entrapment is shown on the overhead banner with the words "Collins Entrapped and a Trip through Wonder Caves of Kentucky." (Dean Snyder Collection.)

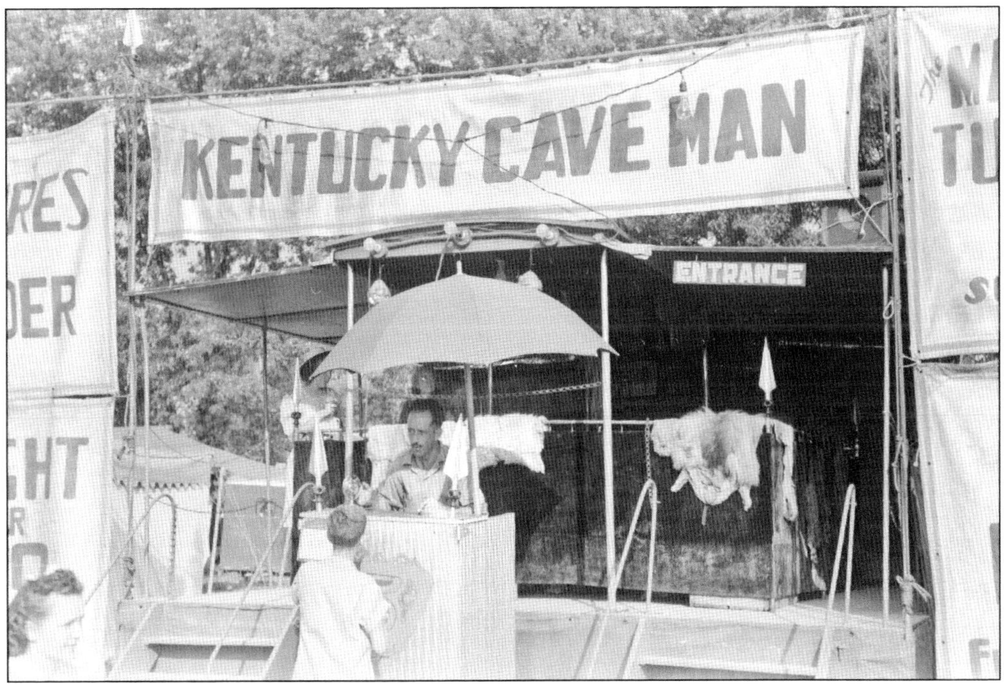

Another show tent was set up at the Shelby County Fair and Horse Show in Kentucky in August 1940. A stuffed cave bat can be seen just below the entrance sign. (Library of Congress.)

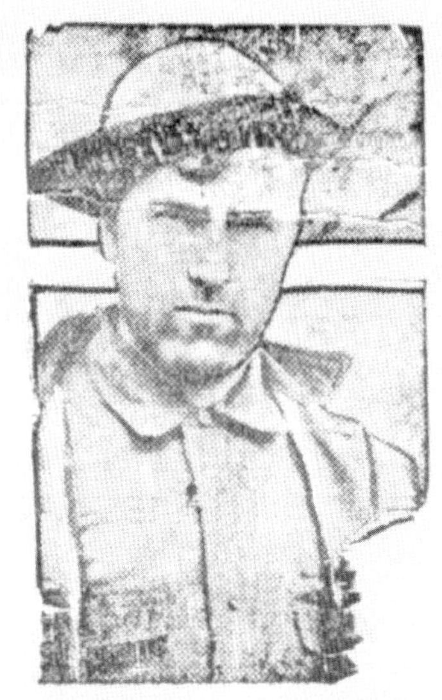

A. B. MARSHALL

"HAMBURGER KING"

From the Blue Grass of Kentucky.

"HERO OF SAND CAVE"

The man who found Floyd Collins at Sand Cave, Ky., Feb. 5-16 1925.

DANVILLE, KENTUCKY

Albert B. Marshall, a native of Italy, was a resident and restaurateur in Danville, Kentucky. He came to Sand Cave as a volunteer—he had previous mining experience—and was included on the crew digging the rescue shaft. He was known as "The Hamburger King" with his food expertise, and his business card also touted him as the "Hero of Sand Cave." (John Benton Collection.)

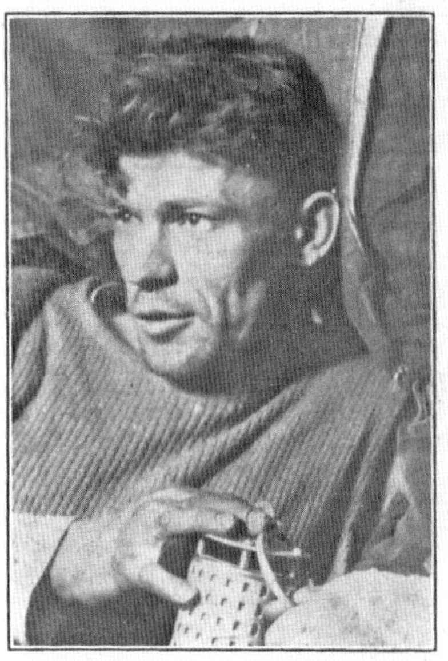

MR. BRENNEN who worked 16 days and nights to rescue Floyd Collins from the cave at Sand Cave, Ky., he being the only man to lay hands on Mr. Collins, after his death.

GIVE WHAT YOU CAN.

Two different "business" cards were used in soliciting donations from individuals for Ed Brenner and Floyd Collins. They both have the message, "Give What You Can." The opportunity to make money off the Collins tragedy went well beyond the tragic event itself. (Both, National Cave Museum.)

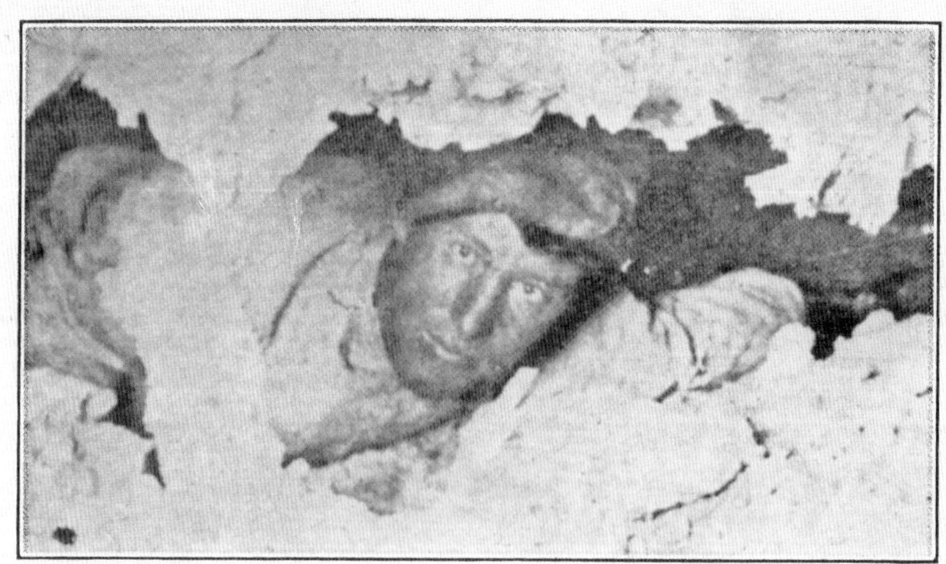

FLOYD COLLINS in a crevice in Crystal Cave Ky., which he discovered. Mr. Collins also discovered Sand Cave and it was in an effort to find a passage way between the two caves that the explorer met his tragic death in Sand Cave.

GIVE WHAT YOU CAN.

Photographer Wade Highbaugh (right) had a major advantage over other photographers at Sand Cave due to the fact that he lived only a mile from the cave. With help from his wife, Annie, and son Udolph, Highbaugh's photographs were developed in his home darkroom and then returned to the scene for anxiously waiting newspaper reporters. Highbaugh is seen here carrying his camera and equipment in July, after the tragedy. (Neville Collection, Cave Research Foundation.)

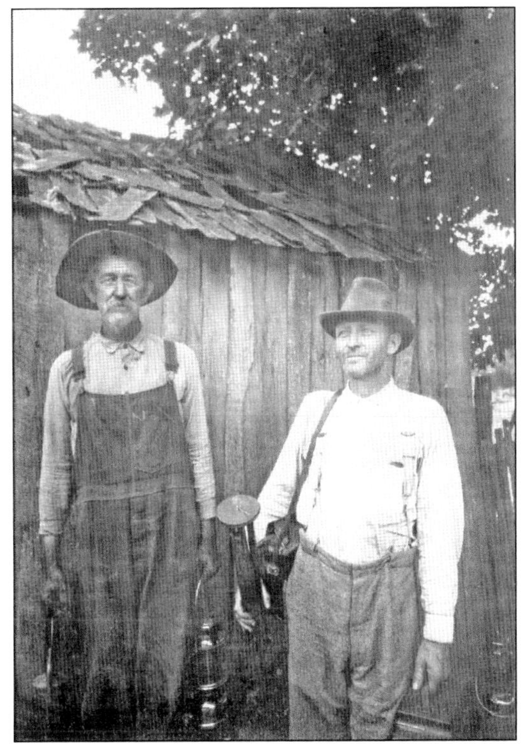

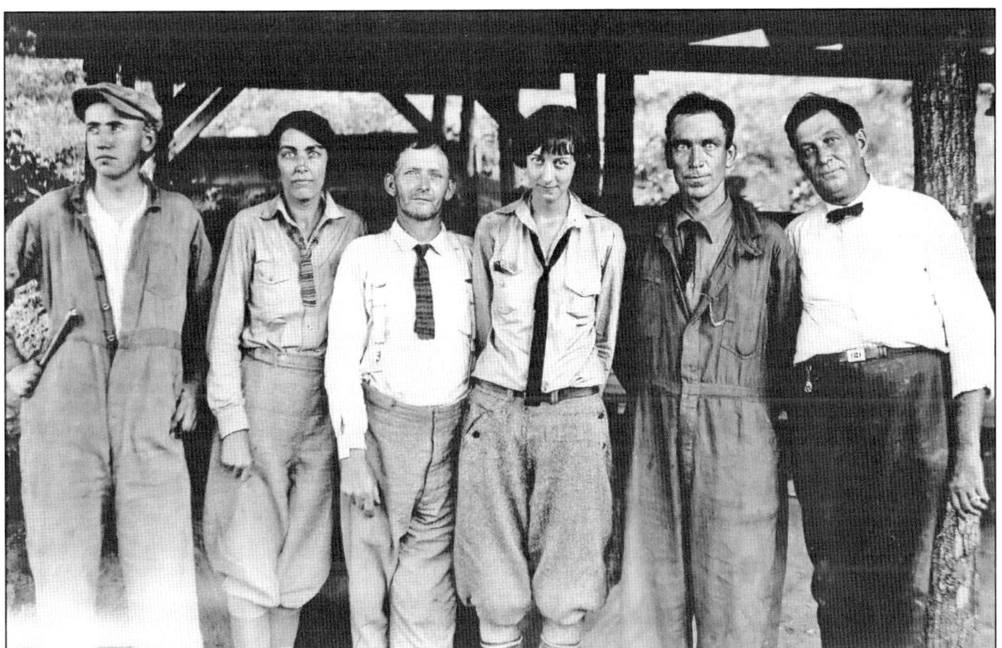

Russell T. Neville (right), a lawyer by trade from Kewanee, Illinois, was also a photographer. Neville took pictures of the Sand Cave area in July 1925, after the Collins entrapment. He made black-and-white movie footage in several of the area's caves using brightly burning magnesium strips for lighting. From left to right are ? Furlong, Neville's sister Hazel, Wade Highbaugh, Neville's daughter Julia, ? Hanson, and Neville. (Neville Collection, Cave Research Foundation.)

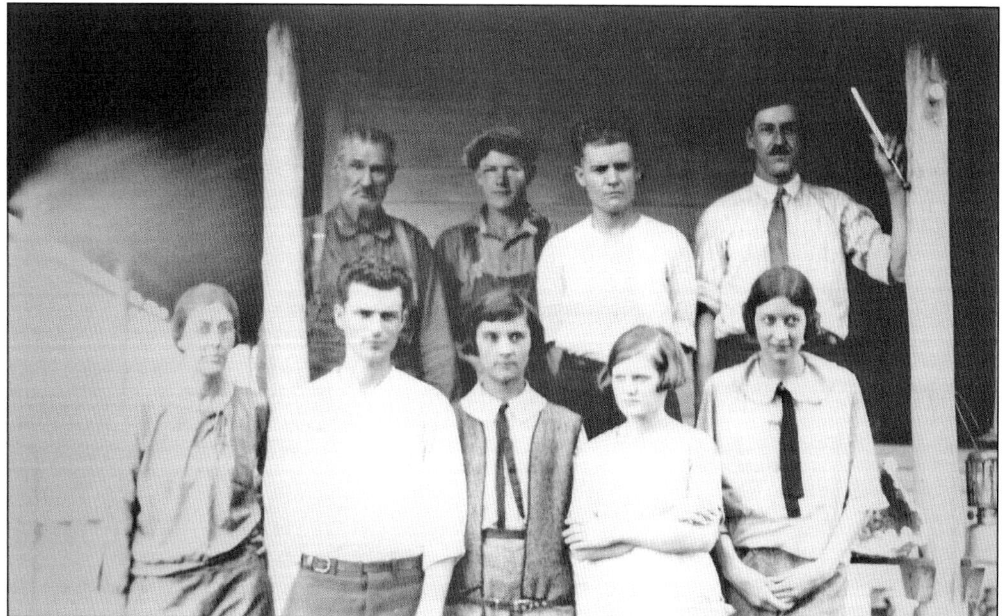

In 1926, members of the Collins family are shown on the porch of the Floyd Collins' Crystal Cave ticket office with photographer Russell T. Neville's sister Hazel (first row, far left) and daughter Julia (first row, far right). Lee and Homer Collins are at top left. (National Cave Museum.)

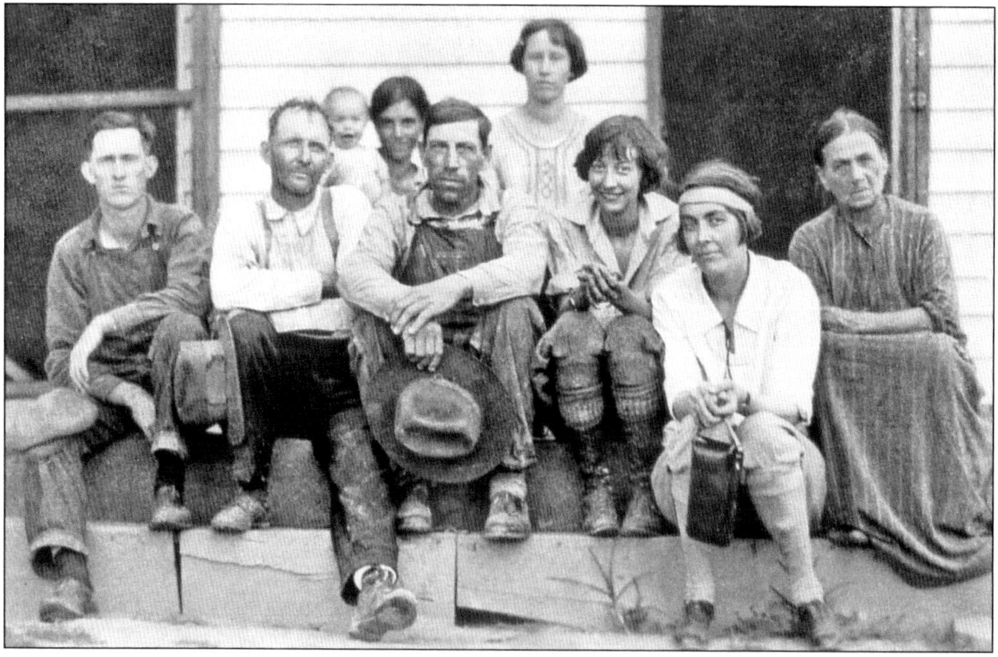

Members of the Collins family are shown on the porch of their home with photographer Wade Highbaugh and Russell T. Neville's sister and daughter. From left to right are (first row) Marshall Collins, Wade Highbaugh, Andy Collins, Julia Neville, Hazel Neville, and Jane Collins; (second row) Janie Collins (holding baby) and Anna Collins. During the Neville family visits to the cave area, Highbaugh assisted Neville in taking pictures of the different caves. (Neville Collection, Cave Research Foundation.)

Great Crystal Cave was owned and operated by the Collins family from 1918 to 1927. Soon after the Collins entrapment in 1925, Lee Collins changed the name of Great Crystal Cave to Floyd Collins' Crystal Cave. In 1927, Lee Collins sold Floyd Collins' Crystal Cave to Dr. Harry Thomas, a dentist in Horse Cave. Thomas owned two other show caves, Mammoth Onyx and Hidden River. Both were located in Horse Cave. Part of the deal was to have Floyd Collins's remains dug up from his present location on the Collins homestead and displayed in Floyd Collins' Crystal Cave in a glass-topped coffin. For the first time, Floyd Collins' Crystal Cave was finally making a profit. A promotional brochure and a copy of the original agreement between Lee Collins and Dr. Harry Thomas are shown. (Right, Richard Hobart Collection; below, Norman Warnell Collection.)

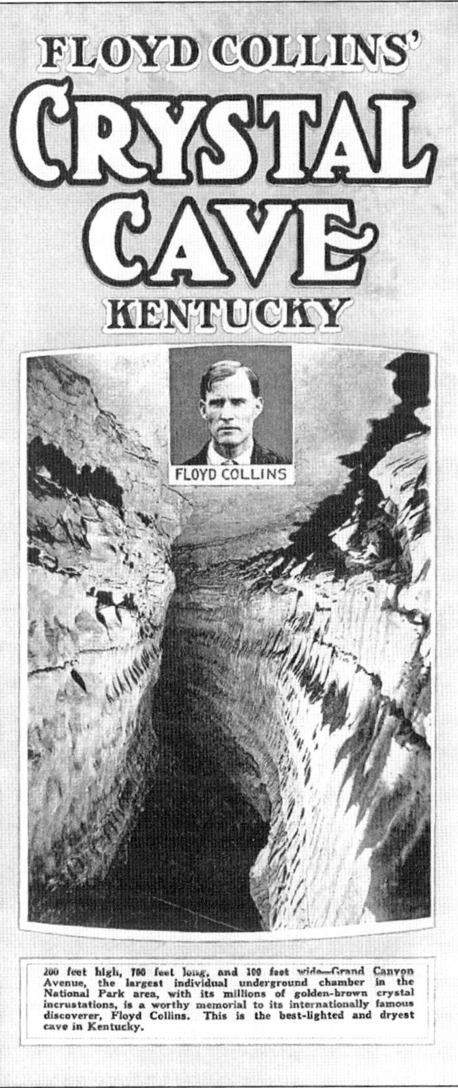

(COPY)

RECORDED in deed book #61,
Page #324. Hart County Court Clerk's office.

WHEREAS, The Great Crystal Cave is situated in the proposed boundary of the Mammoth Cave National Park; and Whereas said Great Crystal Cave was discovered by Floyd Collins, son of Leonidas Collins, who lost his life exploring Sand Cave; and Whereas it is deemed most appropriate that the body of said Floyd Collins should be placed in said Great Crystal Cave as a lasting memorial to him; now, we, Leonidas Collins and his wife, Bena Collins, hereby give and grant to Dr.H.B.Thomas, present owner of said Great Crystal Cave full permission and privilege to place the remains of said Floyd Collins in a glass casket in said Great Crystal Cave so that visitors to said Great Crystal Cave may have the privilege of viewing said Floyd Collins; and the said Dr.H.B.Thomas agrees with said Leonidas and Bena Collins that he will forever reserve said space in said Great Crystal Cave as the permanent resting place of said Floyd Collins, and will preserve the monument and lot 10 x 10 ft. now outside of said cave.

This March 16, 1927.

(Sgd.) Leonidas Collins

(Sgd.) Bena Collins.

State of Kentucky,}
} Sct.
County of Hart, }

I, W.C.Gibbons, a Notary Public, in and for the county and state aforesaid, certify that the above and foregoing instrument of writing was presented to me in my county and duly acknowledged before me by Leonidas Collins and his wife, Bena Collins, to be their free act and deed.

Given under my hand and notarial seal this March 16,1927.

My commission expires October 13, 1928.

(Sgd.) W.C.Gibbons
Notary Public,Hart County, Ky.

(Seal)

State of Kentucky}
Hart County }

I, W.H.Atteberry, Clerk of the County Court for the County and State aforesaid, certify that the foregoing instrument was this day lodged for record, whereupon the same, with the foregoing and this certificate have been duly recorded in my office.

Witness my hand, this 26th day of March,1927.

(Sgd.) W.H.Atteberry, Clerk,
By - C.R.Winn, D. C.

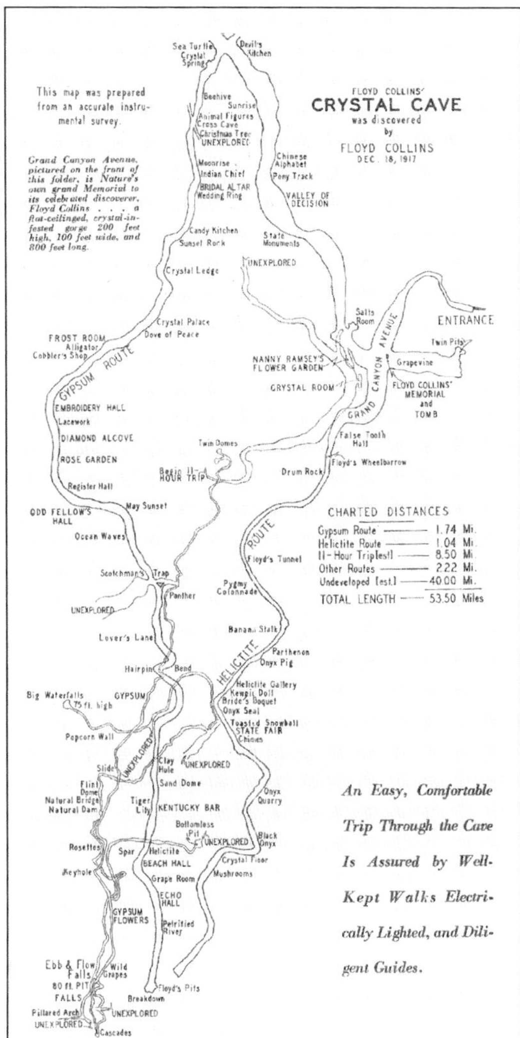

The map of Floyd Collins' Crystal Cave shows two different tour routes that were offered to the general public. Tour route number one, also known as the Gypsum Route, exhibited a display of gypsum flower formations and three large rooms. Tour route number two, also known as the Helictite Route, showed the large passageway known as Grand Canyon Avenue, the Floyd Collins Memorial, and Nanny Ramsey's Flower Garden. Floyd Collins's homemade wheelbarrow and a crude broadax he used to clear away rocks and debris were on exhibit as part of the tour. A promotional flyer for Floyd Collins' Crystal Cave is also shown. (Left, Richard Hobart Collection; below, National Cave Museum.)

A TIP TO TOURISTS

YOUR VISIT TO THE CAVE REGION
IS NOT COMPLETE IF YOU MISS FLOYD COLLINS'

CRYSTAL CAVE

4 MILES NORTH OF MAMMOTH CAVE

If you allow jealous knockers to cause you to miss this cave you have no come back at these knockers.

We Guarantee satisfaction before, or after, you have visited all the other caves. Bring this guarantee with you and if we do not show you what we advertise and if you are not perfectly satisfied your trip costs you nothing.

CRYSTAL CAVE IS SECOND IN SIZE
in the Mammoth Cave Region to Mammoth Cave itself. It has more of a continuous passageway of formation than any other cave in this section, shows the biggest deposit of Gypsum and Crystal Flower Formation and the rarest discovery of Onyx Helectite Formation in Kentucky. We show the greatest variety of formation being shown.

Grand Canyon Avenue, Floyd Collins Memorial, is the largest chamber in this Region. The walls of this Canyon are covered with a Golden Brown Gypsum. Here you hear a Radio 250 ft., underneath the surface of the earth, the effect is like walking into a Cathedral, too georgeous for man to construct. The Cave is illuminated throughout by Floodlights and Reflectors.

ANY TIME

Guide Service Day or Night
Trips From 30 Minutes to 4 Hours

At Crystal Cave you will find an ideal Camping Site, Electric Lights, Wood, good Water, Campers Cottages with Cots, the prettiest Bathing Beach in the Cave Region

ALL FREE

Remember if Crystal Cave were not so good knockers would not be necessary.

H. B. THOMAS, Prop.

Floyd Collins Crystal Cave

See Grand Canyon--Floyd Collins' Memorial

Largest Avenue in the Mammoth Cave National Park Area

The most impressive subterranean phenomenon in the whole Cave Region is GRAND CANYON--Natural Memorial to Floyd Collins--

In FLOYD COLLINS CRYSTAL CAVE

This intrepid, internationally-known Cave Explorer was the first man ever to behold this most spacious corridor found in any of the Caves. Because of its long, gracefully-bending water-cut walls, all covered with brilliant crystalline jewels, it became the pride of his life; and at his request, he sleeps today within this marvelous avenue in a tomb unsurpassed in grandeur by the resting places of the crowned heads of Europe. :: His body is completely mummified, and will be preserved here through the ages.

CAVE VISITORS WHO CARE TO CAN VIEW THE BODY OF FLOYD COLLINS IN HIS MEMORIAL,--GRAND CANYON IN FLOYD COLLINS CRYSTAL CAVE.

THIS CAVE IS ELECTRICALLY LIGHTED WITH 450,000 WATTS OF ILLUMINATION,—MORE THAN FOUR TIMES THE ILLUMINATION IN ALL OTHER CAVES COMBINED.

FIRST IN BEAUTY - SECOND IN SIZE

4 MILES NORTHEAST OF MAMMOTH CAVE - FOLLOW THE SIGNS

These handout cards were used by cave owner Dr. Harry Thomas of Horse Cave to advertise Floyd Collins' Crystal Cave. The card read, in part, "Cave visitors who care to can view the body of Floyd Collins in his memorial." The body of Floyd Collins in the cave was an attraction in itself. (Both, National Cave Museum.)

FLOYD COLLINS' CRYSTAL CAVE

THE HEART OF THE NATIONAL PARK AREA

Not Backed by State Officials but Owned by a Private Citizen and Shown by Native Cave Explorers

NO FINE HOTELS - NO LIVERIED FLUNKIES

BUT---

THE BEST CAVE IN THE AREA

See All of Them, Then Visit Floyd Collins' Crystal Cave--

IF IT ISN'T THE BEST, DRIVE AWAY AND PAY US NOTHING

H. B. THOMAS, Owner

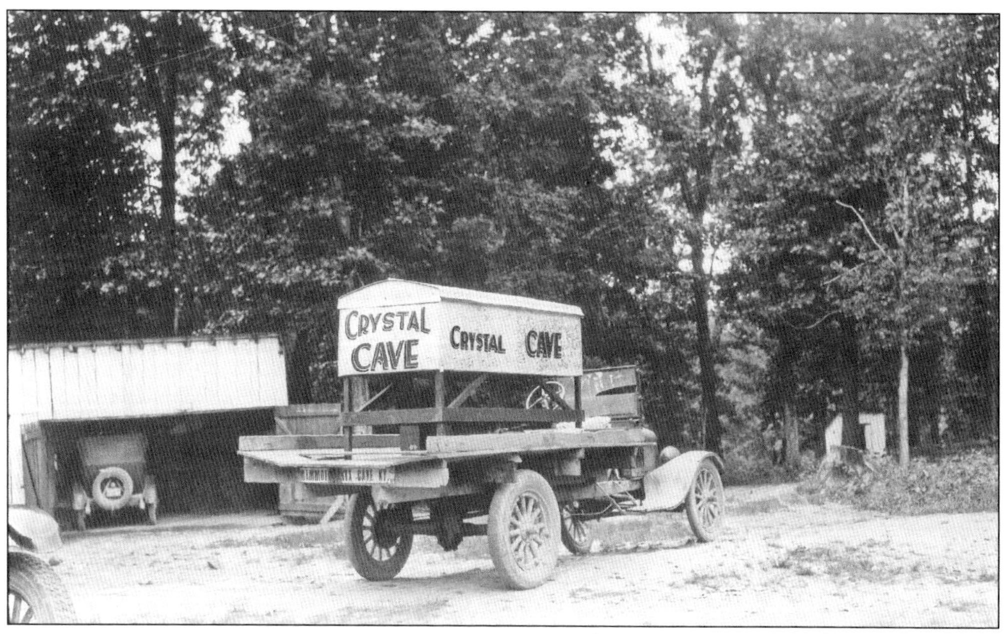

This motor car was used by cave owner Dr. Harry Thomas to advertise Floyd Collins' Crystal Cave. The car was driven around the cave area in order to draw attention to the attraction. Other caves, like Great Onyx Cave, had a similar car. Solicitors from each cave could be found along the roadsides competing with each other for their share of tourist dollars. (National Cave Museum.)

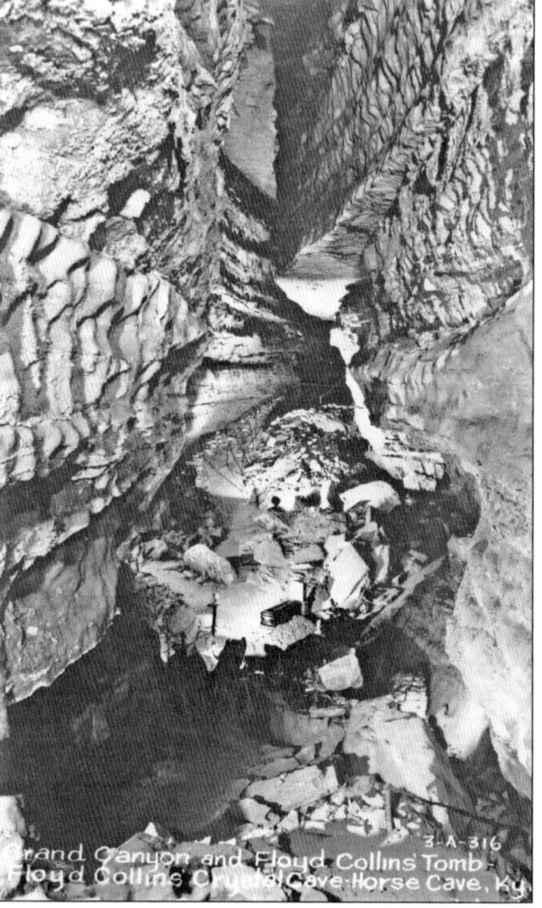

After Floyd Collins's body was removed from the Collins homestead gravesite, considerable embalming had to be done again to the body before it could be placed in the glass-covered casket in Floyd Collins' Crystal Cave. On June 13, 1927, Floyd Collins's casket was placed in the passageway known as Grand Canyon Avenue. This was the third burial for Floyd Collins. (National Cave Museum.)

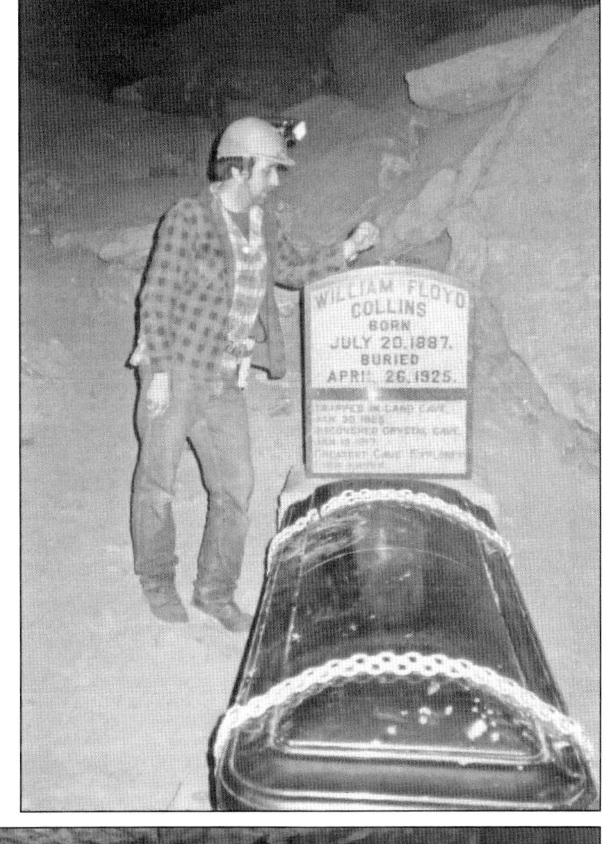

Floyd Collins's body was first displayed in a glass-topped coffin in Floyd Collins' Crystal Cave. After some vandalism in which his body was stolen in 1929, Collins was buried in the cave for the fourth time, this time in a chained casket. Collins historian and coauthor John Benton is shown with the chained casket. (John Benton Collection.)

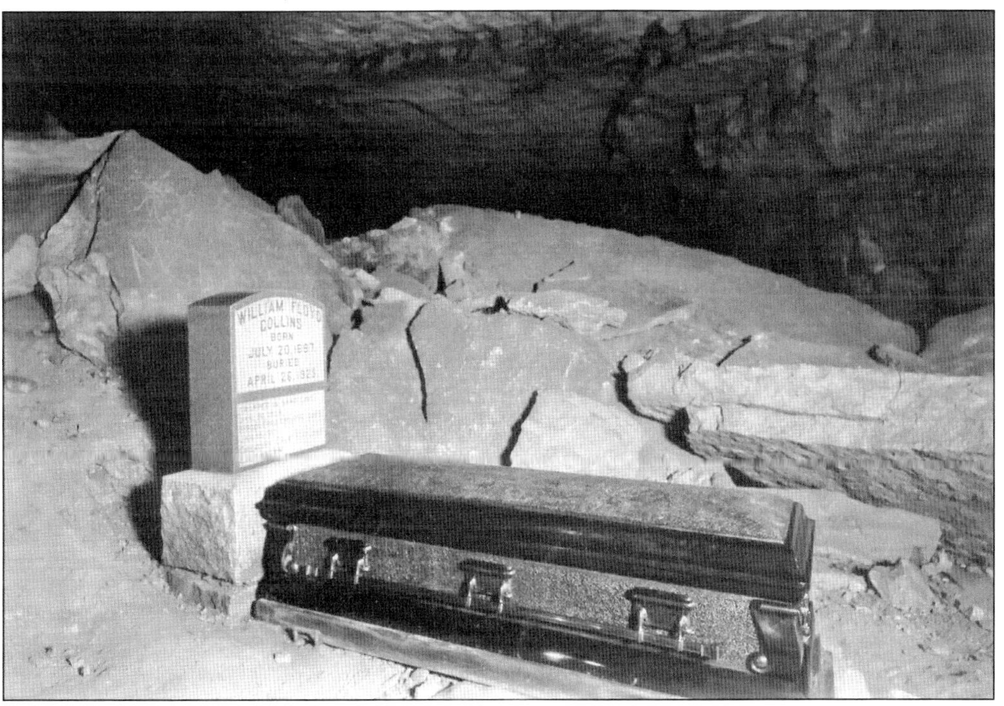

This photograph shows Floyd Collins's casket in Floyd Collins' Crystal Cave. For a tip, visitors were allowed to peek under the lid to view Collins's embalmed body up until the 1950s. Collins had a waxy white face and wore a black suit and gloves. (Neville Collection, Cave Research Foundation.)

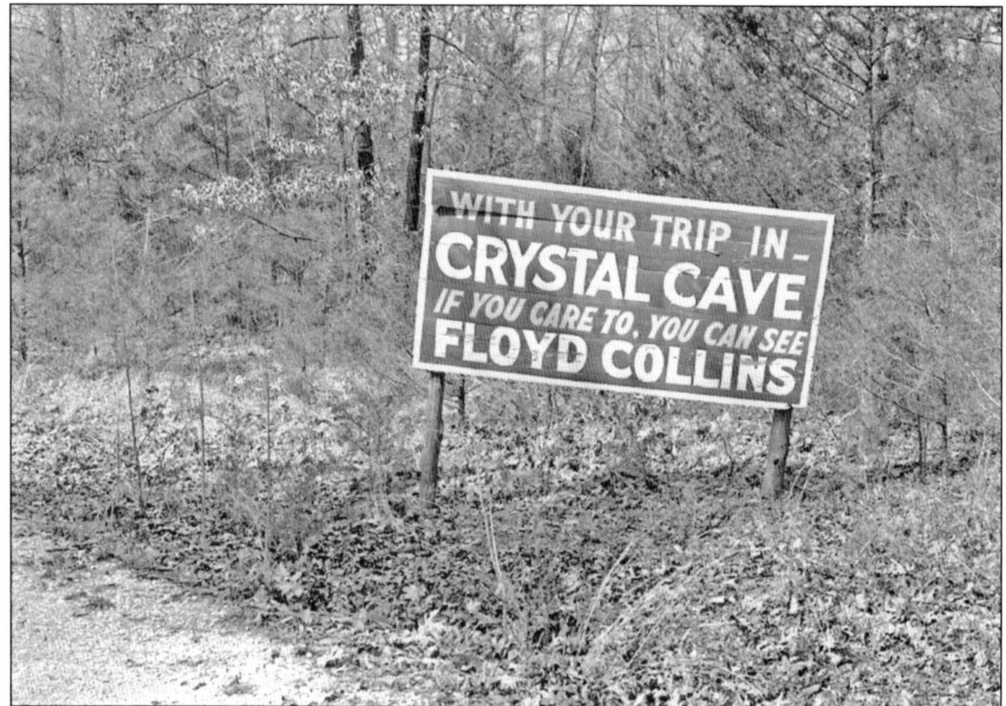

Floyd Collins's brothers sought to void the agreement with Dr. Harry Thomas to display the body of Collins in Floyd Collins' Crystal Cave, but had their lawsuit dismissed. Dr. Thomas had the Collins brothers indicted for burning advertising signs. Floyd Collins' Crystal Cave was operated as a commercial cave by Dr. Thomas and his family from 1927 to 1960. Advertising signs were used by them to entice visitors to the cave. (Both, Mammoth Cave National Park, Kentucky, Park Museum Collections.)

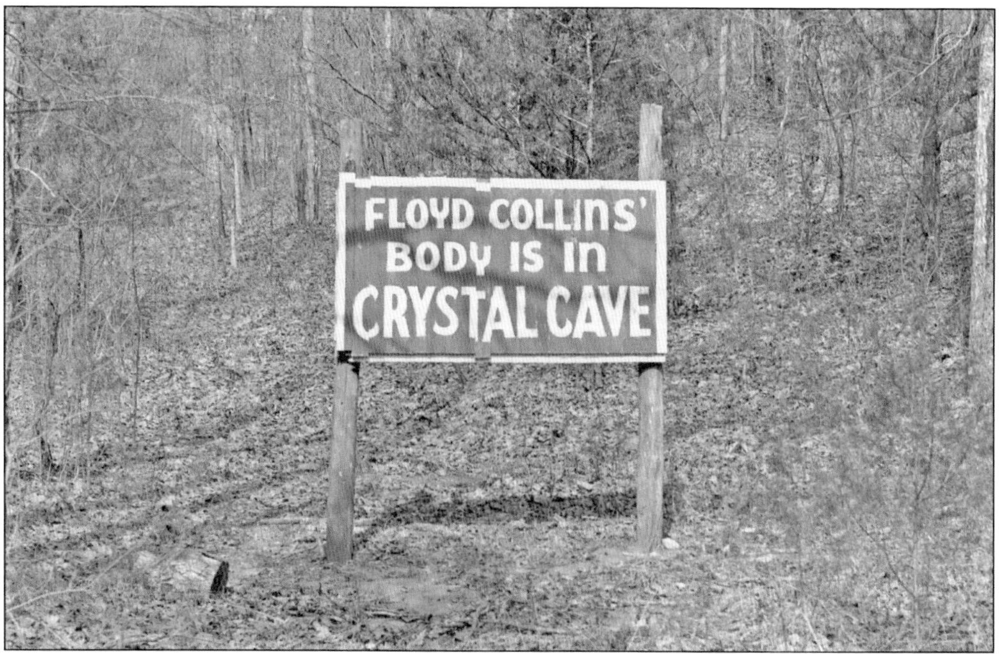

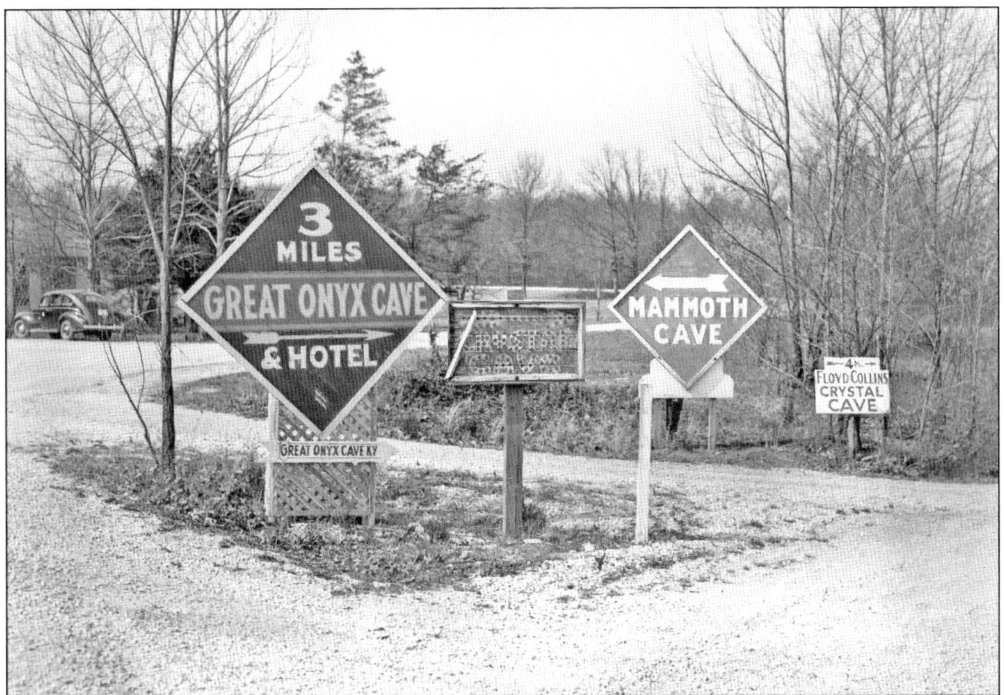

Great Onyx Cave and Floyd Collins' Crystal Cave were located on a narrow gravel road that branches off the main highway to Mammoth Cave. Directional signs are shown in both photographs for Mammoth Cave and for the privately owned Great Onyx Cave and Floyd Collins' Crystal Cave. Mammoth Cave National Park acquired Floyd Collins' Crystal Cave and Great Onyx Cave in 1961. (Both, Mammoth Cave National Park, Kentucky, Park Museum Collections.)

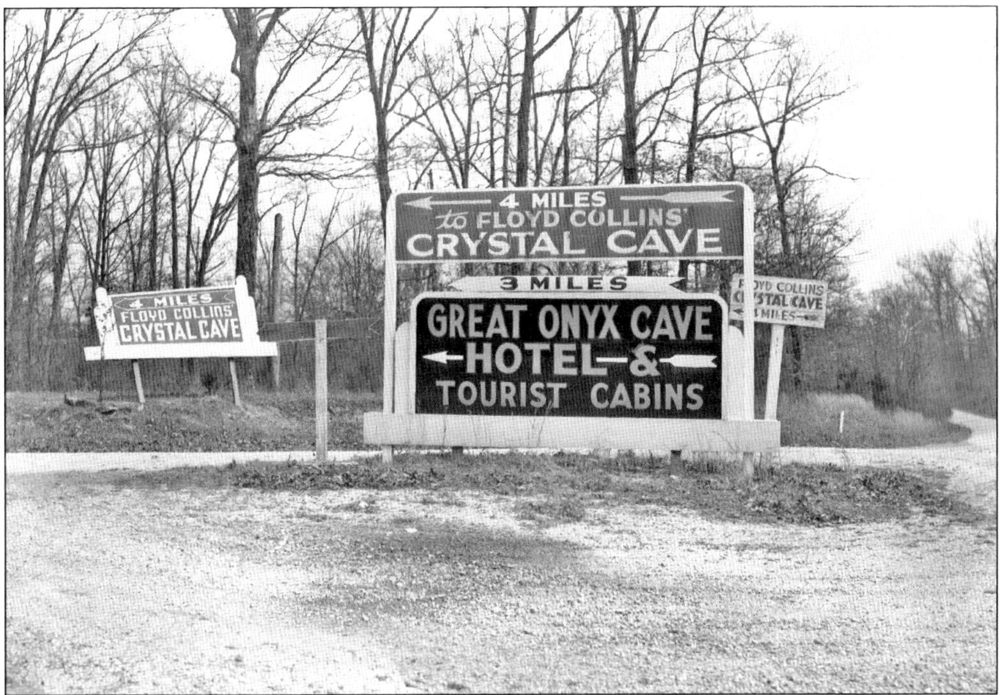

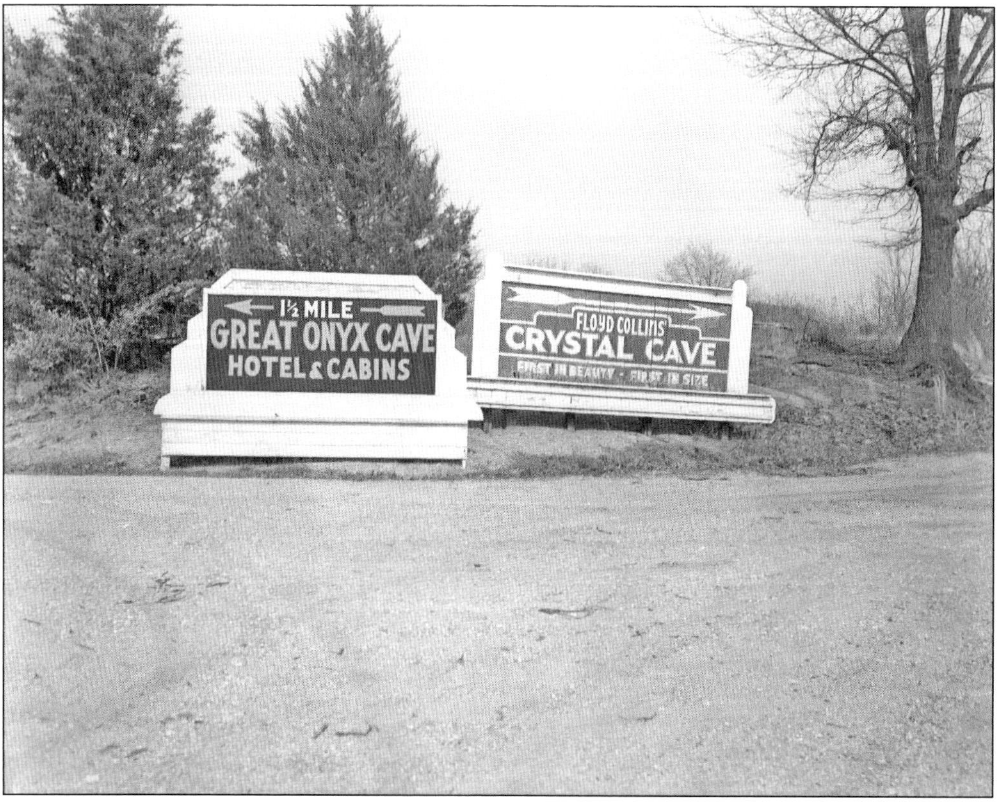

Surrounded by the national park and restricted as they were by the park in the number and size of signs, the private caves never had a chance to develop their true potential as tourist attractions. These large signs near Great Onyx Cave from the 1930s were replaced by one small sign for each cave once Mammoth Cave became a national park. (Mammoth Cave National Park, Kentucky, Park Museum Collections.)

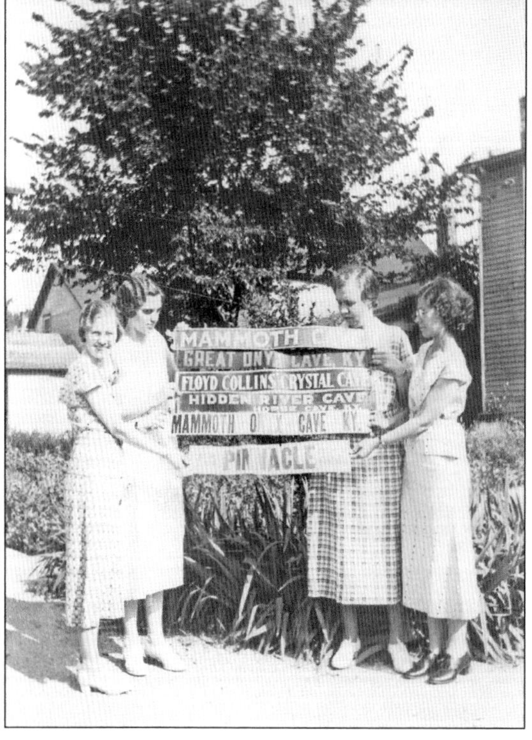

Tourists to the cave area are shown with cardboard signs from the different caves they visited. The caves include Mammoth Cave, Great Onyx Cave, Floyd Collins' Crystal Cave, Hidden River Cave, and Mammoth Onyx Cave. These cardboard signs were affixed to tourist's car bumpers by cave workers. The purpose of the signs was to draw attention to the cave attractions. (National Cave Museum.)

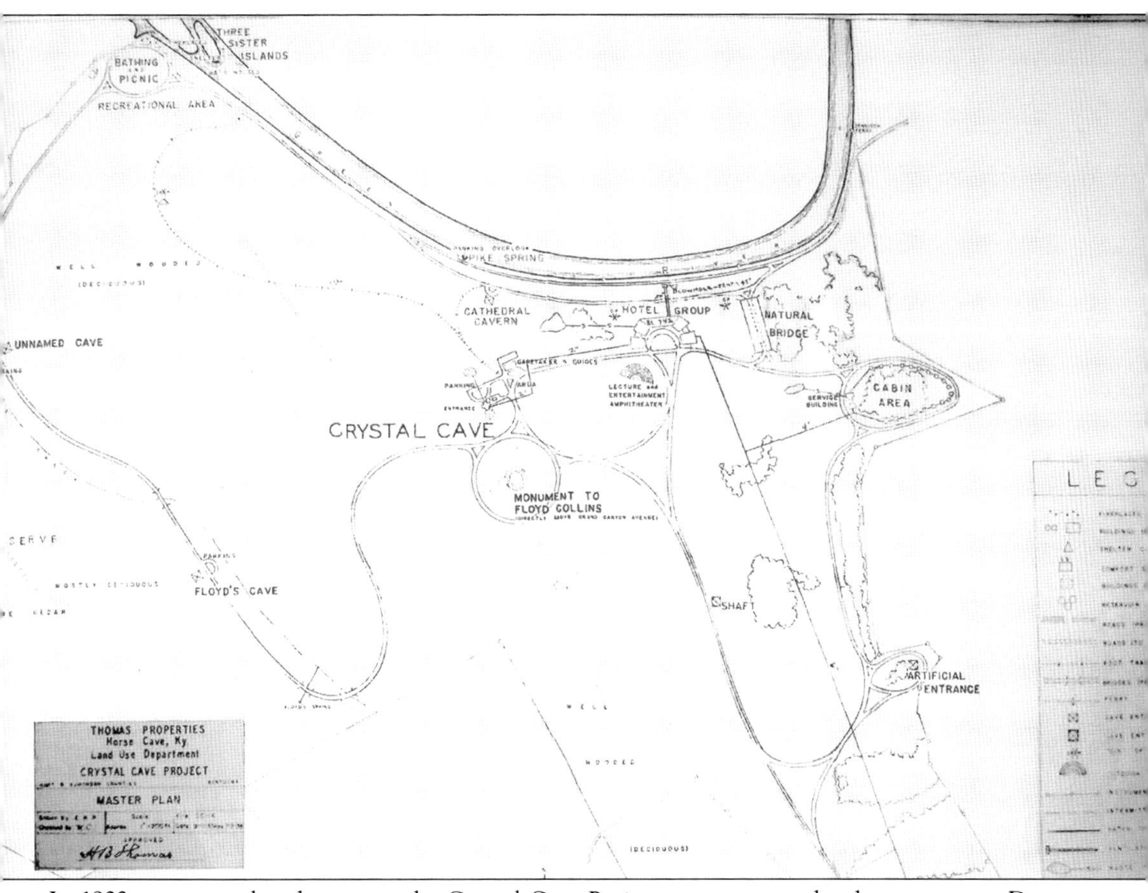

In 1933, a master plan, known as the Crystal Cave Project, was put together by cave owner Dr. Harry Thomas to improve the land surrounding Floyd Collins' Crystal Cave and build a resort to capitalize on Floyd Collins's name. Thomas had a plan to build a monument to the memory of Floyd Collins directly above the Grand Canyon Avenue in Floyd Collins' Crystal Cave, as well as a hotel, cabins, an amphitheater for lectures and entertainment, and a recreational area for bathing and picnicking. Tours were to be given in Floyd Collins' Crystal Cave, Floyd's Cave, and Cathedral Cave, all pictured here. The plan never materialized. (Tom Chaney Collection.)

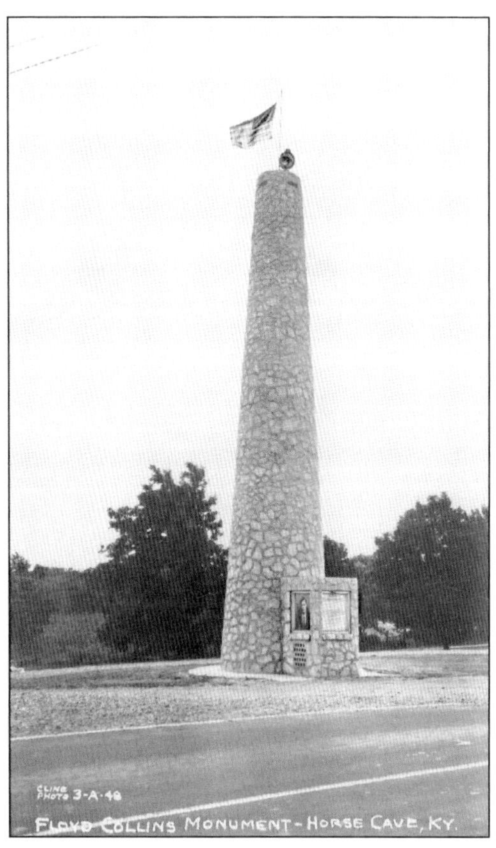

Even though the 1933 master plan at Floyd Collins' Crystal Cave never happened, a memorial to honor Floyd Collins was built by Dr. Harry Thomas in 1939 in the city of Horse Cave. The 30-foot-tall circular monument featured a lighted portrait of Collins on one side and an inscription on the other. The monument was hit by a truck in June 1965 and destroyed, and all that exists of the monument today is the walkway to the base. On one side of the Floyd Collins Memorial is the inscription, "He Lived for an Ideal—In the Search of Earthly Beauty—This he Found In his Discovery of Crystal Cave. He Died for an Ideal—The Ideal of Service Before Self. . . . He elicited greater public sympathy through the world press than any man." (Both, National Cave Museum.)

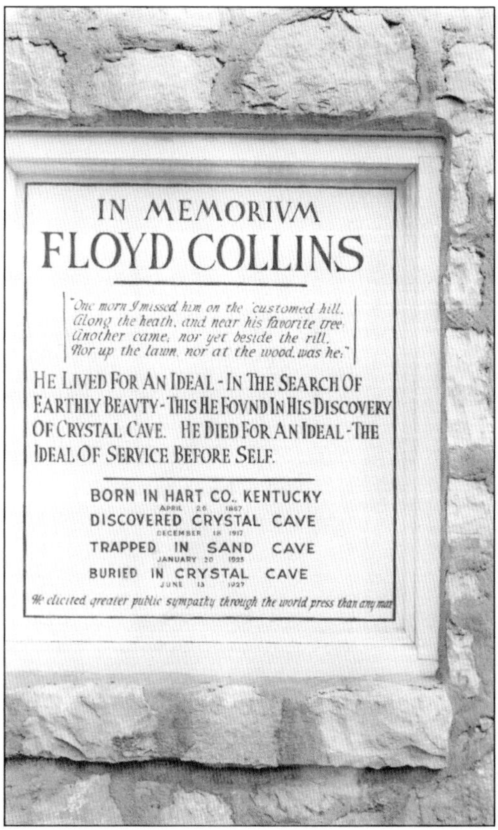

Eight

Other Collins Caves

Using the Collins Name to Profit

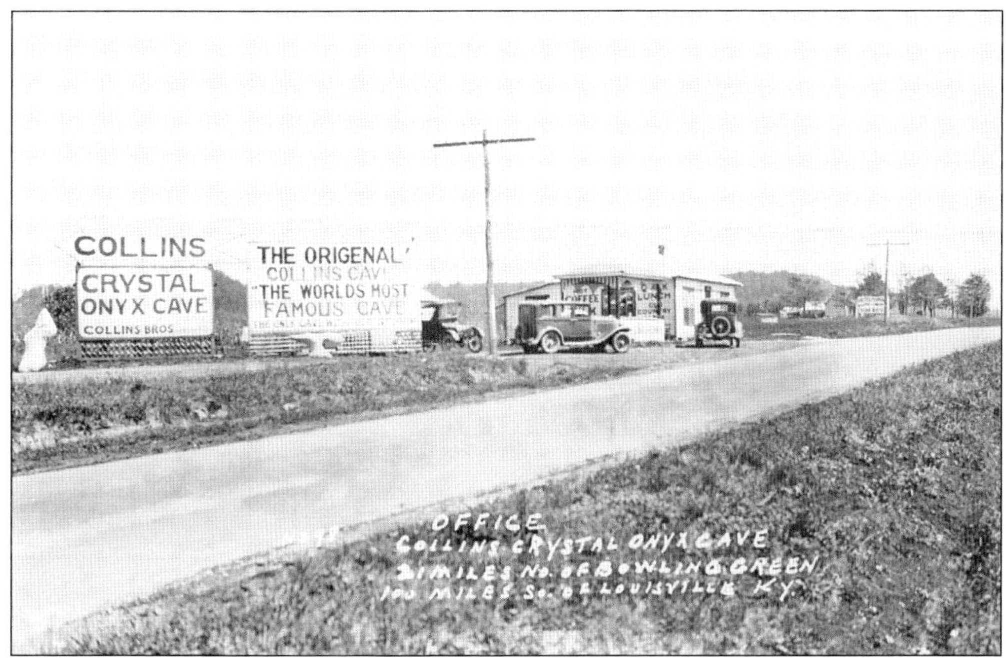

After Lee Collins sold Floyd Collins' Crystal Cave to Dr. Harry Thomas in 1927, the surviving Collins brothers, Andy and Marshall, along with their father, went to a few of the private cave owners along the main highways outside the Mammoth Cave park area and tried to negotiate a deal to operate their caves using the Collins name. One of these caves was Collins' Crystal Onyx Cave. (Richard Hobart Collection.)

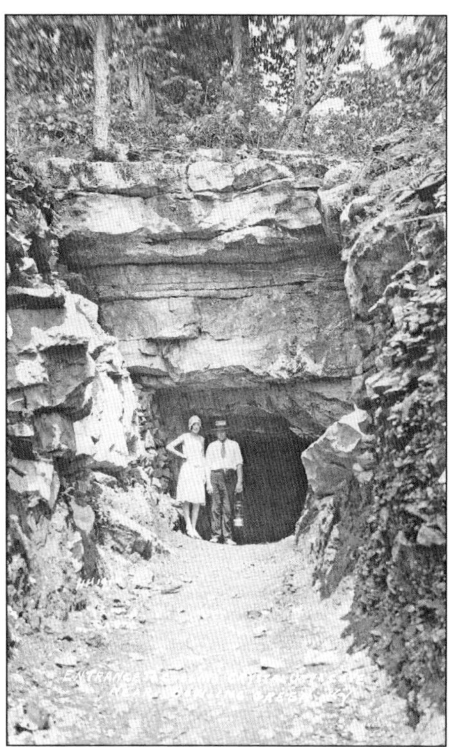

Collins' Crystal Onyx Cave was also known over the years as Andy Collins' Crystal Onyx Cave, Fishback Cave, Little Kentucky Beauty Cave, Old Onyx Cave, and Higginbotham Cave. Andy Collins operated the cave for a short period for the owner, Mrs. Oramus H. Fishback, but it was never a success, and the cave closed in the 1930s. The cave was located near Glasgow Junction (Park City). (Richard Hobart Collection.)

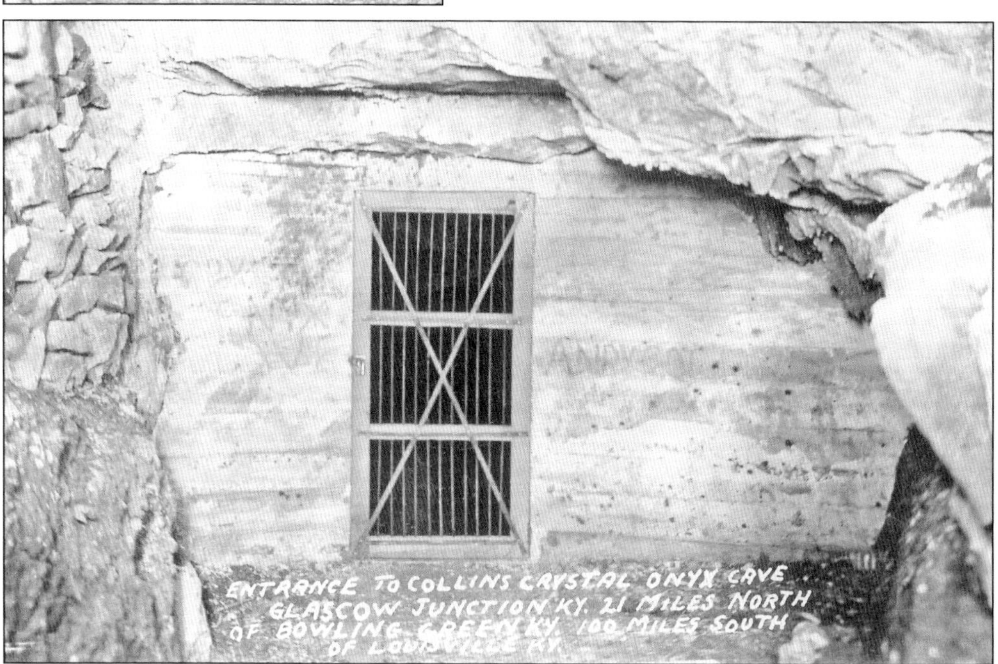

In July 1930, an optional agreement to sell Collins' Crystal Onyx Cave was signed by Mrs. Fishback and five buyers, including Lee Collins. The Floyd Collins Cave Company was formed. Lee Collins tried to get possession of Floyd's casket from Floyd Collins' Crystal Cave to be interred at the Fishback Roadhouse near this cave, but it never happened. Lee Collins married his fourth wife in this cave. (Bob Thompson Collection.)

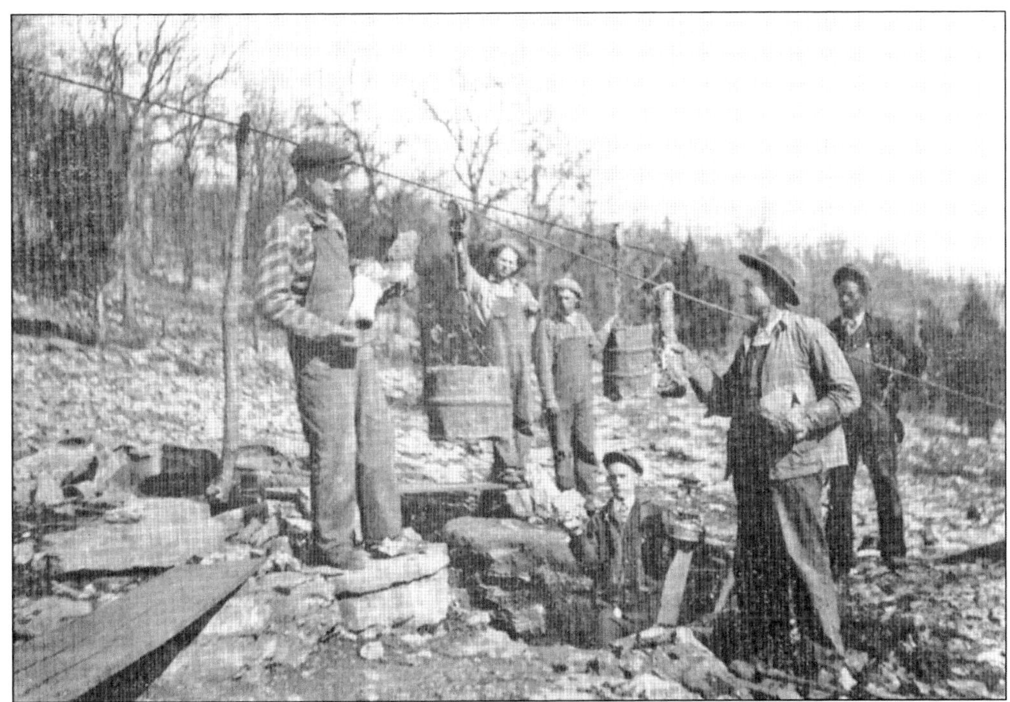

Andy Collins (left) and Otis Turner (second from right) are pictured holding mastodon bones. The Pleistocene cave passage in which the mastodon bones were found was actually too small to be developed into a tourist attraction. However, a nearby cave called Old Doyel's Cave was, at that time, operating as a show cave under the name of Dixie Onyx Cave. It was to this cave that the bones were moved, new brochures were printed, signs changed, and the show cave took on a new name—Collins' Onyx Cave. A closer look at the mastodon bones can be seen at right. (Above, Bob Thompson Collection; right, National Cave Museum.)

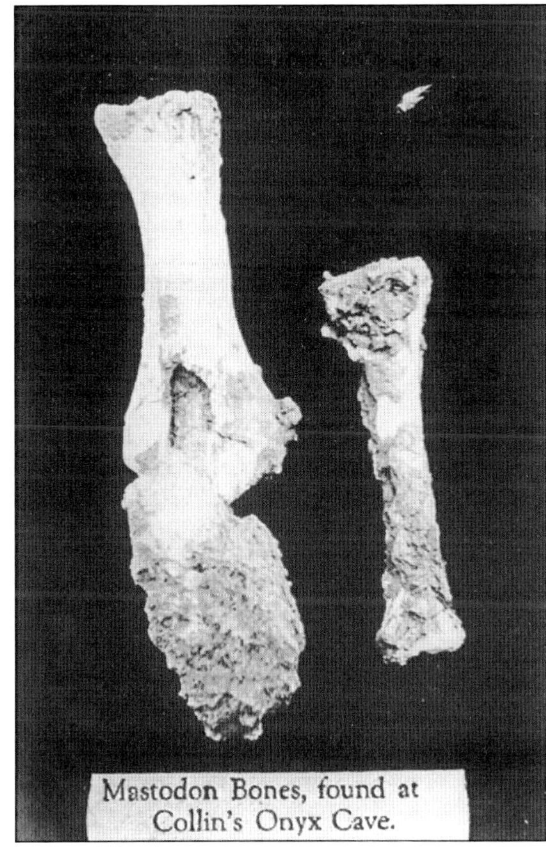

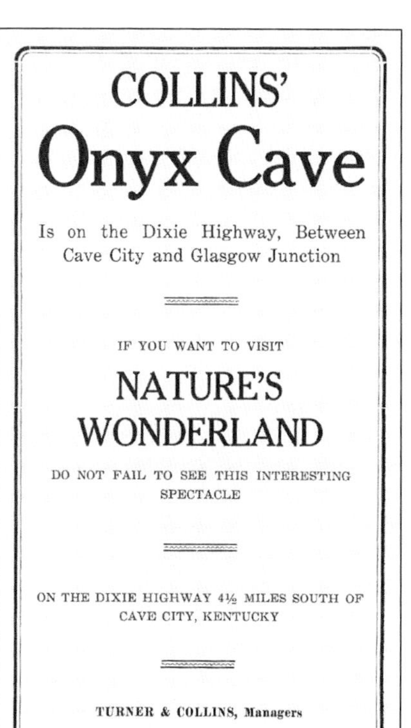

COLLINS'

Onyx Cave

Is on the Dixie Highway, Between Cave City and Glasgow Junction

IF YOU WANT TO VISIT

NATURE'S WONDERLAND

DO NOT FAIL TO SEE THIS INTERESTING SPECTACLE

ON THE DIXIE HIGHWAY 4½ MILES SOUTH OF CAVE CITY, KENTUCKY

TURNER & COLLINS, Managers

R. R. No. 2 Cave City, Ky.

Collins' Onyx Cave (with the mastodon bones) was opened for tours by Andy Collins and Cleon Turner (Otis's son) in 1928. The cave was previously opened in 1925 as Dixie Onyx Cave and was known before that as Old Doyel's Cave. During the winter of 1949, the cave was opened as Show Case Cave. It was never a success. Shown is the cave's only known promotional brochure. (National Cave Museum.)

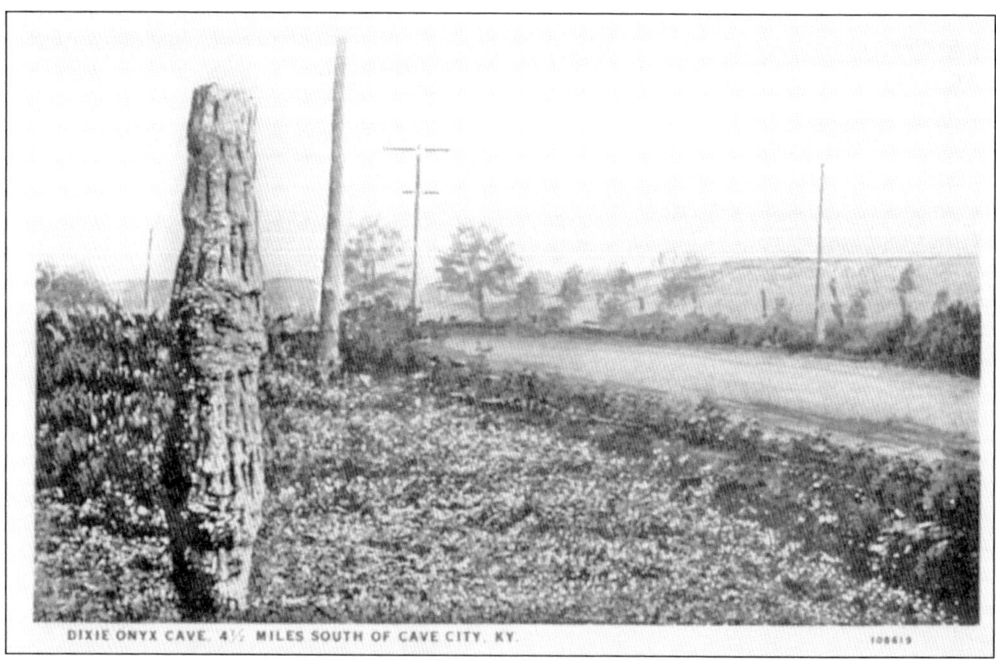

The entrance to Collins' Onyx Cave was just off the main highway between Cave City and Park City. The cave was advertised as "the only cave operated by a brother of the original Floyd Collins." The brochure states that cave trips could "be arranged at any hour, day or night." Note the cave formations standing in the yard. (Richard Hobart Collection.)

Collins' Cave was another cave opened by Marshall and Andy Collins near Horse Cave. It was also known over the years as Marshall Collins Cave. The cave was open for only a short time and was never a success. Pictured on July 22, 1937, are, from left to right, Marshall, Cleona, Anna, and Andy Collins. Note the cave formations that were offered for sale to tourists. (National Cave Museum.)

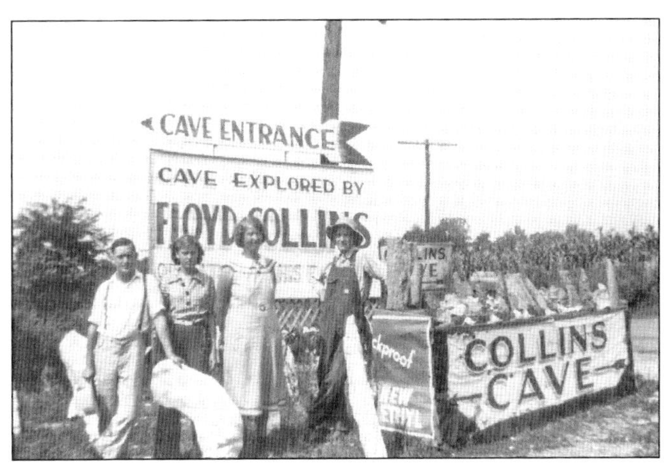

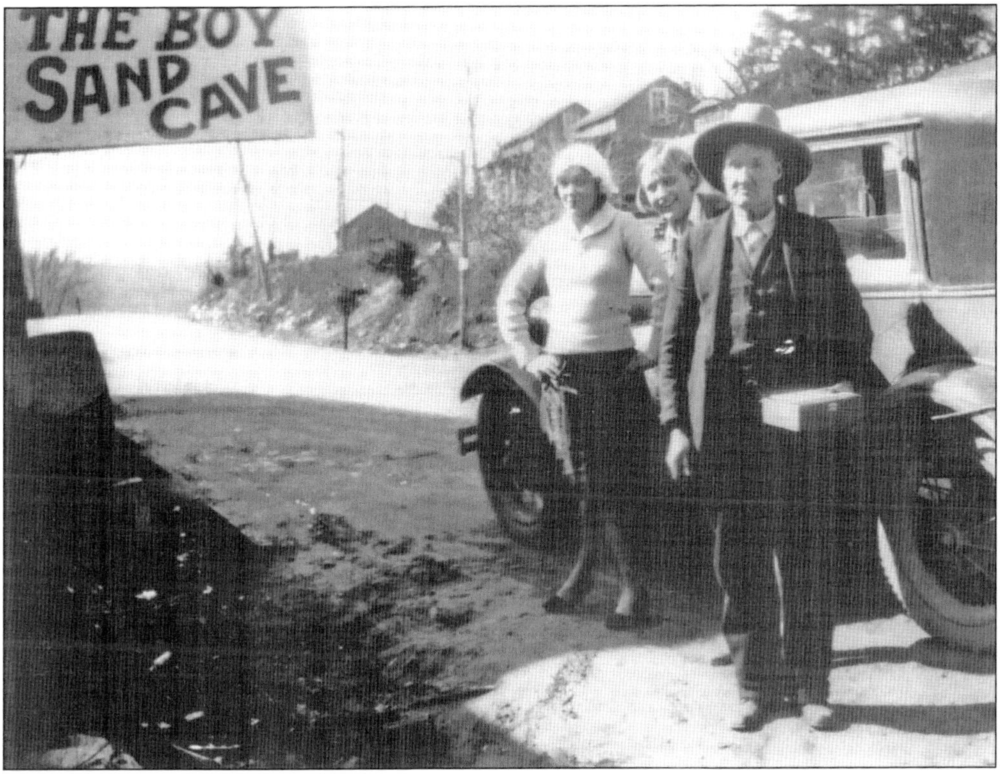

Lee Collins worked for Dr. Harry Thomas in the late 1920s selling cave tickets and souvenirs at a store in Horse Cave. Using a "Sand Cave" sign, Collins is seen here soliciting tourists on the street. Nearby Wonderland Cave was yet another "Collins" cave that had music and dancing outside the cave entrance on weekends. The cave entrance was developed by Lee Collins and his fourth wife. (Pamela Jeter Wilson Collection.)

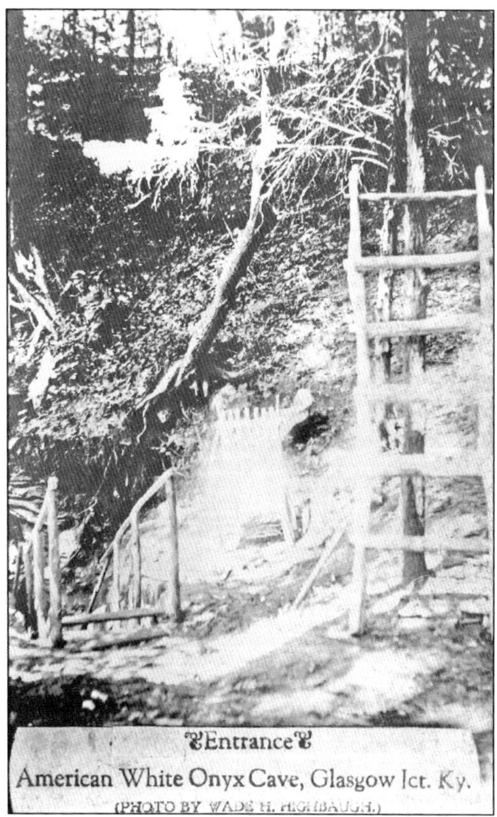

❦Entrance❦
American White Onyx Cave, Glasgow Jct. Ky.
(PHOTO BY WADE H. HIGHBAUGH.)

American White Onyx Cave was also known over the years by the name Vance Cave. This cave was not operated by the Collins brothers but was one of the private caves in the area that was in direct competition with the ones the brothers operated. This cave, open for a short time and run by owner E.G. Vance, was never a success. (Both, Bob Thompson Collection.)

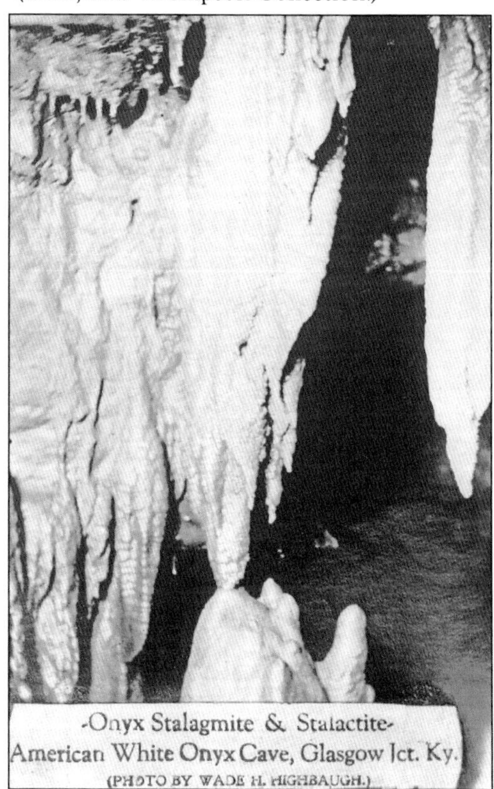

-Onyx Stalagmite & Stalactite-
American White Onyx Cave, Glasgow Jct. Ky.
(PHOTO BY WADE H. HIGHBAUGH.)

Nine

Over 90 Years Later

The Legend and Story Continue

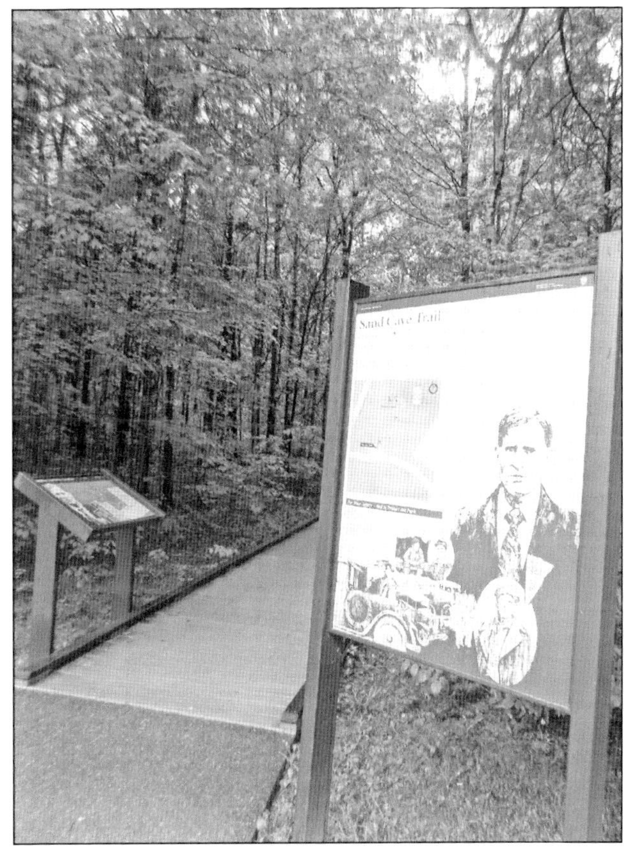

It has been over 90 years since the tragedy at Sand Cave, Kentucky, now inside Mammoth Cave National Park, that eventually claimed the life of Floyd Collins. Floyd Collins is entrenched in the history and culture of the Mammoth Cave area. Probably the area's most famous son, Collins's presence is still apparent today. (Photograph by Bob Thompson.)

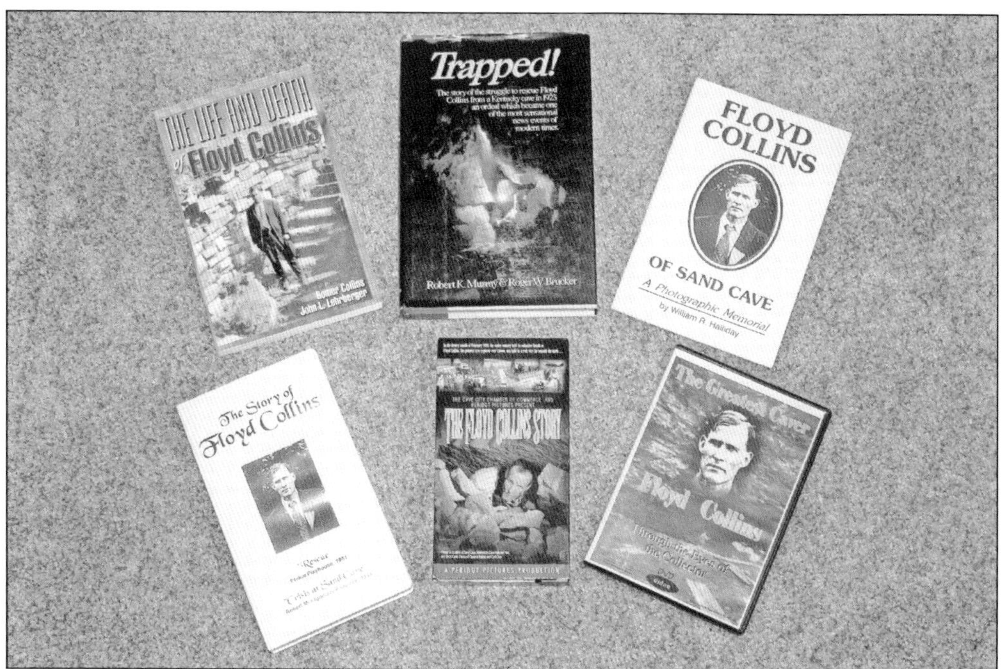

Three books have been written about Floyd Collins in recent times: Roger Brucker and Robert Murray's *Trapped*, William Halliday's *Floyd Collins of Sand Cave*, and *The Life and Death of Floyd Collins* by Jack Lehrberger and Homer Collins. Documentary films were made in 1999 and 2014. An off-Broadway musical continues to make the rounds in multiple cities, and a Hollywood movie on Collins is possible in the future. (Photograph by Bill Napper.)

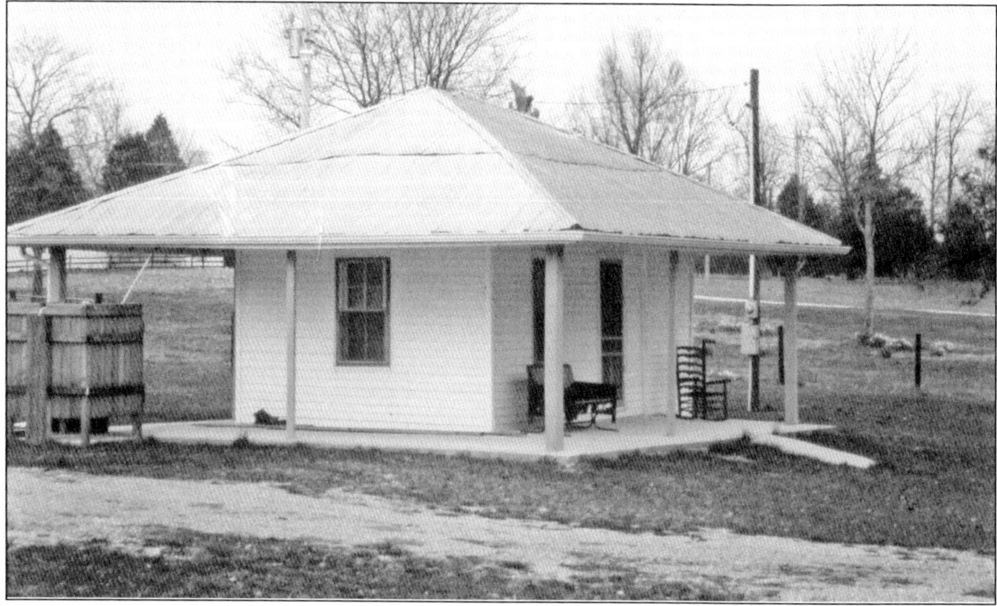

Sand Cave today sits at the eastern boundary of Mammoth Cave National Park. The National Park Service maintains a short boardwalk trail that leads to an overlook view of the cave. Just southeast of the Sand Cave site sits the old Sand Cave ticket office on the former Bee Doyel farm. The old office is on private property but can be viewed from the road. (Photograph by John Benton.)

Displays of Floyd Collins memorabilia can be seen at the American Cave Museum in downtown Horse Cave, Kentucky, and in the dental office of Dr. Tim Donley in Bowling Green. Records, postcards, photographs, brochures, pennants, sheet music, old newspapers, and other items are shown at these museums, including a chair (below) from the Horse Cave dental office of Dr. Harry Thomas that Floyd Collins sat in. (Both photographs by Bob Thompson.)

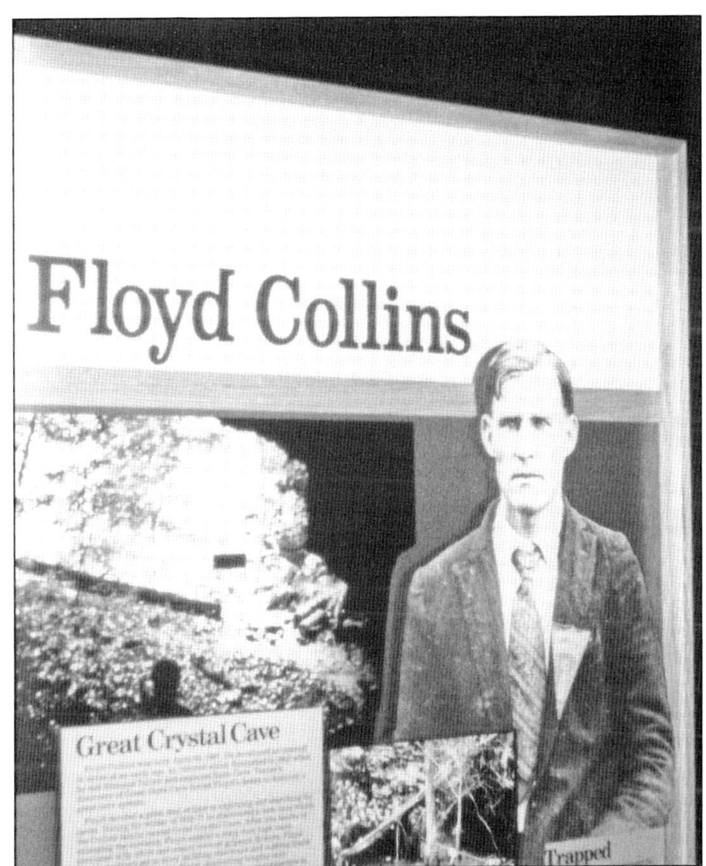

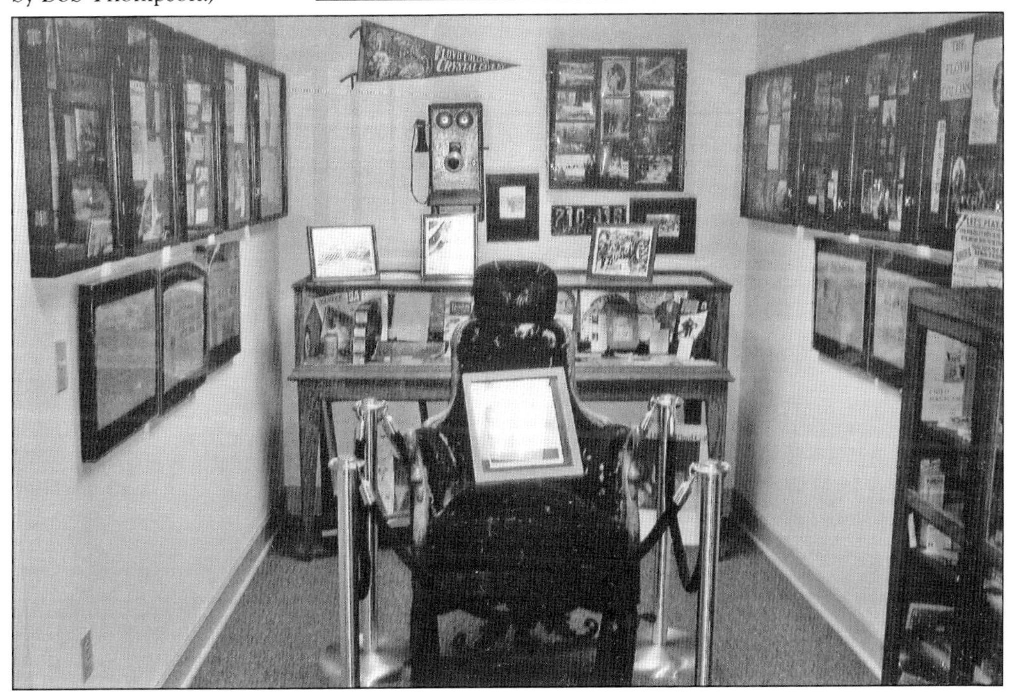

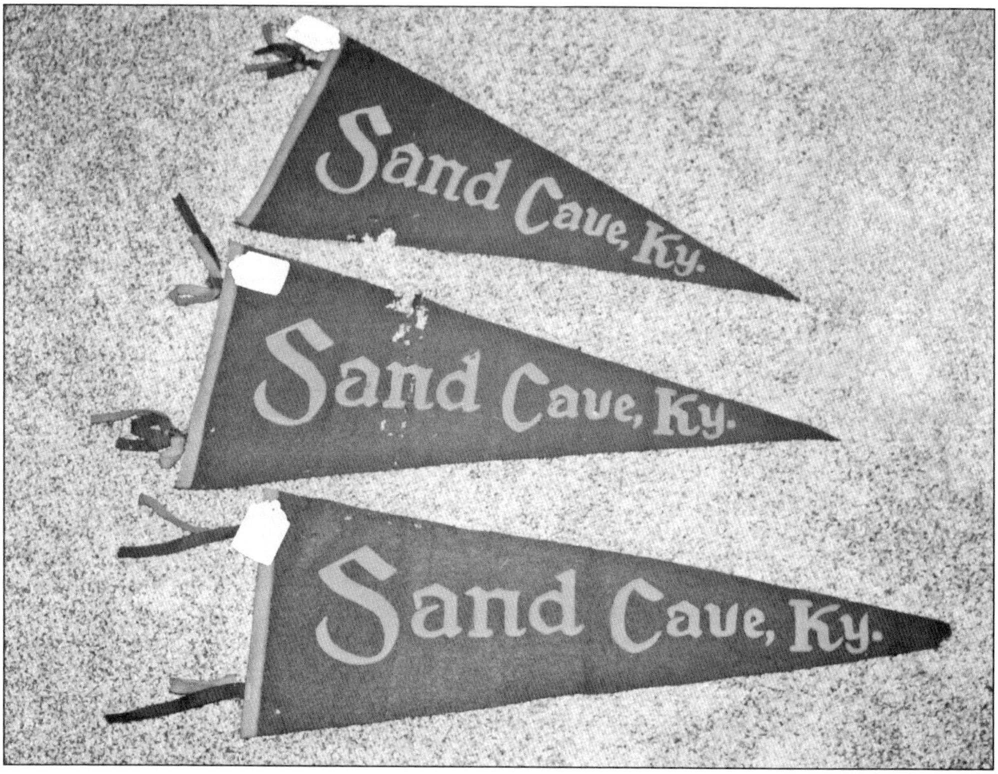

Souvenirs of Sand Cave are highly sought after by collectors, including these rare Sand Cave pennants and a Floyd Collins/Sand Cave rock formation. Sand Cave owner Bee Doyel sold these handmade souvenirs at his ticket office for only a couple years after the 1925 tragedy. (Both photographs by Bill Napper; above, National Cave Museum; below, Scott Cundiff Collection.)

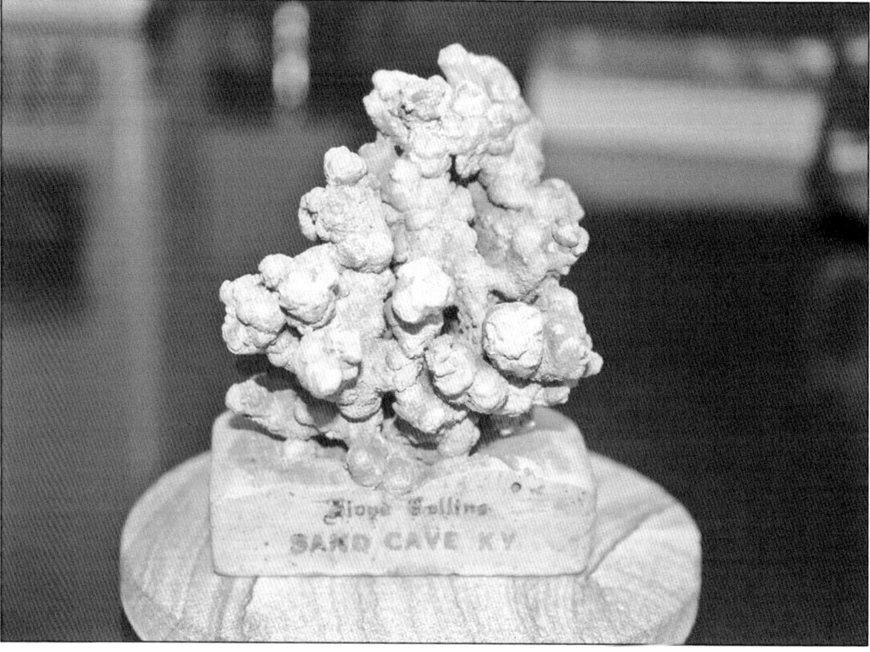

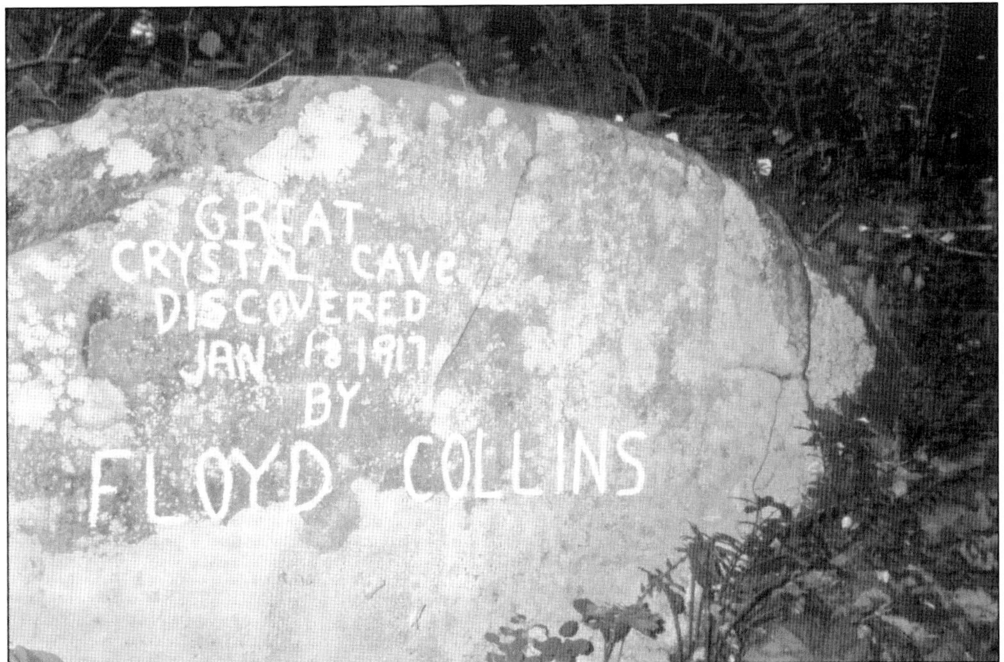

This rock sits outside the entrance steps to Floyd Collins' Crystal Cave and was probably added when Dr. Harry Thomas owned the cave after 1927. This worn etching is barely legible today, and the date (digitally enhanced) is in question. The date of December 17, 1917, is also possible. (Photograph by John Benton.)

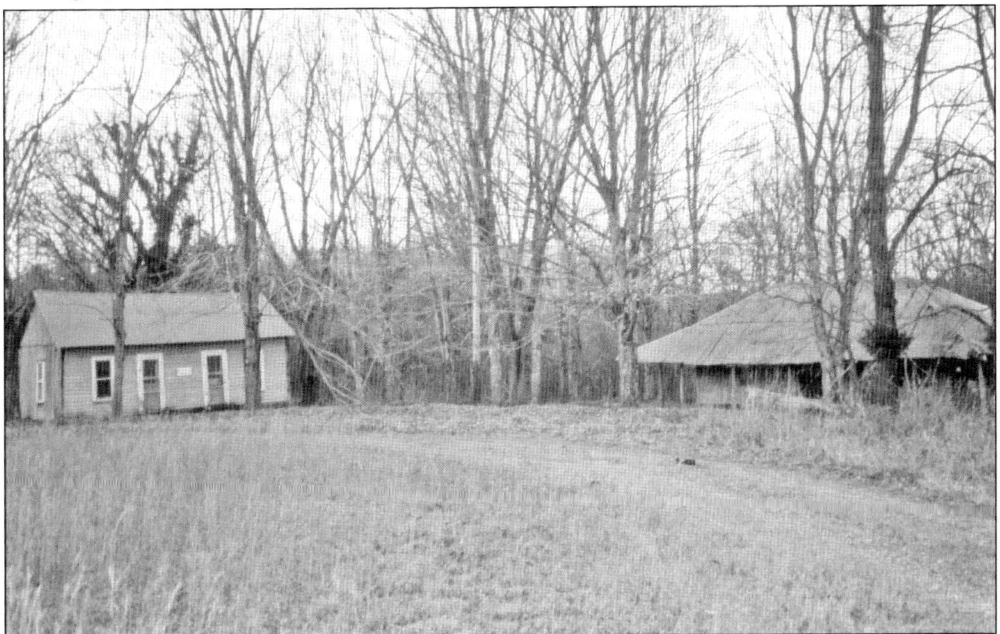

In 2005, the National Park Service started a preservation project to stabilize the Floyd Collins' Crystal Cave ticket office and Collins homestead buildings to protect these historic structures, which are both over 50 years old. A gravel lane, usually gated, winds for over a mile to the old Collins farm and these structures. (Photograph by John Benton.)

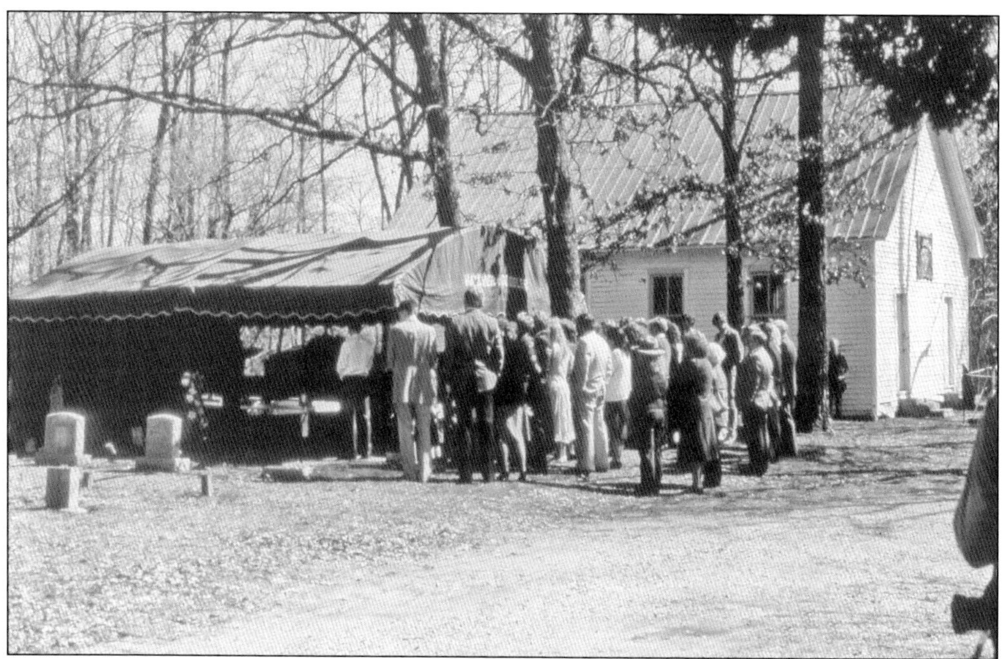

Floyd Collins's body remained in Floyd Collins' Crystal Cave until the National Park Service reburied him in 1989 at the Mammoth Cave Baptist Church Cemetery on Flint Ridge Road in Mammoth Cave National Park at the request of the Collins family. This was the fifth and final burial of Floyd Collins. The first was inside Sand Cave in February 1925. In April 1925, the Collins family paid to have the body safely removed and reburied near the Floyd Collins' Crystal Cave ticket office. In 1927, Dr. Thomas purchased the cave and had Collins reinterred inside Floyd Collins' Crystal Cave for his third burial. The fourth time was after the body was stolen in 1929 and then reburied back in Floyd Collins' Crystal Cave once it was recovered. The fifth and final time was in 1989 where Collins is today, the cemetery at Mammoth Cave Baptist Church. (Both photographs by Alex and Jenny Hicks; John Benton Collection.)

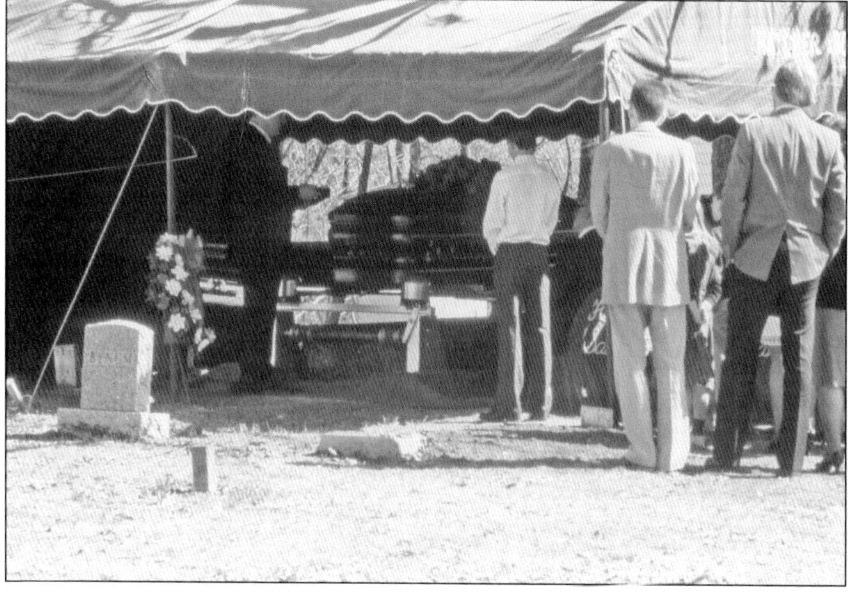

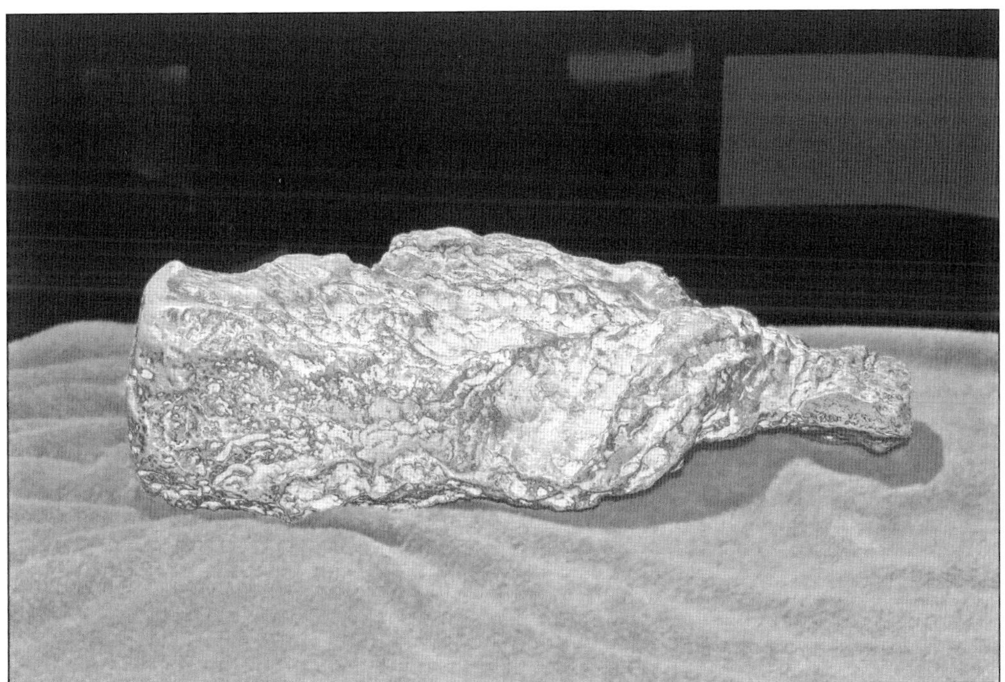

The 27-pound rock that trapped Floyd Collins is occasionally displayed at events by its private owner. It was shown at the July 1999 world premiere of the documentary film *The Floyd Collins Story* in Cave City, at the Mammoth Cave Hotel event *Roots in the Cave* in November 2013 (pictured), and at the 2016 Floyd Collins Remembered exhibit at the Cave City History Center. (Photograph by William Gross Magee.)

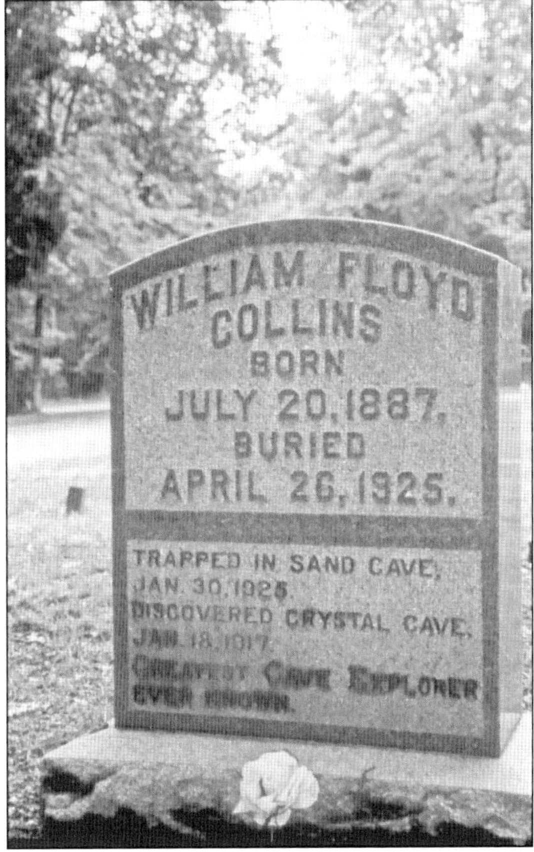

Floyd Collins was buried for the last time at the Mammoth Cave Baptist Church Cemetery on Flint Ridge, inside Mammoth Cave National Park. Here lies the most famous person that people have probably never heard of, Floyd Collins, "the greatest cave explorer ever known." (Photograph by John Benton.)